Ontario's Niagara Parks

A History

BY

George A. Seibel
Niagara Parks Historian

Olive M. Seibel, B.A.
Editor

THE
NIAGARA
PARKS
COMMISSION
Ontario

Published by
The Niagara Parks Commission
1985
Revised January 1987

Seibel, George A. (George Alfred)
Ontario's Niagara Parks

Includes Index.
ISBN 0-9691082-3-0

1. Parks — Niagara River Region (N.Y. and Ont.) — History.
I. Seibel, Olive M. (Olive Marguerite)
II. Niagara Parks Commission (Ont.)
III. Title.

FC3065.N52S43 1985   333.78'3'0971   C85-093000-6
F1059.N5S43 1985

Book design and layout by David J. Dick, Set•All Typesetting, Wellandport, Ontario
Maps by Erna Jahnke
Typeset by Commercial Photo Copy Ltd., St. Catharines, Ontario
Set•All Typesetting, Wellandport, Ontario
Printed and bound in Canada by Ainsworth Press Limited, Kitchener, Ontario

FOREWORD

It gives me great pleasure to endorse this revised edition of Ontario's Niagara Parks written by George A. Seibel. This history book was originally published by The Niagara Parks Commission in their Centennial year of 1985 with James N. Allan as Chairman. You will find in this edition updated information on Ontario's Niagara Parks.

Although The Niagara Parks Commission has changed considerably since 1885, the two founding principles of the Park remain unchanged. They are, first, to provide those wishing to view and enjoy the splendour of the Falls an opportunity to do so with ease, and second, to maintain the Parks on a financially self-sustaining basis. The Niagara Parks Commission is pleased to be able to provide numerous free facilities for both local residents and millions of people who visit Niagara Falls yearly. Since my appointment as Chairman of the Commission in May of 1986, the Commission has begun construction on a new Recreational Trail. This trail will run from Lake Erie to Lake Ontario, parallel to the Niagara River. Improvements continue in other areas of the Park in programs of preservation, restoration, Parks expansion and beautification.

May you enjoy many hours of reading in this new edition of Ontario's Niagara Parks.

Pamela Verrill Walker, Chairman
The Niagara Parks Commission
April 1987

AUTHOR'S PREFACE

In October 1981, the Niagara Parks Commission on the recommendation of its Centennial Committee, accepted my proposal, made on behalf of the Niagara Falls Heritage Foundation, to write the story of Ontario's Niagara Parks for the 100th Anniversary. My proposal was for a popular history of the areas now under the jurisdiction of the Niagara Parks Commission, from the beginning to the present. Each area or individual attraction of the Parks was to be treated separately.

I would like to acknowledge individuals who provided articles on subjects in which they are expert: Donald E. Loker, Local History Specialist, Niagara Falls New York Public Library, who supplied material on the Illumination; George Dalby, Niagara Parks Superintendent of Parks, who checked horticultural information and provided articles on Horticulture, the School of Horticulture and the Greenhouse and Conservatory; Ann Boyer, Curator of Battlefield House, Stoney Creek, who wrote the Battlefield House and Stoney Creek Battlefield story; George Bailey, Niagara Parks Director of Public Relations and Advertising who wrote the history of the Niagara Parks Police. Material submitted was edited and some changes were made.

My appreciation is extended to Robert W. Welch for the use of information included in his unpublished thesis: "The early years of the Queen Victoria Niagara Falls Park Commission: a study of the development of an Ontario Government Park at Niagara Falls, 1873-1893". This thesis was written for Mr. Welch's Master of Arts degree at Queens University, Kingston, in 1977. Frequent reference was made to Ronald L. Way's *Ontario's Niagara Parks — A History,* published by the Niagara Parks Commission in 1946 and revised in 1960.

I wish to thank my fellow members of the Niagara Falls Heritage Foundation: Robert L. Coombe, Jack A. Sampson, William Sauder, Robert F. Smith and the late Winston C. Fischer, who served as secretary-treasurer for thirteen years from 1971 to 1984.

My work on this book was made easier by the extensive research done by Betty Braaksma and Sheila Tonet for the Niagara Falls Heritage Foundation, in the course of Canada Works and Employment Development Projects. As a result of their research in old guide books on Niagara Falls, the Annual Reports of the Queen Victoria Niagara Falls Park Commissioners and the Niagara Parks Commission, an extensive card file of research material was compiled. Eventually this file will be available to other researchers through the Local History Department of the Niagara Falls Ontario Public Library.

Information was supplied by A. Blake Robertson, former owner of the Niagara Spanish Aero Car; Christine Mosser, Librarian, Canadian History Department, Metropolitan Toronto Library; Miss Heather Wright, Dunnville Library; Mrs. Sheila Wilson, St. Catharines Public Library; Inge Saczkowski, Local History Librarian, Niagara Falls Ontario Public Library; Louis McDermott, Fort Erie, Ontario. The co-operation of the following people is gratefully acknowledged: Larry Weiler, Archivist, Government Records Section, Archives of Ontario; Mrs. Beryl Way, Kingston, Ontario; Pat Speck, Secretary to the General Manager, Niagara Falls Bridge Commission; Lorne C. Featherston, Fort Erie Public Library; J.S. Montgomery, Niagara Falls; the Reference Staff at the Niagara Falls Public Library.

Geological information contributed by Albert H. Tiplin to the Map of the Whirlpool, the Map of the Niagara Glen and the *Visitor's Guide to Ontario's Niagara Parks,* was used in this history.

The following Department Heads and staff of the Niagara Parks checked articles and made helpful suggestions: James Harris, Superintendent of Engineering; David Gillis, Architectural Technologist; George Dalby, Superintendent of Parks; William Hutton, Properties Manager; Roland H. Barnsley, Superintendent of the School of Horticulture; Robert F. Brooker, Controller; Lorne E. Burns, Attractions Manager; William Glashan, Superintendent of Golf Courses; Tim Shaughnessy, Manager, Old Fort Erie.

Dr. Philip Downie read the rough and finished manuscripts, making helpful revisions. Mary Richards typed manuscripts from rough copy — often very rough. Robert D. Barnett, Historical Technologist, chairman of the Niagara Society for Industrial History, checked metric conversions. All the maps in this book were drawn by Erna Jahnke for the Niagara Falls Heritage Foundation in 1981, and revised by her in 1984.

Inge Saczkowski, Local History Librarian, Niagara Falls Public Library, organized the style of the references. Dorothy Van Slyke, Chief Librarian of the Niagara Falls Public Library was responsible for the index, organizing and checking the hundreds of individual references before the final index was completed. Their contribution is gratefully acknowledged.

I would like to thank James N. Allan, Chairman, and the members of the Niagara Parks Commission for choosing me to compile this 100th Anniversary History of the Niagara Parks. Manuscripts were submitted for correction and comments on current administrative procedures, to Donald R. Wilson, General Manager of the Niagara Parks, and Malcolm Cushing, Assistant General Manager. They read the manuscripts and attempted - with limited success - to keep me from writing at great length about every event that ever took place within the confines of the present Parks. Their co-operation helped me to avoid making errors in matters not covered by the Annual Reports.

The encouragement and co-operation of George Bailey, Director of Public Relations and Advertising for the Niagara Parks Commission, has been invaluable. Throughout the three years that this book was in progress, he cheerfully accepted unusual demands on his personal time. He always succeeded in finding that extra picture we needed and suggested many ways in which we could make the book more interesting. Only Olive and I can fully appreciate his contribution.

This book was a joint effort, with my wife Olive working along with me through all its phases. She was editor, rewrite specialist, proofreader and layout critic. Because of her insistence there are more pictures than if the choice had been left to me alone.

Our hope is that the book will bring back pleasant memories to those who knew the Parks in days gone by. A younger generation of readers will become aware that where there were pioneer settlers' farms, water-powered grist mills and an iron foundry, unsightly commercial buildings and military battles, there are now beautiful parklands — theirs to enjoy.

George A. Seibel
Niagara Parks Historian

January 1, 1985
Niagara Falls, Ontario, Canada

ACKNOWLEDGEMENTS

Pictures from several photographic collections were used for the first time. The F.H. Leslie Collection of photographs which is in the care of the Niagara Falls Review, is one. I would like to thank W. Bruce Leslie, Gordon Murray, publisher of the *Niagara Falls Review,* Clive Jacklin, News Editor, Gabrielle Herbison, Librarian, and Ron Roels, photographer, for their co-operation in making these pictures available.

Photos taken by Edwin "Eddie" Hodge are also included. Mr. Hodge was employed by the Hydro Electric Power Commission in Niagara Falls and for many years, during the 1920's and 1930's, he took hundreds of pictures for the Niagara Parks Commission. These pictures are in the Niagara Parks Archives. Eddie Hodge's pictures of Jean Lussier and his trip over the Horseshoe Falls in a ball are included, courtesy of Eddie's sister, Helen Hodge.

Harry Mottershead took colour pictures of current scenes in the Niagara Parks and copied old pictures in colour, from coloured lantern slides, and old postcards. Photographs copied by Winston Bain for the Niagara Falls Heritage Foundation were used.

Photographs were contributed by: Ontario Hydro, Chris Norman, Picture Archivist, Kipling Archives; M.S. Hanson, Advertising Co-ordinator, Ontario Hydro; K.R. Macpherson, Archives of Ontario, Toronto; Dr. Herman Sass, Ph D., Senior Librarian, Buffalo and Erie County Historical Society; Herbert C. Force, who permitted the use of his prize picture of the Whirlpool Rapids Raft Ride — "Man Overboard"; Ralph Grant, Great Gorge Trip and Daredevil Gallery; Donald E. Loker, Local History Specialist, Niagara Falls New York Public Library; Mark Francis, Editor, and Alan Johnson, Librarian, *Niagara Gazette;* John Burtniak, Technical Services Librarian, Brock University, who made his post card and stereograph collection available; Frank Simon, Vice-President and General Manager, and Captain L. McGinn, Maid of the Mist Steamboat Co. Ltd.; Northway Gestalt Corporation, Toronto; Anthony Bannon, Buffalo, N.Y.; George H. Forman, Buffalo, New York; Jerry L. Kearns, Library of Congress, Washington, D.C.; Dr. and Mrs. F. Kellar, New Orleans, Louisiana; Willis E. Beese, Niagara Falls.

The author and the publisher are grateful to the following who provided colour transparencies without charge for use in this book: Gerard F. Hunnealt, Loan Officer, and Lise Gobeil, Reference Assistant, Picture Division, Public Archives of Canada, Ottawa; David B. Kotin, Head, Canadian History Department, Metropolitan Toronto Library Board; Mrs. N.P. Naud, Hirschl Adler Galleries, New York, New York; Patricia C. Geeson, Rights and Reproductions, National Museum of American Art, Smithsonian Institute, Washington D.C.; Anne B. Tully, Historic Sites Assistant, New York State Historic Sites Bureau, Waterford, New York; G. Rosenmund, Department of the Army, Washington, D.C.; N.E. Frank and Tom Robbins, New York Power Authority; Walter Haldorson, Superintendent, Niagara National Historic Parks, Niagara-on-the-Lake, Ontario.

Colour transparencies were obtained on loan through the co-operation of: Jane Abbot, Audio Visual Services, Royal Ontario Museum, Toronto; Ann Adams, Registrar, Amon Carter Museum, Fort Worth Texas; John C. Dunn, Director and Galen R. Wilson, Manuscript Curator, William L. Clements Library, the University of Michigan, Ann Arbor; Rebecca Tiger, Assistant Registrar, Corcoran Gallery of Art, Washington, D.C.; Susan Campbell, Head, and Monique McCaig, Reproduction Rights and Sales, National Gallery of Canada, Ottawa; Nicki Thuras, Assistant to the Director, Addison Gallery of Art, Phillips Academy, Andover Mass. Many of the colour photos credited to the Niagara Parks Archives were taken by Gordon Counsell.

TABLE OF CONTENTS

Preface 1

The Early History of Europeans in the Niagara Area 3

Early Tourism 6

The Front 12

The Niagara Falls Park — Its Establishment 22

Queen Victoria Park 27

Dufferin Islands 61

Oak Hall 73

The Hollow 77

Cedar Island 81

Table Rock House and Scenic Tunnel 83

Refectory 93

King's Bridge Park 101

The Maid of the Mist 105

Maid of the Mist Incline 111

Maid of the Mist — Roger Woodward 115

Illumination 117

Ice Bridge 127

Stunters 135

Power 152

The Scow 163

The Horseshoe Falls — Recession — Diversion — Remedial 166

Whirlpool Rapids 174

Niagara Spanish Aero Car 186

Whirlpool 196

Niagara Glen 203

Queenston Heights Park 213

Navy Island 237

The Mackenzie Rebellion and Navy Island 239

Niagara Parkway — Chippawa to Fort Erie 243

Mather Park — Mather Arch 251

Niagara Parkway - Queenston to Niagara-on-the-Lake 254

HISTORIC SITES AND RESTORATIONS

Old Fort Erie 258

Fort George, Navy Hall, Butler's Burying Ground 265

McFarland House and McFarland Park 269

Stoney Creek Battlefield and Battlefield House 272

Drummond Hill Cemetery and Lundy's Lane Battlefield 278

HORTICULTURE

Horticulture 281

Greenhouse — Conservatory 285

Oakes Garden Theatre and the Rainbow Gardens 293

School of Horticulture 303

Floral Clock 309

Lilac Gardens 311

RECREATION

Recreation in the Parks 313

Queen Victoria Park — Picnic Grounds 315

Whirlpool Golf Course 319

Miller's Creek Campsite and the Marina 324

Charles Daley Park 328

ADMINISTRATION

Administration 332

Finance 336

Index 338

Preface

One hundred years have passed since the birth of Ontario's Niagara Parks. The enlightened foresight of Ontario's Provincial Government in establishing 62.2 ha (154 acres) of public parkland in the area adjacent to the Horseshoe Falls, has resulted in the 1130 ha (2792 acres) of parkland we have today including the 56 km (35 miles) of parkway along the Niagara River from Lake Erie to Lake Ontario. The original concept of the Provincial Government and the Park Commission was only to acquire and preserve lands immediately adjacent to the Falls. The present day Niagara Parks include historic sites, golf courses, picnic grounds, marina, campgrounds, swimming beaches, restaurants, gift shops, a horticultural school and gardens. As well as the Falls, many scenic attractions are within the Parks system - the Whirlpool, the Rapids and the Niagara Glen.

Before the creation of the Queen Victoria Park Commission in 1885 and the establishment of a public park, the area around the Falls was overrun with commercial enterprises. A motley collection of buildings crowded right up to the gorge bank, leaving only room enough for a narrow carriage road between the Ferry Road and Table Rock. The unwary visitor was accosted by cab-men, runners and persistent concessionaires, competing for his dollar. It was impossible to view the natural wonders of Niagara without unwanted interruptions. The creation of the public park - Queen Victoria Park - ended this.

When the Queen Victoria Park Commissioners selected the land for the new park, they found it necessary to expropriate some property. The price to be paid for the properties was referred to the Provincial Arbitrators. The Commissioners then had to devise a financial scheme for the payment of the arbitration awards and to provide funds for the improvement and maintenance of the new Park, because their mandate from the Provincial Government required that the Park be financially self sufficient. The system of tolls and fees they imposed for the use of various Park facilities proved to be inadequate. It was not until the 1890's when franchises were given to private enterprise to operate concessions in the Park, to operate an electric railway and to build electric generating plants, that the Park became financially self-supporting.

The Commissioners kept pace with the increased demands made on their resources, demands brought about by the popularity of the automobile. New roads were built connecting Queen Victoria Park with the parks at the Niagara Glen and Queenston Heights. Parking lots and picnic areas were built to accommodate the motoring public. From 1934 a program of restoration and improvement was carried on. During the economic depression of the 1930's the Commission, in conjunction with the Federal and Provincial Governments, took advantage of the skilled labour available due to lack of work in the construction and allied trades. This program continued until 1940 when the Second World War was in progress.

At the same time that construction and restoration was going on the Commission was embroiled in litigation with the International Railway Company over the amount to be paid by the Commission to the Railway Company for the railway facilities abandoned in 1932. In 1934 an initial award in favour of the Railway Company of one hundred and seventy nine thousand one hundred and four dollars plus costs was made by the Provincial Arbitrators. In 1942 after numerous appeals to the Privy Council in London, the International Railway Company received a much higher award. This award plus interest and legal fees incurred by the Parks Commission brought the total cost of the award to one and a half million dollars. Including the cost of improvements and restorations in the Park, the Commission was left with a staggering debt, almost four million dollars at the end of 1942. It took fourteen years of judicious management for succeeding Commissions to make payments on the debt and carry out necessary improvements and required maintenance before the debt was fully repaid by the end of 1956.

Throughout the first one hundred years of the Niagara Parks existence the Commission's policy was "to provide an opportunity for Park visitors to view the Falls, the gorge, and the river, under the most pleasant condition and circumstances possible". In 1969 the Commission's goals were described as follows:

1) To maintain, preserve, and enhance the beauty and surroundings of the Canadian Niagara Falls and the Niagara River, from Fort Erie to Niagara-on-the-Lake.

2) To develop, operate and maintain a system of park and recreation areas, historic sites and educational facilities which complement the natural wonders of the Niagara Falls and the Niagara River, and which will facilitate and add to the visitor's enjoyment.

3) To provide those wishing to view and enjoy the splendour of Niagara Falls an opportunity to do so with ease.

4) To provide a broad range of educational opportunities for people in the fields of horticulture, geology, natural history, and the history of the Niagara Frontier.

5) To continually seek new methods and means for improving the visitor's experience when visiting the Falls area.

6) To encourage complementary uses of lands adjacent to the Parks System, and to work with other groups and agencies who have compatible interests in the Park area.

7) To insure a suitable first and/or last impression for the many millions of foreign visitors to Ontario and to Canada crossing the borders along the Niagara Frontier.

8) To encourage and promote the development of the tourism industry in Ontario and Canada.

9) To pursue the self-sustaining nature of the Parks System while recognizing the limitations of compatible and suitable revenue-producing facilities and the long range need for capital improvements.

The present Niagara Parks Commission is continuing the policy of the Commissions of former years, in carrying out a program of preservation, restoration, commemoration, beautification and attraction, for the enjoyment of the millions of Park visitors from all over the world. As you read through the pages of this book recording the progress in the Niagara Parks over the past one hundred years, you will realize how faithfully successive Commissions have carried out their mandate.

The Early History
of Europeans
in the Niagara Area

The first written mention of Niagara Falls was made by Jacques Cartier who left France in May of 1535 on an exploration journey. Reaching the St. Lawrence River he named it after the Saint of the same name. Here he enquired of the Indians about the source of the river and was told "that after ascending many leagues among the rapids and waterfalls he would reach a lake 140 to 150 leagues broad (Ontario), at the extremity of which the waters were wholesome and the winters mild; that a river emptied into it from the south, which had its source in the country of the Iroquois; that beyond the lake he would find a cataract (Niagara) and portage, then another lake (Erie) about equal to the former, which they had never explored".[1]

Samuel de Champlain, who came later, in 1608, recorded in his book *Des Sauvages* what the Indians on the St. Lawrence told him about the waterfall, but Champlain never visited it. Later, in 1615, Champlain's interpreter and agent, Étienne Brûlé went into the interior of North America and lived among the Indians. He was the first white man to see Lakes Ontario, Erie, Huron and Superior. It is possible that he reached the Niagara River and saw the Falls, but he left no records.

The Franciscan friar, De la Roche Daillon crossed the Niagara River near what is now Lewiston in 1626. Jesuit Father Gabriel Lalemant in his *Relation* of 1640-41 - a Relation was an annual report sent back to Jesuit headquarters in France - refers to the Niagara River as Onguiaahra, the celebrated river of the Neutral Nation. The name

Onguiaahra appears on maps as early as 1640. This name and the later, present version, Niagara, probably derived from the attempts of the early Jesuit missionaries to establish a written equivalent for the Iroquoian word. The generally accepted meaning of the name is "The Strait".[2]

The first direct mention of the Falls of Niagara was made by Le Sieur Gendron, a Doctor of Medicine who lived among the Huron Indians for many years. He wrote about the Falls in 1644 in letters sent back to his friends in France. In 1660 these letters were published in book form, *Quelques Particularités du Pays Des Hurons en la Novelle France*. In one of the letters Gendron describes the Falls but does not mention having visited them. He wrote: "Almost due south of the Neutral Nation one discovers a great lake about 200 leagues around, called Erié, which is formed by the discharge from la Mer Douce (Lake Huron). At its far end it plunges over a waterfall of terrific height into a third lake called Ontarié, but which we call Lac St. Louis. As the water rushes among the great boulders at the foot of the falls the spray forms a stone, or rather petrified salt, yellowish in colour, which is very effective in the cure of sores, fistules, and malignant ulcers.

"In this direful spot there dwell also certain savages who live off elk, harts, wild cows, and every kind of game, that the rapids carry away and among the rock. They catch them thus without chase - more than enough for their own provision and for that of travellers, with whom they trade these Erian stones (called thus after the lake), who then carry them away

Hand-coloured engraving from a copy of Hennepin's Nouvelle Découverte, *1697 which belonged originally to William III of England to whom the book is dedicated.*

Metropolitan Toronto Central Library

a. *The Place where a Piece of Rock was broken from, which while standing turns the Water of Obliquely across ye Fall as in Popple's Map.* A View of the Fall of Niagara. b. *Two Men passing over ye east Stream with staves.* c. *The Indians reascending their Ladder.*

Buffalo and Erie County Public Library

A View of the Fall of Niagara. From the Gentleman's Magazine February 1751.

and distribute them among the other tribes".[3]

The Iroquois Federation challenged French occupation in 1648 by invading the territory of the Neutral Indians where the French had their missions and trading posts. A period of unrest and conflict resulted, which disrupted the fur trade and the work of the missionaries. It was not until the Iroquois were subdued by the French in 1667, that the *coureurs de*

bois were able to move along the western trails once more. The missionary explorers followed; the Jesuits, the Sulpicians from Montreal and the Recollets, all undertook a series of explorations. A Sulpician expedition, led by a former cavalry officer, François Dollier de Casson and Bréhand de Galinée accompanied for part of the way by a young La Salle, became the first Europeans known to have entered the Niagara River from Lake Ontario. They were also the first to winter on Lake Erie in 1669-70 and the first to make adequate surveys along the shores of both lakes.[4]

Galinée wrote in 1669: "We found a river, one-eighth of a league broad and extremely rapid, forming the outlet of communication from Lake Erie to Lake Ontario . . . . This outlet is 40 leagues long, and has from 10 to 12 leagues above its embouchure into Lake Ontario, one of the finest cataracts, or falls of water, in the world, for all the Indians of whom I have enquired about it, say, that the river falls at that place from a rock higher than the tallest pines, and that is about 200 feet. In fact we heard it from the place where we were, although from 10 to 12 leagues distant, but the fall gives such momentum to the water, that its velocity prevented our ascending the current by rowing, except with great difficulty. At a quarter of a league from the outlet where we were, it grows narrower, and its channel is confined between two very high steep rocky banks, inducing the belief that the navigation would be very difficult quite up to the cataract. Our desire to reach the little village called Ganastogue Sononotoua O-tin-a-oua prevented our going to view the wonder which I consider as so much greater in proportion as the River St. Lawrence is one of the largest in the world".[5]

It was Robert Cavelier, Sieur de la Salle who was to be a party to the "discovery" of Niagara Falls, even though he was not to be the one to see them first. La Salle came to New France in 1666 and became involved in voyages of exploration and fur trading. He established a trading post at Cataraqui, now Kingston, Ontario. In 1678 King Louis XIV of France authorized La Salle to search for an inland route to the Gulf of Mexico, and to establish forts and trading posts along the route of his exploration.

In 1678 the advance party of this expedition, led by La Salle's lieutenant, La Motte, and including Father Louis Hennepin a Recollet priest in the party, set sail from Cataraqui in late November. They arrived at the mouth of the Niagara River on December 6, and on the morning of December 7, proceeded upriver to make a landing on the west bank.[6] They were looking for a suitable place on the Upper Niagara River to build a boat which would take them through the Upper Lakes to the source of the Mississippi. They climbed the escarpment and then travelled along the bank of the Niagara Gorge. Later on that same day they came upon the Falls of Niagara. They went on and that same night set up

camp at the mouth of what is now the Welland River. Father Hennepin in his book *Nouvelle Découverte* published in Utrecht in 1697 wrote: "We lay that Night near a River, which runs from the Westward, within a League above the Great Fall of Niagara . . .".[7]

Hennepin's book included a description of the Falls and an engraving by J. Van Viene. This is the first published picture of Niagara Falls. To Father Louis Hennepin, therefore must go the credit of being the first European to see, describe and depict the Falls of Niagara.

Hennepin's exaggerated description of the Falls, describing them as 183 m (600 ft.) high, was not disputed until 1750 when Peter Kalm's account, accompanied by a sketch, appeared in the *Gentleman's Magazine,* January 1751. Kalm wrote: "Monsieur Morandrier the king's engineer in Canada, assured me, and gave it me also under his hand, that 137 feet was precisely the height of it; and all the French Gentlemen who were present with me at the Fall, did agree with him, without the least contradiction: it is true, those who have try'd to measure it with a line, find it sometimes 140, sometimes 150 feet, and sometimes more; but the reason is, it cannot that way be measured with any certainty, the water carrying away the line".[8] Although Kalm had nothing to do with the sketch that accompanied the article, it is quite evident that the engraver based his work on Kalm's description. It is considered to be the first picture after Hennepin to be based on an actual sight of the Falls.[9]

The British capture of Fort Niagara in 1759-60 ended French domination in the area. Through the writings of the French priests, traders and explorers, Niagara Falls became known to Europeans before Jamestown and Plymouth Rock. The expansion of the British influence brought articulate travellers who wrote descriptive accounts of their visits, which were published and distributed in England, generating more interest in this natural wonder. Depictions of Niagara Falls improved when done by British officers who had been taught drawing and water colour painting by drawing master Paul Sanby, R.A. as part of the course of study at the Royal Military Academy in England.

The invention of lithography which allowed widespread sale in England of lithographic views of the Falls, heightened public awareness of the Cataracts. This sparked an interest in the natural wonder and increased the desire of many to visit the Falls of Niagara.

Early Tourism

Early travellers wishing to see the Falls had to come down from the high bank by way of a crude path which wound through one of the many gullies which scarred the bank. Then they carefully picked their way through the swampy terrain on their way to the gorge bank. Suddenly the path came to an end and they found themselves out of the dense undergrowth and upon a flat bare rocky ledge, Table Rock, where the whole panorama of the Falls and the gorge came into view. It was a dramatic moment - they had heard the roar of the Horseshoe Falls, felt the spray - now they saw the Falls in all their majestic grandeur. It was an awe-inspiring sight.

Monsieur J.C. Bonnefons visited Niagara Falls in 1783 and his natural curiosity led him to find his way down the side of the gorge wall to the base of the Horseshoe Falls. From here he ventured behind the falling water. He descended the cliff by hanging on to roots and branches and using rocky ledges as footholds. It took him an hour to reach the bottom. He was tired and drenched from the rain-like spray, but his curiosity led him farther. Finding himself close to the base of the Falls he walked toward it: "I passed over a shingle of flat rock, which led me under the sheet of falling water . . . I found myself in a cavern which appeared to be about 40 ft. by 20 ft. and its depth was scarcely more than 15 ft. . . . I was unable to go further because of large clefts which I was unable to cross. I had to retrace my steps."[1]

The Table Rock was a large shelf of bare rock which had once been part of the crest of the Horseshoe Falls. It was left high and dry when the Horseshoe Falls receded some time in the early 1700's. The surrounding area, all along the lower bank, was a heavily wooded cedar swamp, which was flooded at times when the river rose due to high winds and heavy rainfall. The swamp was kept wet at all times by the many springs which flowed out of the base of the high bank.

As early as 1791 a log hut situated on the high bank above the Horseshoe Falls, served as an inn. It was described as "the only place of accommodation . . . for travellers of the day to refresh themselves". The Duke of Kent, Queen Victoria's father, visited the inn on his journey to the Falls of Niagara in 1791: "The Royal Party alighted (from horseback) and partaking of such refreshments as the house afforded, followed an Indian path through the woods to the Table Rock overlooking the Horseshoe Falls".[2]

The site of this inn was included in the 80 ha (200 acres) Crown Grant of Land to Francis Ellsworth in 1798. Ellsworth sold his land to William Dickson. He in turn rented to Charles Wilson the property on which the inn stood. Wilson continued to operate an inn and tavern there from 1808 until his death in 1812. His wife carried on the business until 1818.[3]

In 1818 William Forsyth, an American entrepreneur who emigrated to Canada from Buffalo, purchased the former Ellsworth tract from William Dickson and took over Mrs. Wilson's old tavern. Immediately he began to take advantage of the commercial possibilities of this location. In 1818 he built a stairway down the side of the gorge wall at Table Rock, and in the same year in co-operation with Parkhurst Whitney,

National Collection of Fine Arts, Smithsonian Institution

The Great Horseshoe Fall, Niagara. An oil painting by Alvan Fisher, 1820.

the proprietor of the Eagle Tavern on the U.S. side, began operating a row boat ferry service across the Niagara River below the American Falls.[4] In doing so Forsyth was breaking the law. He was encroaching on Crown property. When the area was first surveyed in 1786 by Augustus Jones, the Crown surveyor, a strip of land one chain in width was reserved all along the gorge bank as the property of the Crown (a chain is equivalent to 20 m or 66 ft.). It was referred to by various names, the Chain Reserve, Crown Reserve and Military Reserve. Forsyth's stairway and ferry service were unauthorized uses of the Chain Reserve.

In 1822 Forsyth razed the old tavern and built the Pavilion Hotel, six stories high. From its outside galleries and windows facing east, a fine view of the Horseshoe Falls - albeit a partial view because of the trees - and the Upper Rapids was to be had. John Brown built a hotel a year or two later, farther south on the Portage Road near the present day site of the Loretto Centre. A fierce rivalry sprang up between Forsyth and Brown, tempered at times when the two co-operated as they did in promoting the first organized stunt at Niagara Falls in 1827, when the condemned schooner "Michigan" was sent over the

Horseshoe Falls with a "cargo of wild animals".

Forsyth's desire to control all hotel business at Niagara Falls led him to a rash act in 1827. He built high board fences on either side of his property and extended them across the Chain Reserve to the edge of the gorge wall, thus shutting off access to Table Rock and the Horseshoe Falls. Only those who stayed at his Pavilion Hotel were allowed to approach Table Rock and the Horseshoe Falls.

Lieutenant-Governor Sir Peregrine Maitland was incensed at Forsyth's action in fencing off the Chain Reserve and on May 18, 1827 Maitland sent Captain Philpotts and a troop of Engineers to tear the fence down. Forsyth replaced the fence and Maitland had it torn down again. There ensued a long and complicated court action which ended in 1833, with Forsyth the loser. Forsyth, disgusted, and in debt for his legal costs, sold his property in 1833 to the Honourable Thomas Clark M.P. and Samuel Street and moved to Bertie Township.[5]

Clark and Street were influential merchants and mill owners who had alerted the Lieutenant-Governor to Forsyth's infringement on the Chain Reserve. After Lieutenant-Governor Maitland moved Forsyth

The stairway and path to the foot of the gorge near Table Rock, Niagara. Water colour by James Pattison Cockburn, 1827.

The Pavilion Hotel at Niagara Falls, September 30, 1830. Water colour by James Pattison Cockburn.

The first building at Table Rock, circa 1830.

Niagara Parks Archives

off the Reserve, Clark and Street applied for permission to occupy it themselves and on August 31, 1827 a lease was signed with Clark and Street allowing them to occupy the Crown property. Forsyth was given notice not to trespass.[6]

Clark and Street took over Forsyth's stairs. Immediately they sub-let the stairs and the right to conduct people behind the Horseshoe Falls, to W.D. Wright, then later to Isaiah Starkey. Clark and Street began to erect several buildings on the Reserve in violation of the terms of their lease. Lieutenant-Governor Sir John Colborne who succeeded Maitland in 1828, sent a troop of Engineers to stop the work, as Maitland had tried to stop Forsyth. The officer in charge was aware of the fate of his predecessor, Captain Philpotts, who was being sued by Forsyth, so he issued a warning only. It was to no avail, the construction continued. Clark and Street subsequently instituted two lawsuits, one against the Officer of the Engineers and the other against the Government. Their influence in the District was so great that they obtained a favourable verdict, with damages of 500 pounds against the Crown. Clark and Street retained undisputed possession of the Reserve at the Horseshoe Falls.[7]

One of the buildings they erected contained dressing-rooms where tourists were outfitted with water-proof clothing for the trip Behind the Sheet, that is, behind the Horseshoe Falls. The other was a shelter built at the top of the stairway, containing a barroom. No charge was made to go down the stairway, but there was a charge for the use of the water-proof clothing. It was expected that the tourists would spend money at the bar. At one time a sign at the site advertised "Starkey's Refreshment Rooms". Ice cream and lemonade were available as well as liquor.[8]

After they purchased Forsyth's property in 1833, Clark and Street joined forces with Lieutenant-Colonel John Murray, James Buchanan, James Robinson, the Honourable William Allan and the Honourable James Dunn, to form the City of the Falls Company, to carry out a land development project on the 162 ha (400 acres) tract of land. The City of the Falls Project was an ambitious scheme with two declared aims, one believable, the other suspect. First it was to be a money-making venture and second it was to be an effort to preserve the area around the Falls from vandalism and commercial enterprise. The promoters' idea of preservation was to subdivide the property into lots which were then divided among the partners, who expected to sell them for a huge profit. Advertisements were placed in newspapers encouraging prospective buyers to purchase lots in the project and hold them in anticipation of a speculative profit. Choice lots had a 15.2 m (50 ft.) frontage on the Chain Reserve with a roadway planned to run on the Chain Reserve along the gorge bank.

The City of the Falls was to be a resort and as it was fashionable at the time for people visiting summer resorts to take "baths" for health reasons, the promoters felt that people would be attracted to the area if baths were available for invalids and others who wished to take them. In 1835 they built the Bath House, a hydropathic centre with a Pump Room probably comparable to today's whirlpool baths. It also had an Assembly Room for dancing. To provide water for the Bath House, a mill dam and an undershot water wheel were erected on Table Rock. Water was forced up the high bank at a rate of 364 litres (80 gallons) a minute through wooden pipes, bound with iron hoops, to a standpipe reservoir located in a tower on the summit level. From there water would be gravity fed to the Bath House. The water wheel was put in operation but the wooden pipes burst under the pressure of the water being forced through them.[9] The Bath House was without water and was never used for the purpose intended. It was destroyed by fire in the 1840's. The City of the Falls scheme collapsed when, after an extensive advertising campaign, only a few lots were sold. The Company's management was inefficient and it became involved in litigation with the Government over rights to the Chain Reserve. All of the original investors lost heavily. All that remains today of the City of the Falls Project in Queen Victoria Park are

the names of two of the shareholders, who are commemorated in Murray Street and Robinson Street.

The City of the Falls Company operated the Pavilion Hotel beginning in 1833 but the Pavilion was soon eclipsed by the new Clifton House. The Clifton House was built by Harmanus Crysler and opened in 1835 on the Ferry Road on the site of present day Oakes Garden Theatre. The property was originally part of the 162 ha (400 acres) of Crown land granted to Philip George Bender in 1790. Bender settled here in 1782 or earlier, and the Bender family is generally acknowledged to be Niagara Falls' first settlers. The Bender land grant adjoined the Ellsworth Crown Grant. It extended along the River from a point close to what is now Robinson Street to within 1.2 km (.75 mi.) of the present Whirlpool Rapids Bridge. In the early 1800's Bender sold part of his land to Christopher Boughner who operated a farm on it.

In the early 1830's Captain Ogden Creighton, a retired British Army Officer, bought 21 ha (52 acres) of Boughner's farm including the land which was

The Clifton Hotel on the Ferry Road, circa 1835. Water colour by Sir Henry W. Barnard.

Sigmund Samuel Collection Royal Ontario Museum

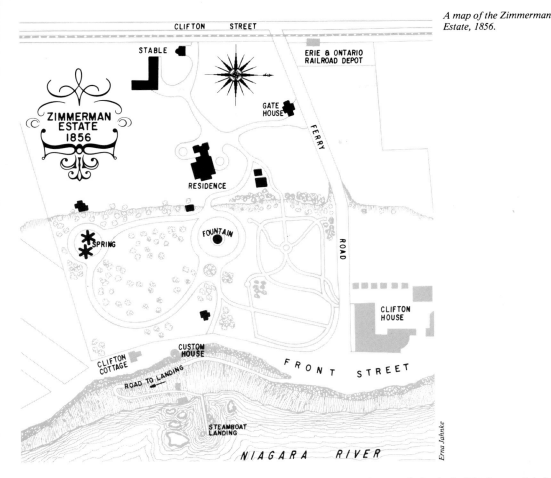

A map of the Zimmerman Estate, 1856.

south of the Ferry Road and within the boundaries of the present Queen Victoria Park. In a letter dated York U.C. 1832, sent to Mrs. E. Lyon in England, Sir John Colborne, the Lieutenant-Governor of Upper Canada, wrote: "Captain Creighton . . . has bought property at the Falls of Niagara and intends to build and give his residence the name of Clifton. The spray from the Cataract is to be the gentle dew of his garden."

In the late 1840's Samuel Zimmerman purchased Captain Creighton's "Clifton Estate" from Creighton's widow. Zimmerman, an American from Pennysylvania arrived in the area in 1842. A shrewd businessman and a contractor, he made a quick fortune from construction contracts, building locks on the Second Welland Canal and laying roadbed and tracks for the Great Western Railway. He began to plan an elaborate estate of his own on the Creighton property. He built stables and a house in which to live while his

great mansion was being built. The lower plain below the high bank, in what is now Queen Victoria Park was laid out with paths and shrubs and trees were planted. A fountain was built, activated by the gravitational force of the spring water coming out of the base of the high bank.

Gate Houses were built at the entrances to his estate, one on the Ferry Road and the other on the lower level close to the Toll Road along the gorge bank. The latter was to become the first Administrative Office of Queen Victoria Park. Zimmerman died tragically in a train accident at the Desjardins Canal in 1857. His property was sold to J.T. Bush, who then sold off the property below the high bank in smaller lots. On these the new owners erected buildings including a small hotel, greenhouses and a livery stable. These lots below the high bank were expropriated by the Queen Victoria Niagara Falls Park Commissioners in 1887.

The Front

The area around Table Rock and the Horseshoe Falls was to change and become the scene of unprincipled competition for the tourist's dollar. In 1827 Thomas Barnett built the first substantial building in the area, about 91 m (300 ft.) south of Table Rock. In it he established a Museum. Then he built a stairway down the gorge wall alongside the stairway operated by Isaiah Starkey, and conducted visitors Behind the Sheet in competition with Starkey. In the early 1840's Barnett built his second Museum, a frame building with a rough cast exterior, at the foot of the Murray Street ravine. At the same time he opened a zoological annex in the old distillery on the north side of Murray street, opposite the new Museum. An undated account written prior to 1844 reported that the Museum contained upward of 5,000 specimens: "There are bipeds, and quadrupeds, birds, fishes, insects, reptiles, shells and minerals and Indian curiosities, all regulated to delight the eye and improve the understanding and mend the heart. Of the birds, beasts, fishes and insects, several hundred species were caught in the vicinity of the Falls."[1]

In 1844 Saul Davis who came from the Buffalo area, built the Prospect House on a site south of Barnett's new Museum. About the same time other businesses were established along the Chain Reserve near Table Rock and conditions became so bad that a visitor wrote in 1847: "Now the neighbourhood of the great wonder is overrun with every species of abominable fungus - the growth of rank bad taste, with equal luxuriance on the English and the American sides - Chinese pagoda, menagerie, camera obscura, museum watch tower, wooden monument and old curiosity shops."[2]

In 1852 the St. Catharines, Thorold and Niagara Falls Toll Road Company, headed by William Hamilton Merritt, petitioned the Ordnance Board for permission to construct a macadamized road, which would be a toll road, on the Chain Reserve from the Ferry Road to Table Rock. The Ordnance representative who inspected the site noted: "The Chain Reserve at this point occupies about 9 acres. Its intrinsic value is nothing, being mostly bare rock."[3] He had no objection to the application and noted further "a road already had been partly formed along the Chain Reserve by the Suspension Bridge Company without the permission from Ordnance." He recommended that permission be granted. The road was called Front Street and the portion within today's Queen Victoria Park, extending from Murray Street to Table Rock, was called "The Front".

In 1853 Saul Davis turned over the management of the Prospect House to his cousin Colonel Isaacs. He then built a hotel which he called Table Rock House immediately south of Barnett's Table Rock House, that is, between Barnett's Table Rock House and the Table Rock, thus effectively cutting off Barnett's customers. In this location Davis could intercept any potential customers of Barnett's. The resulting competition between Davis and Barnett became so fierce that before it was over, it would include a homicide, the destruction of stairways by

Addison Gallery of American Art

The old distillery at the bottom of the ravine, where Thomas Barnett established the zoological annex to his Museum. John Maude wrote in his Visit to the Falls of Niagara in 1800 *"Descending a very steep and difficult road, I came to a deserted distillery, where I stopped to recover my breath, and to allay my thirst at an excellent spring." This view is from a water colour, circa 1815, by William Dunlap.*

vandalism, fire and explosives, and the harassment and abuse of visitors. The cost of photographs, souvenirs and going Behind the Sheet was misrepresented and the tourist who didn't readily pay the exhorbitant prices demanded was threatened and abused both verbally and physically. Visitors who wanted only to enjoy close-up the scenic beauty of the Falls, were victimized. The Front became notorious as a tourist trap.

An example of how some tourists were treated is recorded in testimony given under oath by George Loveridge at the libel trial *Saul Davis vs The Hamilton Evening Times 1868.* In the Spring of 1867 The Times ran a series of stories on Saul Davis in which Table Rock House was called "the den of the forty thieves". Davis sued the newspaper for libel

and on November 6, 1868 the trial was held in St. Catharines. In 1860 Davis had been given a lease from the Crown to use the Chain Reserve for a stairway and to pass tourists Behind the Sheet, on condition "that he allow all persons free access to the Falls by the pathway at the foot of the Rock (Table Rock) and at all times pass people down his stairway for a charge not to exceed 25 cents."[4] Davis did not fulfil the terms of the lease.

Loveridge's testimony at the trial, examined by Mr. Gibson: "I reside at Churchville in the State of New York . . . and on 3rd July, 1866, in company with Lyman Carter and four ladies, I visited the Falls; we engaged a cab to drive from the Bridge to the Falls, without asking to be taken to any particular place; we were driven up to the steps of Table Rock Hotel, and

The Prospect House on the Front was sometimes patronized by royalty. In January, 1879, Her Royal Highness Princess Louise and her husband, His Excellency the Marquis of Lorne, Governor-General of Canada, stayed in the Royal suite during a four day visit to Niagara Falls. In 1888 the Prospect House with its outbuildings, including stables, a chicken house, an ice house, a wood shed and outside toilet facilities, was sold at auction. The buildings were demolished and the Annual Report of the Commissioners for 1888 reported: "as soon as the weather permitted, filling up the large cellars and levelling and seeding down the grounds . . . followed, and by the beginning of June all the wooden buildings which had so scarred the beauty of the place were removed and nature invited to resume her more perfect work".

Barnett's Table Rock House with Saul Davis' Table Rock House at the right, circa 1860.

Table Rock House, built by Saul Davis in 1853. From a photograph by William Notman.

pressingly invited into the house, being told the House was free of charge; we went to the observatory, on descending, we were met by . . . (porters) on the second floor, who invited us to put on oil cloth suits to go under the Falls by the circling stairs, saying at the same time there would be no charge; and that it was all free; the ladies were pressed off into one room, and the gentlemen into another; shortly after one of their females came and told us the ladies were anxious to go under the Falls; when after a great deal of pressing we put on the suits, we were taken to a point in the hall where the ladies could see us and thinking that we

wanted them to go under, after a great deal of hesitation they also put on clothing, and went down the stairs, and we proceeded under the Falls; on returning, the ladies made purchases to the extent of eight or ten dollars; stayed in the neighbourhood of Table Rock about two hours. Saul Davis invited us into the hotel to register our names; we did so; a young lady had charge of the register book; after the registry, the lady demanded twelve dollars; asked how this could be as the . . . . (porters) had said there was nothing to pay; she said it was a charge whereon the Government received one-half; about five or six .

Table Rock and two stairways down the gorge wall, circa 1840. An oil painting by Guerlok Rock.

Niagara Parks Archives

Thomas Barnett's Museum, built in 1859 at a cost of $150,000, on the site of the present day Victoria Park Restaurant. With its colonnade front and upper balcony surrounded by a Corinthian facade, its architectural design surpassed all other buildings on the Front.

. . (porters) came around, and on our telling them that they had previously stated there was no charge, they used profane language, and said we lied; shook their fists in our faces, and spoke very excitedly . . . I then told them what I thought of them and was about to depart, when a . . . (porter) stood in a defiant attitude at the door and refused to allow us to leave; as I approached him he pushed me nearly across the room; then he swung both fists in my face and said ' - - - (expletive deleted), you can't go out of that room without paying what I ask'; a gentleman who was with me named Lyman Carter, attempted to go out, and he was treated in the same way; two . . . (porters) put their fists under his nose, telling him he could not go out until he paid $12.00; about this time I offered $4.00 in payment; then I enquired if I could send a message to a policeman, magistrate or the American Consul; the reply was I had to pay the $12.00 American currency; my friend paid the $12.00 and we were allowed to pass out; the ladies in my company were very much excited and afraid; it was only to allay that excitement that my friend Carter paid the $12.00."[5]

The Times was able to amass a veritable mountain of evidence to support its condemnation of Davis. Not all the people who offered to come to testify could be accommodated, only a few were chosen. They were representative of the people from all over the United States, mainly from New York State and Pennsylvania who had been subjected to Davis' abuse. The verdict went in favour of the newspaper. Saul Davis lost the suit.

In 1859 Barnett moved the building which housed his Musuem and erected a new Museum building on the same site at the foot of the Murray Street ravine. Under the terms of the joint lease granted to Barnett and Davis in 1860, Barnett had the right of passage along the talus, up to and behind the Sheet of Falling Water at the Horseshoe Falls. To allow his patrons to get down the gorge bank in front of his new Museum Barnett claimed that he had "at great expense . . . spent some $2,000 in having his present stairs cut out of solid rock, which he gives the public free use of." From the bottom of these steps there was a pathway along the top of the talus which went past Davis' stairway to the foot of the Horseshoe Falls where people were guided Behind the Sheet. Mrs. Davis, on hearing of Barnett's claim, countered with a sworn statement that Barnett's "stairs" actually formed a roadway which Barnett had cut into the gorge wall in front of his new Museum, to make a grade for a "horse-railroad" by which he brought up blocks of limestone from the lower river to the upper level. She claimed that Barnett had the limestone cut and fashioned by his masons to be used in the building of his Museum. When he finished quarrying the limestone, he cleared the grade, forming a pathway, which was used by his patrons to get to the talus path.[6]

Davis soon ignored the terms of the joint lease which allowed Barnett the right of passage on the talus slope to the Horseshoe Falls. He put up a "wall", actually a stone fence with a gate, at the northern boundary of his property and extracted a fee from Barnett's customers who had to go through his area to reach the foot of the Horseshoe Falls. He closed the gate in 1861 when Barnett refused to pay.[7]

Barnett complained and the joint lease was cancelled in 1862, when the citizens of Clifton supported Barnett with a signed petition charging Davis with "alleged fraudulent practices, extortions and ill treatment of visitors." Davis could no longer legally use his stairway nor take people "Behind the Sheet". Barnett now had a monopoly, his customers passed unhindered along the talus path, past Davis' property to the Horseshoe Falls.

Davis immediately began to use his stairway again without authorization and trouble brewed. The *Niagara Falls Gazette* of April 23, 1865 reported this incident: "Mr. Saul Davis' stairway down the bank at Table Rock - Canada side - was burned down one night last week. Of course it was set fire to by someone unfriendly to Mr. Davis. People who have been duped there, an e are said to be many - will

Table Rock and the Front looking towards Barnett's Museum, circa 1862. Robinson's Pagoda is at the left, a lattice work tower enclosing a stairway which led to an observation platform. The top of Saul Davis' stairway is in the left foreground. The Clifton Hotel located on the site of present day Oakes Garden Theatre is in the background. A photograph by William Notman.

Niagara Falls New York Public Library

Looking toward the Front from the Ferry Road. The toll road runs along the top of the cliff. J.T. Brundage's livery stable is in the upper centre. Barnett's Museum, Saul Davis' Table Rock House and the other buildings along the Front are in the distance, circa 1870's. From a stereograph by B.W. Kilburn.

say 'served him right'. Saturday morning the Davises came to Mr. Barnett's staircase with a party and insisted on using the stairs free. Mr. Barnett objected, demanding the same charge of Davis as of others. Davis marshalled his forces and a large row seemed imminent, when the Davis party withdrew deeming discretion the greater part of valour.''

Davis was enraged. He had his runners circulate rumours among the tourists that Barnett's pathway was unsafe. The Gazette of April 23, 1865 reported further: "This week under the plea of rebuilding, Davis has been industrious in throwing stones and dirt over the bank and evidently for the purpose of preventing people (Barnett's patrons) from appoaching nearer to the sheet of water.'' He went on doing this all through the 1865 tourist season. It was not until December 19, 1865 that a restraining order was placed on Davis, preventing him "from excavating or interfering with the cliff or bank, from throwing masses of rock down the said cliff.''[8]

In 1866 Davis once again obtained a lease for his stairway, but in the same year it was sold on a writ of execution to settle a debt. The purchaser was Rolland Macdonald, Thomas Barnett's standing counsel. Macdonald transferred the lease to Barnett who once again had complete control of the descent to the bottom of the gorge at the Horseshoe Falls. Barnett now had two leases and in 1869 he arranged to have both leases cancelled and replaced by one lease which gave him full control of the talus slope on the Chain from his Museum to the Horseshoe Falls.

In 1867 at Confederation, the Reserve came under the jurisdiction of the newly created Province of Ontario. Davis erected a new stairway and began taking tourists Behind the Sheet in 1869, claiming that he had received authority from the Province of Ontario.

Barnett and Davis employed runners and guides, some of them enforcers and "heavies". An ugly incident occured in 1870 which would damage

The first recorded rock fall from Table Rock occurred in July 1818. Other sections broke off in 1828 and 1829. This sketch depicts the great fall of June 26, 1850 when a large mass 61m (200 ft.) long and 18m (60 ft.) wide fell into the gorge below. A cab driver who was washing his omnibus on the rock at the time narrowly escaped with his life. Subsequent falls in 1853, 1876 and 1897 left Table Rock as only a slight promontory. Finally in 1935 what was left of the overhang was blasted off. Table Rock remains today in name only.

Niagara Falls New York Public Library

Barnett's image. Both Barnett and Davis were photographing tourists, using the Falls as a backdrop. Edward Davis, one of Saul's sons, also took photos from a point at the head of the Ferry Road. To reach his "business location" Edward Davis had to pass in front of Barnett's Museum, now the location of the Victoria Park Restaurant, pulling his photographic cart behind him. On the evening of June 25, 1870, Davis was passing Barnett's Museum when he was attacked by a group of Barnett's men "throwing sticks and stones and an iron hatchet".[9] In self defense and fearing for his life, Edward Davis drew a pistol and fired it among his attackers, wounding one man who subsequently died. Davis was tried for homicide and acquitted. Thomas Barnett was reprimanded by the court and judged responsible for instigating the harassment of Edward Davis.

Davis' lawyers found a loophole in Barnett's lease. Barnett had been paying his rent to the Office of the Secretary of State in Ottawa, and continued this practice after Confederation when the Reserve came under the control of the Province of Ontario. It was 1872 and the rent should have been paid to the Province of Ontario. As Davis was persona non grata in the eyes of the Provincial Crown Lands Department, his wife applied for a lease, claiming that the Davis property had been transferred to her name in 1867. In the memorandum submitted by Mrs. Davis' lawyers to the Crown Land Department, to support her request for the cancellation of the Barnett monopoly she wrote: "Prior to the granting of the Barnett lease in 1866 when the Davises were deprived of the privilege, three different stairways were destroyed by violence - one was chopped down, one was blown up by gunpowder and a third set fire to in the night."[10]

Through all this turmoil, Barnett was the one who suffered most financially. He made nominal charges for his Museum and his Behind the Sheet concession. Davis was prospering by overcharging people. Barnett, in an attempt to restore his finances, planned a grand promotion for 1872 - a Buffalo Hunt and Wild West Show with Wild Bill Hickok. The event was set for August 28-30 but it was a fiasco,

only about two thousand people were in attendance. Barnett lost more than $20,000 on the affair. This was the beginning of his financial downfall.

Things got worse as the years passed. On November 6, 1876 the *Niagara Falls Gazette* reported that "Thomas Barnett, the proprietor of Barnett's Museum over the river, sold his stock of buffaloes, consisting of three full-grown animals and a calf, to an agent of P.T. Barnum the famous showman. The sum realized from the sale was $700."

In 1877 Barnett's Museum and other buildings went on public sale to satisfy his debts. Saul Davis, his arch enemy, purchased all of Barnett's property and so took virtual control of the Front. Davis operated the Museum and other concessions on the Front for ten years without competition before the Queen Victoria Park Commissioners took over. The Commissioners, after due consideration and in need of the income, allowed Saul Davis to operate Table Rock House and the Museum under strict supervision until the Spring of 1888 just before the opening of Queen Victoria Park.

Niagara Falls New York Public Library

The American Falls from Canada, circa 1870. From a stereograph by C.L. Pond. There are cows grazing in the centre foreground. The Front View House is at the right.

The Niagara Falls Park Its Establishment

Over the years various people have been credited with the first suggestion that the area around the Falls of Niagara should be made into a public preserve. It is not easy to choose one person, either from the United States side, or from the Canadian side, to whom this credit should be given.

Actually the idea that the area adjacent to the Falls should be set aside, occurred to many of the early travellers, who recorded their thoughts in letters and articles which were often published. One of these was the Duc de Rochefoucault-Liancourt who visited the Falls of Niagara in 1795. His account of the visit is more of a complaint than a description: "It is much regretted that the government of a people which surpasses all other nations in fondness for travelling and curiosity should not have provided convenient places for observing this phenomenon from all possible points of view".[1]

E.T. Coke in 1832 was possibly the first to make a positive suggestion: "Tis a pity that such ground was not reserved as sacred in perpetuum; that the forest trees were not allowed to luxuriate in all their wild and savage beauty about a spot where the works of man will ever appear paltry".[2]

No action resulted from Coke's comments, nor from the great numbers of others that were made in the next twenty years. It fell to Frederic Church, the renowned American landscape artist, to initiate the movement that would result in the establishment of public parks in both Canada and the United States. Church came to Niagara Falls in 1856 and took up a

position at the crest of the Horseshoe and made preliminary sketches for his painting of the Horseshoe Falls. While he was here he became annoyed and upset by the rampant commercialism and other unwelcome intrusions which detracted from the natural beauty of the Falls. He left after his sketching was completed, obsessed with the idea that the area around the Falls should be set aside as a public park. Church was one of the most renowned landscape artists in the United States and he was much sought after as a guest for social events. At these affairs he met people of means and influence. He took every opportunity to talk about the desecration of the area around the Falls of Niagara and to try to gather converts to his cause - the establishment of public parks at Niagara Falls.

Church found a ready supporter in Frederick Law Olmstead, a successful landscape architect. Olmstead wrote in 1879: "I have myself been an occasional visitor to Niagara for forty-five years. My attention was first called to the rapidly approaching ruin of its characteristic scenery, by Mr. F.E. Church about ten years ago. Shortly afterwards, several gentlemen, frequenters of the Falls met at my request to consider this danger, one of them being a member of the Commission now reporting on this subject".[3] Olmstead was referring to William Dorsheimer who was at the time District Attorney for the Northern District of New York, later to become Lieutenant-Governor and a United States Congressman.

Olmstead later wrote a letter to Thomas Welch,

first Superintendent of the State Reservation at Niagara Falls, recalling the incident: "While rambling on Goat Island with Mr. Dorsheimer and Mr. Richardson I brought the subject before them . . . I cannot fix the date but have an impression that it was September 1869. It can be determined by finding when Mr. Dorsheimer, Mr. Richardson and I were registered on the book of the Cataract House". The date was later confirmed as being August 7, 1869.[4]

Olmstead, Dorsheimer, Richardson and Church kept the public park scheme in mind, discussing it at every opportunity with anyone they thought could help. Then Church conceived the idea of appealing to the Governor-General of Canada, Lord Dufferin, as a way of getting Canadian co-operation. How he contacted Lord Dufferin is described in a letter Church wrote to Welch: ". . . A long time has elapsed since the idea occurred to me that Niagara Falls should be reserved as a Park . . . The importance of having the co-operation of Canada finally determined me to take advantage of the kind services of William H. Hurlbut, Esq., then editor of the *New York World* and a friend of Lord Dufferin, who wrote to him on the subject. I opened the matter to several of my friends who received it with so much enthusiasm that I was glad to leave it in their hands for such action as they deemed advisable, but no publicity was given until Lord Dufferin alluded to it in a speech."[5]

Considering the evidence, the honour of being the first proponent of the public park scheme should belong to Frederic Church. However, Lord Dufferin, Governor-General of Canada, should get credit for making the first public suggestion, followed by the first official action toward the improvement of conditions at Niagara Falls.

In 1878 Lord Dufferin spoke to the Ontario Society of Artists at Toronto. Near the end of his speech he put in his endorsement for a public park at Niagara Falls: "And now, gentlemen, before I sit down there is another topic to which I would for a moment refer. I am about to confide to you a mission which, though not directly in your line, is sufficiently connected with your pursuits to justify me in demanding your assistance. In your neighbourhood there exists, as you are aware, one of the most wondrous, beautiful, and stupendous scenes which the forces of nature have ever constructed. Indeed so majestic is the subject, that though many skillful hands have endeavoured to transfer it to canvas, few have succeeded in adequately depicting its awe-inspiring characteristics. I allude to the Falls of Niagara. But I am further sure that everyone will agree with me in thinking that the pleasure he may have derived from his pilgrimage to so famous a spot, whether as an artist or a simple tourist, has been miserably marred and defeated by the inconvenience and annoyance he has experienced at the hands of the various squatting interests that have taken possession of every point of vantage at the Falls to tax the pocket and irritate the nerves of the visitors, and by whom - just at the moment when he is about to give up his whole being to the contemplation of the scene before him, as he is about to feel the inspiration of the natural beauties around him, - his imagination and poetic faculties are suddenly shocked and disorganized with a demand for ten cents. Some few weeks ago, I had

Niagara Falls, an oil painting by Frederic Edward Church, 1857.

the good fortune to meet His Excellency the Governor of the State of New York, and I then suggested an idea which had long been present to my mind, that the Governments of New York and of Ontario or Canada should combine to acquire whatever rights may have been established against the public, and to form around the Falls a small public international park ... Nothing could have been more gratifying or gracious than the response which His Excellency the Governor of New York was good enough to make my representations, and he encouraged me to hope that, should a fitting opportunity present itself, he and his government might be induced, if not to take the initiative in the matter, at all events to co-operate heartily with our own in carrying out such a plan as I have sketched. Nowhere in the world are all the arrangements connected with pleasure grounds better understood than upon this continent. You possess quite a specialty in that respect, and if on either side of the river the areas adapted for such a purpose were put under the charge of proper guardians, and the present guides organized into an efficient and disciplined staff, it would be a source of increased gratification to thousands and thousands of persons. Now of course we all know that what is everybody's business is nobody's business, and notwithstanding the all-embracing energy of my honourable and learned friend upon my right, it is not the kind of thing which probably would have come to the notice of his Government unless the matter was previously agitated by some powerful interest. It is for this reason that I take the opportunity of addressing an audience who I am certain will sympathize with such a project on this subject, and of urging upon them, the advisability of bringing their influence to bear in the direction I have suggested".[6]

Oliver Mowat, the Premier of Ontario, was the "honourable and learned friend" who was seated upon Lord Dufferin's right. Mowat became interested in Lord Dufferin's proposal and eventually presided over the creation of the public park on the Canadian side at Niagara Falls.

Lord Dufferin immediately wrote to Governor Robinson of New York State asking him to lend his support in the effort to convince the Governments of Canada and the United States to join together in the legal and prompt removal of the commercial interests around the Falls and of forming on either side of the river an "International Park" with a staff of the necessary guides and guardians.[7] Dufferin also wrote to the Ontario Government, appealing for their support. This ended Lord Dufferin's participation in the public park scheme, his term as Governor-

General came to an end and he left Canada by the end of 1878.

At the opening of the New York State Legislature in Janurary 1879, Governor Robinson strongly recommended that Lord Dufferin's suggestion be given support. The Legislature took action and directed the Commissioners of the State of New York to report on the project and gave them the authority to confer with the representatives of either the Dominion of Canada or the Province of Ontario. The Commissioners first act was to appoint James T. Gardiner, Director of the State Geological Survey, and Frederick Law Olmstead, the distinguished landscape architect, to visit and assess the area adjoining the Cataracts on both sides of the river and make recommendations as to how the proposed park scheme should be put into effect. They carried out the inspection and in 1879 brought in their report which had particular reference to the American side.

The United States Board of Commissioners of the State Survey adopted the report and then met with members of the Ontario Cabinet in September 1879. Maps showing the proposed areas of the Parks on both sides of the river were displayed. The suggested land acquisitions outlined in this report were much the same as those eventually chosen. The Ontario representatives expressed their support but claimed that the Dominion Government should assume the cost of establishing the park since it claimed jurisdiction over most of the lands involved. From this point the Canadian project would come to a halt for three and a half years, while the United States scheme would be carried on, proceeding by fits and starts until the New York State Reservation at Niagara Falls would become a reality in 1885.

A Bill to authorize the acquisition of lands for a State Reservation at Niagara Falls was brought before the Legislature of New York State in 1880. It passed the Legislature but not the Senate. In 1881 a similar Bill was introduced but because of the incumbent Governor Alonzo Cornell's opposition the Bill was abandoned. The greatest obstacle to the park scheme was callous indifference. On one occasion, after listening to an eloquent and impassioned description of the shoddy conditions around the Falls, Governor Cornell is reported to have said: "Well, the water goes over just the same, doesn't it?"[8]

The movement for a public park was reinforced by an appeal made in 1880 in the form of memorials addressed to Governor Cornell and to the Governor-General of Canada by citizens of the United States and Canada, together with residents of other lands.

The Canada Southern Railway at Niagara, an oil painting by Robert Whale, 1870.

The National Gallery of Canada, Ottawa

Among the prominent men who signed their names to the memorials were: Carlyle, Emerson, Longfellow, Whittier, Holmes, Lowell and Ruskin.

Lord Dufferin was succeeded as Governor-General by the Marquis of Lorne. In 1883 the new Governor-General wrote an article, accompanied by illustrations, which put forward the desirability of a public park around the Falls. In June of the same year in Toronto, he addressed the Royal Academy and the Ontario Society of Artists, and brought up the matter of a public park at Niagara Falls: "There is only one other subject I would like to mention . . . it is one mooted by Lord Dufferin in this very place . . . some years ago. He asked me when I came not to lose sight of it, but to push it upon all possible occasion. I allude to the formation of a national park at Niagara."

In 1882 Grover Cleveland became Governor of New York State. The public park supporters waited until 1883 before they brought in a Bill entitled "An Act to Authorize the Selection, Location and Appropriation of Certain Lands in the Village of Niagara Falls for a State Reservation; and to Preserve the Scenery of the Falls of Niagara". The Bill passed both the New York State Legislative Assembly and the Senate. On April 30, 1885 it was signed into law by Governor Hill.[9]

A Board of five Commissioners including William Dorsheimer, was appointed to select the lands required for the new Reservation. The Commissioners selected 166.7 ha (412 acres) of land including Prospect Park, Goat Island, and Bath Island. Appraisers were appointed and on the basis of their report, the Supreme Court of New York set the value of the property at $1,452,810.40 including arbitration and other incidental costs, for 45.3 ha (112 acres) of land out of the water and the buildings occupying the property.[10] After a difficult battle, the legislation was passed providing State funds to pay the arbitration awards. Governor Hill, successor to Governor Cleveland, signed the appropriation legislation on April 30, 1885, the last day for approval allowed by law. The newly acquired New York State Reservation was formally opened for public use on July 15, 1885.

While the Americans were going through their process of establishing the State Reservation at Niagara Falls, New York, a peculiar battle was being waged between the Ontario and the Dominion Governments in Canada. Premier Oliver Mowat of Ontario was interested in seeing a public park established on the Canadian side of Niagara Falls but the vociferous opposition he was receiving from the Conservative Party and their supporting newspapers made him disclaim all responsibility for establishing the park. In New York State the newspapers, no matter what their political persuasion, were in support of the public park project at

Niagara Falls. Mowat was kept constantly informed of the progress being made on the American side but he could not report in return any similar progress on the part of his Government.[11]

Ownership and jurisdiction over the Chain Reserve, the Crown Land along the river bank which was surrendered to Upper Canada by the Ordnance Branch in London in 1852, was important to the establishment of a park. While it was presumed that Crown Lands had reverted to the Province of Ontario at Confederation in 1867, neither the Provincial nor the Dominion Government wanted to accept responsibility for the land. Both levels of Government were saying that they could not establish a park because they did not have control of the Chain Reserve.[12]

The Ontario Government sought to prove its case by pointing out that the Niagara River was a navigable waterway and an International Boundary and so was under federal jurisdiction. The Dominion Government countered by saying that the Chain Reserve had passed to the Ontario Government at the time of Confederation and in that year, the Ontario Government had given leases along this Chain Reserve to Saul Davis and Thomas Barnett.[13]
In February of 1880 Premier Mowat introduced legislation entitled: "An Act Respecting Niagara Falls and the Adjacent Territory", in an attempt to force the Dominion Government to action. This bill would allow the Dominion Government to expropriate land as needed to add to the Chain Reserve for the purpose of establishing a Federal Park at Niagara Falls. The Act was passed on February 24, 1880. Mowat thought that with the passing of this Act he would safely and firmly place the matter of a public park at Niagara Falls in the Dominion Government's lap. He was mistaken, as time would tell.

The Dominion Government's response to Mowat's tactic was the appointment of a Federal Niagara Falls Park Commission, a Commission that would turn out to be only a sham. John A. Macdonald, the Prime Minister, was afraid to take the initiative to establish a national park at Niagara Falls because of opposition he knew would come from the Maritimes and Quebec. The formation of a public park at Niagara Falls was stalled.

Three and a half years were wasted while both Governments stood their ground. Private entrepreneurs wanting to develop the Park for their own gain soon took advantage of the indecision shown by the two levels of Government. They submitted proposals for the development of a private park on land that would be leased from the Provincial Government. The Canada Southern Railroad helped bring matters to a head. The Railway was building its line in 1883 along the high bank above the Falls and it was rumoured that the Company wanted to build a bridge over the gorge between the Clifton House and the Falls. The spectre of a bridge in this location with an adjoining railway yard was enough to arouse public attention. The Canada Southern Railroad for its part was not projecting a good public image. It had proprietary rights allowing it to cut down trees and throw earth over the bank, which it did in the area above the Horseshoe Falls, destroying the wooded hillside with the earth fill which it refused to haul away because it would cost too much money. The public became alarmed at this despoliation of the high bank and at what might happen in other areas if the Government didn't take over and establish a pubic park.[14]

Mowat was finally moved to action and on December 15, 1884 he asked Casimir Gzowski to be chairman of a possible Ontario Government Niagara Falls Park Commission. Gzowski agreed to act. The Premier was spurred to further action when two railway proposals were put forward, to construct a railway coming into Niagara Falls from Queenston. Both proposals had the possibility of being primarily land speculation schemes and to forestall them, Mowat on March 20, 1885 introduced the "Niagara Falls Park Act - An Act for the Preservation of the Natural Scenery about Niagara Falls." The Act's object was to procure valuation of the land required for Park purposes. The Act left open the question of private or public ownership of the proposed park and it included a provision which would allow the transfer of any Commission acquired lands to a private company if the Provincial Government so desired.

Queen Victoria Park

The Niagara Falls Park Act was passed by the Ontario Legislature on March 30, 1885. On April 25, Colonel Casimir Stanislaus Gzowski, John W. Langmuir and John G. Macdonald were appointed Commissioners. The new Commissioners possessed extremely high qualifications for the task assigned them. Colonel Gzowski's engineering accomplishments and John Langmuir's business experience in particular were to be a great asset to the people of Ontario when they were applied to the task at hand – the establishment of Queen Victoria Park.

The Commissioners' first task was the selection of land for the Park. The natural topographic features of the area around the Falls marked out what should constitute the Park. It remained for the Commissioners to fit their selection of the lands into the finances available.

A survey was made of the area which was finally decided upon, described in the 10th Annual Report for the Queen Victoria Park Commissioners, 1895, as follows: "From the Clifton House southwards, following the general direction of the river, and at a distance of about 300 yards from the edge of the rocky wall of the gorge, there is a beautifully wooded escarpment rising over 100 feet above the general level of the plateau immediately adjacent to the gorge, and leading up to the general level of the table land between the two lakes. This escarpment is clearly defined up to and beyond the head of the rapids and it was decided that a better boundary could not be chosen to delimit the territory reserved for a park. The intention of the Commissioners was at

first to select a line embracing the whole of the escarpment, but it was found that the adjoining proprietors put a very high value on the land forming the very edge of the bluff, and in consequence a line a little below the top of the escarpment was chosen; thus securing to the park the slope with its wealth of foliage, while at the same time all commanding views obtained from the table land above were retained by the owners, and their demands for compensation for the portion taken below the table land made less onerous. The lands thus selected comprised a total area of some 154 acres and embrace all the land from the escarpment already described, to the river, including Cedar Island, the Dufferin group of islands, and the talus under the cliff from the Clifton House southwards to the margin of the Horseshoe Falls".[1]

An Order in Council was passed on December 14, 1885 confirming the Commissioners' selection of land for the new Park, and authorizing them to employ experts to value the lands and buildings. The appraisal was completed in January, 1886, but the Commissioners were able to settle with only two of the owners. The purchase prices for the other nineteen properties were referred to the Provincial Arbitrators under the provisions of the Public Works Act of Ontario. At the end of 1886, when the Arbitrators reported, the total amount of the arbitration awards was $436,813.24.

The Commissioners then recommended that the Provincial Government should authorize the issue of $525,000. of forty-four year bonds bearing 4% interest, with principal and interest guaranteed by the

The Arbitration Awards for the lands and buildings acquired for Queen Victoria Park.

Owner's Name	Amount Awarded	Amount Offered by the Commissioners
Bush	$34,000	$27,500
Lyman, Moore	2,900	1,675
Tench, E.A.	8,000	5,500
Tench Jr.	1,500	1,000
Robinson, Eliz.	3,600	3,500
Robinson, W.	3,600	3,500
Brundage, J.	15,050	11,388
Buchanan, W.O.	21,767	17,861
Wood, Peter	14,000	11,400
Newton, W.	400	400
Clarke, P.S.	2,500	1,500
Buchanan, Estate of Jas.	1,550	1,000
Buchanan, Estate of R.S.	5,600	7,120
Davis, Saul	102,500	98,750
Davis, Ellen	35,000	25,000
Davis, Prospect House	37,500	37,500
Gladstone, Mrs.	8,252	6,500
Toll gate	3,900	2,500
Macklem, S.	100,000	26,175
Canada Southern R.R.	150	100
Vanderbilt	860	450
Brett	250	250
	$402,879	$290,569

Awards made later to J.T. Bush, and to the St. Catharines, Thorold and Niagara Falls Toll Road Company brought the total to $436,813.24.

Province, and to form a charge against the revenues of the Park. The money raised by the bond issue would be used to purchase the lands and to do the necessary renovations and improvements. The Commissioners' mandate under the 1885 Niagara Falls Park Act was now complete.

The Government approved the recommendations put forward and in order to implement them the "Queen Victoria Niagara Falls Park Act" was passed on April 23, 1887[3], reappointing the three Commissioners as a corporation called "The Commissioners for the Queen Victoria Niagara Falls Park." A fourth Commissioner, John A. Orchard of the Town of Niagara Falls was appointed soon afterwards. The Act provided that the lands already selected, as well as other lands that might be acquired, should be vested in the Commissioners as trustees for the Province of Ontario. In their corporate

capacity they were also authorized to issue and sell debentures not exceeding $525,000. and to apply the proceeds of their sale to the purchase of the lands and to making necessary improvements.[2]

Wide powers were vested in the Commissioners regarding the collection of tolls, making of by-laws, the appointment of superintendents or managers, gardeners, workmen, etc., although their decisions were subject to the approval of the Lieutenant-Governor.

On May 5, 1887, the Commission appointed James Wilson, a civil engineer, to be Superintendent of the Park. The Commissioners arranged for a temporary loan while the bonds were being prepared, to pay for the properties of which immediate possession could be taken. The whole bond issue was sold at a premium of 1.0184% realizing $534,667.14. The Commissioners were now able to pay the arbitration awards and they took possession of the various properties early in the summer of 1887.

Work was begun at once. The larger buildings such as Table Rock House, Prospect House and the Museum all had outbuildings - stables, chicken coops, ice houses, summer kitchens and in the case of the Museum a monkey house and a bear pit. Most of these undesirable buildings were removed. The Prospect House, with its outbuildings, was auctioned off. Saul Davis and his family were allowed to retain possession of both Table Rock House and the Museum until their new Museum was built on the U.S. side. They were allowed to sell off any merchandise in stock but were not allowed to order or stock any new merchandise in their fancy goods stores. Saul Davis was allowed to operate the "Behind the Sheet" attraction until March 1888, under strict scrutiny of the Commissioners. The old Barnett Table Rock House adjoining Table Rock House was lowered and roofed to serve as a drive shed for the protection of the carriage horses while the cab drivers' fares were going "Behind the Sheet". Street's Pagoda, the observation tower on Cedar Island, was removed and the building which stood at its foot became a gatekeeper's residence. The bridges connecting Cedar Island with the mainland were strengthened and the road leading to the Cynthia Islands, now called the Dufferin Islands, was improved.

Gate houses made of cedar bark, were built at the entrances to the Park. The main gate located on the Ferry Road opposite the Clifton House, was called Mowat Gate in honour of Oliver Mowat, Premier of Ontario. The gate at the southern entrance to the Park was named Dufferin Gate in honour of Lord

Dufferin, former Governor-General of Canada. There were also smaller gates at Robinson Street and Murray Street. Turnstiles were installed at all entrances to provide an accurate count of each day's attendance.

With so many facilities available for the use and enjoyment of today's visitors to Queen Victoria Park, it is hard to imagine that earlier conditions were quite different. When the Act forming the new Park was passed in 1885, there were no sanitary facilities, no drinking water, no barrier fence along much of the gorge bank, and no facilities to tie up horses except those on private property. There was only a dusty macadamized road along the edge of the gorge. It had been a toll road until 1876, when the Toll Road Company removed the toll booths rather than repair the road. When the Queen Victoria Park Commissioners took over in 1885 they began negotiations for the purchase of the toll road which was owned by the St. Catharines, Thorold and Niagara Falls Toll Road Company. It was not until 1887 when the Provincial Arbitrators rendered their decision, that a price was established for the road. The Commissioners paid $4,000 for a piece of roadway that was in deplorable condition.

The Commissioners decided to abandon the portion of the road that ran along the cliff between the entrance of the new Park and the bottom of the Murray Hill Ravine at the Museum. A new road was built in 1887, "a substantial roadway of graceful alignment and easy gradient, sweeping in an easy curve past the Superintendent's office and close to the large pond where a drinking trough will be provided for horses, then to a junction of the old road in front of the Museum Garden".[4] The new road which was macadamized, was 5.5 m (18 ft.) in width, wide enough for two carriages to pass. The existing road through Queen Victoria Park today, though much wider, generally follows this original route. At the same time what was left of the old toll road along the edge of the gorge between the Murray Street ravine and the northern boundary of the Park was removed and fill was added to level it off. A broad gravel walkway was laid out in its place. This same walkway is in use today.

The Park grounds remained open to the public during the renovations and construction, but this did not hamper the work. By the middle of May, 1888, work was far enough advanced to allow for the "opening" of the Park on May 24, Victoria Day. No official opening ceremonies took place at that time but leading citizens of the Town of Niagara Falls expressed a desire to show their appreciation for the establishment of the Park and asked if they could

Mowat Gate with gatekeepers, circa 1890. The turnstiles were there to record the number of visitors to the Park.

Margaret Cadham.

Niagara Parks Archives

Inspiration Point observation shelter constructed of cedar and decorated with cedar bark, circa 1895.

provide an official opening. Permission was granted.

The Town Committee headed by John J. Bampfield, took advantage of the troops stationed at Niagara-on-the-Lake, to have a grand civil and military display on June 21 in honour of the Park. Refreshment booths were set up after permission was reluctantly granted by the Commission - their plans for the new Park did not include provision for selling food or refreshments within the Park boundaries. The military display was held on the "Flats" beyond Cedar Island, the area which Chairman Gzowski had set aside for sports and games. An estimated 13,000 visitors enjoyed the spectacle and the improvements made to the Park grounds.

One of the problems that arose soon after the Park opened, was centred around the tolls charged to cross the Cedar Island Bridges in order to view the Upper Rapids and to visit the Dufferin Islands. Criticism of the tolls appeared in the newspapers of the day. *Toronto Saturday Night* on June 9, 1888 reported: "The general impression has been that the Niagara Falls Park was to be a National one. The American Park is free because it was bought with State money for the enjoyment of the people. The Canadian Park, bought with Ontario money, likewise

for public enjoyment, isn't free. Surely this is contrary to the intention of those who voted for the Act in the Ontario Legislature. Whilst the main park is free, the 'Islands are preserved' to the tune of 10¢ for pedestrians and 50¢ each for vehicles. On the 24th of May it is said that 457 vehicles and 1,400 people passed in at the main entrance but a large number of those went no further than the main Park. On the same day the International Park on the American side is said to have held 10 to our 1. We don't say that the tariff is totally responsible for this but it is a potent factor . . . We fail to see much difference between the doings of the Queen Victoria Park Commissioners and those of the individual owners of the Islands under the old system . . . A National or Provincial Park should be entirely free for the people".[5]

Newspapers of the day reflected strong political bias. As the Park came into being under a Liberal Government, it is not surprising that opposition Conservative papers would be very critical, even to the point of not reporting exactly how the Park was financed - saying that it was "bought with Ontario money". They did not explain that it was borrowed money that had to be repaid out of future Park revenue, while the State Reservation on the U.S. side

Park Whistler

The bridge to Cedar Island, circa 1890. The Town of Niagara Falls waterworks pumping station at the left by the crest of the Falls was built in 1889 and remained in this location until it was demolished in 1937. The water intake for the pumping station is on the river bank below the small building just above the mainland side of the bridge.

John Burtniak Collection

Protective iron pipe railing at the Horseshoe Falls . The bare rock in the foreground was formerly part of the river bed.

of the Niagara River was under no such obligation. In 1892 tolls to the Islands were abandoned, not because of public pressure, but because so little revenue was derived from them.

There was no protective railing or wall along the top of the cliff in 1885, except for a section of split rail fence or a loosely constructed stone wall placed here and there in front of the various business establishments which occupied the area before the Com-

missioners took over. There was one section of open railing made of 2.5 cm (1 in.) gas pipe around the Horseshoe Falls and Table Rock placed there by the Town of Niagara Falls. In 1889 this pipe railing was extended to run along the whole length of the Park to the New Suspension Bridge.

The provision of drinking water for the visitors' refreshment and for horses was a problem easy to solve. There was a plentiful supply of fresh water, coming from the many springs which flowed out of the base of the high bank. In 1888 six drinking fountains and a water trough for horses were installed. The fountains were gravity fed, the spring water came out of the base of the high bank, passed through a wooden box filled with loose gravel, which acted as a filter, and then flowed freely through a pipe to the fountain, where it gathered in a pool. Two tin cups were provided, and the thirsty visitor dipped his cup into the pool and got his cool drink. Each fountain was enclosed in an arbour made of cedar bark, arranged to look like a wigwam.

One of the first lavatories was a small wooden structure on the edge of the cliff near Inspiration

The Indian Spring in Queen Victoria Park, circa 1895, from a stereograph by George Barker.

Niagara Falls, New York Public Library

Point, about 305 m (1000 ft.) north of the Museum. In 1901 a new and much larger building was erected there, constructed of "lasting materials" and flushed by a constant stream of spring water which flowed through the lavatory then dropped over the cliff on its way to the river below.[6]

It was not long before the Commissioners had a "parking" problem. The number of Sabbath School and church picnics had increased - these picnickers came in horse-drawn wagons. These and other visitors to the Park from nearby communities wanted better facilities for their horses and carriages. In 1901 the Commissioners built a drive shed of iron pipe frame covered with corrugated steel and with a gravel floor. It was big enough to shelter twenty carriages and had a tie-up yard capable of holding forty additional teams and wagons. Located just north of the present day bandshell, it solved the parking problem at that time.

Travellers coming to the Queen Victoria Park on the Canadian side had a problem which didn't exist for those going to the Niagara Reservation on the U.S. side. The Bridge Street train station on the Canadian side was several miles from the Queen Victoria Park. On the U.S. side the New York Central Railway Station was close to the U.S. Park and the American Falls. Most of the hacks which met

the trains at the Bridge Street station were owned by James T. Brundage who was antagonistic to the new Queen Victoria Park. His livery stable property had been expropriated when the Commissioners took over the new Park area; he received less for his property than he thought it was worth; the new Park was in competition with Brundage's Whirlpool Rapids Park, the Queen Victoria Park Commissioners' fee for their elevator was less than the fee Brundage charged for his Incline Railway at the Whirlpool Rapids; and finally Brundage's drivers were also unhappy as cabs were not allowed to come into the new park empty to pick up customers and commissions were no longer paid for bringing fares to the "Behind the Sheet" attraction. As a result of these grievances Brundage and his hackmen retaliated against the Queen Victoria Park by not taking their fares there. They picked up fares at the Great Western Station on Bridge Street, took them first to Brundage's Whirlpool Rapids Park then across the Suspension Bridge to view the Falls from the State Reservation on the U.S. side. By the time Brundage and his drivers were through with them, visitors were tired and had spent their money. Not many tourists who passed through Brundage's hands went on to visit Queen Victoria Park.

Consequently, anticipated revenue was less than estimated, only $4,000. in the first seven months of operation rather than the $41,000. they had expected in 1888. From data available it was estimated that the amount spent by each person, visiting the various points of interest in Niagara Falls prior to the establishment of Queen Victoria Park, was not less than $1.50. In the first seven months of the Park only 2½¢ per person, not $1.50, was spent in Queen Victoria Park. In 1889 it was only 2¼¢ per person. It became apparent that new sources of revenue would have to be found if the Park were to be self supporting.

On November 8, 1890, Chairman Gzowski wrote a confidential letter to Premier Mowat: "By estimating receipts for October 1890 to April 1891, as they were for the same period in 1889 ... there will be sufficient funds to meet all current expenditures but there are not funds to meet the half yearly interest on the bonds falling due in England on June 1, 1891, amounting to $10,000. The Commission recommends that the amount required to pay the half yearly bond coupons be provided by the Government".[7] The worst had happened, the Commissioners were forced by circumstances to ask the Provincial Government for more money. If the newpapers ever got wind of this, the controversy over the tolls to the Islands would be a tempest in a tea pot compared to the

A Niagara Park and River Railway car in Queen Victoria Park opposite Inspiration Point, circa 1895. From a postcard by The Buffalo News Co. Buffalo, N.Y.

storm they would raise over this.

The first source of new revenue the Commission considered was the granting of a franchise for the operation of an electric railway along the river from Queenston to Chippawa. The Commissioners felt that an electric railway would solve a number of pressing problems, each of which had financial implications. It was felt that an electric railway would circumvent the hackdrivers who were still persistently opposing the Park and taking their fares someplace else. It would also provide a convenient and economical means of reaching the Park and hopefully those excursionists who were landing at Lewiston and going on to the Niagara Reservation on the U.S. side, would get off the lake boats which would be docking at Queenston when the railway was built, and come by the electric railway to Niagara Falls and Queen Victoria Park. Last but not least, the franchise fee would pay the half-yearly bond interest each year.

On December 4, 1891, after protracted negotiations, a franchise for the construction and operation of an electric railway was granted to Messrs. E. B. Osler, H.C. Hammond, Wm. Hendrie and R.B. Angus, who were incorporated as the Niagara Falls Park and River Railway Company. The Commissioners undertook to secure all the land required

for the railway right-of-way and to furnish all the water necessary for the generation of the electricity required to operate the line. The Company for its part agreed to pay an annual rental fee of $10,000.[8]

Construction began in 1892 and a voltage electrical problem arose. The Railway Powerhouse being built just south of Table Rock at the Horseshoe Falls, was the pioneer electric power station on the Canadian side. It operated on a 19 m (62 ft.) head of water and produced direct current at a voltage of from 600 to 660 volts. The voltage was kept steady by diverting power, when necessary, through resistances.[9] The Company's engineer was not certain that the voltage would be strong enough at the end of the line at Queenston to pull the cars up the Heights. To transmit electricity for such a long distance, about 13 km (8 mi.), was an untried venture.

They proposed to the Commissioners that they be allowed to operate the line as a steam line from Queenston to the Whirlpool and from Dufferin Islands to Chippawa. Only the section of the line from the Whirlpool to Dufferin Islands would be electric. The Commissioners refused the proposed change. The Railway Company solved the problem by building a steam operated booster station on the river bank at Queenston, to maintain the voltage and provide the power to pull the electric cars up the

Niagara Falls Park and River Railway cars and trailers lined up at Queenston Docks to take passengers from the "Chippewa" to Queen Victoria Park, circa 1900.

Heights. The booster station was used between June 1 and September 10 each year during which time the railway did 75% of its business. It continued in operation until improved transmission techniques made it obsolete.[10]

The Niagara Falls Park and River Railway began operating on May 24, 1893 with a single track line. It carried 354,000 passengers from the Queenston Docks to Queen Victoria Park in the first year. The line was double-tracked in 1894 and carried 499,015 passengers. In the same year it was extended past Chippawa to Slater's Dock to pick up excursion traffic coming from Buffalo by the river steamers.

The Commission's financial problems would seem to be over. People were coming to the Park in sufficient numbers to provide the needed revenue. The hack drivers were not able to intercept the electric railway passengers, so they all came to Queen Victoria Park. The large number of people passing Queenston Heights and Foster's Flats on their way to Queen Victoria Park led the Com-

missioners to make plans for the development of these areas as outlying parks. Once again the Commission would need money for development.

When the Park opened in 1888 the Commissioners planned to operate the "appliances" (concessions) such as the Hydraulic Lift and the trip "Behind the Sheet" themselves. The Hydraulic Lift was built to replace Saul Davis' old wooden stairway. The Commissioners hired two guides, outfitted them in green uniforms, to conduct visitors "Behind the Sheet". In 1889 the Commissioners had experimented by awarding Samuel Barnett a franchise to operate a restaurant in the old Museum, and John Zybach a franchise for photographic privileges at Table Rock. The Commission now decided to increase revenue from these franchises by re-arranging the terms under which the restaurant and photographic concessions were leased and to combine them with the business of conducting visitors "Behind the Sheet". Advertisements solicited bids from responsible parties. J.T. Brundage, the Park's old nemesis had

Construction of Number 2 conduit of the Ontario Power Company April, 1910. The International Railway Co. Powerhouse is in the foreground, the Municipal Waterworks pumping station in centre and Table Rock House on the left.

sold his Whirlpool Rapids Park to the Niagara Falls Park and River Railway Co. and was looking for another enterprise. He joined forces with John Zybach and they submitted a bid for the advertised franchise. On June 6, 1893 the firm of Zybach and Brundage was awarded an exclusive franchise for ten years, with rights to the Hydraulic Lift, the "Behind the Sheet" attraction, the photographic business and the use of the Museum building as a restaurant, for $8,200. a year. The contract also included the right for a second ten year renewal at a rental to be agreed upon or settled by arbitration. Brundage's fortunes were now allied with those of the Queen Victoria Park Commissioners.[11]

After considering many possible solutions to the Park Commission's financial problems, the Provincial Government passed an Order in Council allowing the Commissioners to borrow the money required for the bond interest from the Imperial Bank of Canada.[12] The Commissioners went further into debt and were allowed to run an overdraft at the bank. John Langmuir, who had replaced Sir Casimir Gzowski as

Chairman on June 19, 1893, was afraid that the Imperial Bank would ask for the overdraft to be paid. In 1894 the Legislature passed a Bill allowing the Commission to float a new bond issue for $75,000.[13] The overdraft was paid off and the July 1894 bond interest payments were met. The money left after everything was paid, was deposited in the Commision's bank account. Money came in from the new leases and soon the Commission had a surplus.

The third and largest source of revenue for the Park Commission would come from granting franchises for the use of Niagara River water within the boundaries of the Park, for the generation of hydro electric power. The construction work which took place during the erection of the power plants resulted in almost complete disruption of the Park, from south of Table Rock to Dufferin Islands. This area was torn up in some way or another over a period of almost 30 years from 1892 until 1918, when the last conduit for the Ontario Power Plant was laid from Dufferin Islands to the area in front of the Refectory.

In 1903 the Superintendent reported that there

Construction for the Ontario Power Generating Station. Hydraulic Elevator at the right, Dufferin Cafe, former Barnett Museum and present site of the Victoria Park Restaurant in the background.

This 1917 view shows the gateway built at the lower entrance to the Park in 1906 after the original cedar bark gateway located further west, deteriorated and had to be demolished. From 1906 until 1922 it was called the "principal gate". In 1922 after the death of Sir Oliver Mowat the gateway was dedicated to him and renamed the "Mowat Gate" although he had earlier requested that his name not be associated with this gateway to the Park. In 1936 this gateway was dismantled and set up at the entrance further west on Clifton Hill, at the site of the original cedar gateway of 1888.

Edwin H. Hodge

The observation area at the Horseshoe Falls in the 1920's.

were 6 km (4 miles) of roads in Queen Victoria Park of which 3 km (2 miles) were impassable due to power plant construction. During the construction of the Ontario Power Company Powerhouse it was necessary to cut into the rock bed in front of the Refectory to install the penstocks and the underground distributor which would carry water from the conduits to the penstock openings. In 1908 when the area was filled in, a brick road was built from the Refectory to the Horseshoe Falls, where a loop was made to allow carriages to turn around and drive back. The rock base was rough and undulating around Table Rock, and so the low spots were filled in and a smooth roadbed was laid, with rubble from the conduit excavation. The bed for the brick road was excavated to a depth of 30.5 cm (12 in.), a 16.5 cm (6½ in.) concrete pad was laid and a sand cushion 4 cm (1 in.) thick was uniformly laid and compacted, to receive the 10 cm (4 in.) paving brick. The brick, a vitrified yellow clay fire brick was purchased from New Cumberland, West Virginia. Overseeing the building of this road was James Wilson's last job as Park Superintendent. He resigned on April 6, 1908. He was replaced by John H. Jackson, A.M.E.I.C., O.L.S. who was appointed Acting Superintendent, then confirmed in the position on January 27, 1909. In 1920 the brick road was extended to the bridge spanning the intake for the International Railway Company powerhouse (former Niagara Falls Park and River Railway Powerhouse). The yellow brick road was a feature of this area of the Park for many years.

The 1925 Annual Report said: "Although the roads have been widened from time to time, added room has not kept pace with the growth of traffic. The parking problem is difficult to solve, in the narrow width which physical conditions have imposed on a considerable area of Queen Victoria Park. To cope with this situation it will be necessary to completely redesign the roadway system from Clifton Hill to a point south of the Horseshoe Falls".

In 1926 a new roadway was built from the Park entrance to the Refectory 20 m (66 ft.) wide with intervals of grass covered boulevard in the centre. The bottleneck in the Table Rock area was cleared when old Table Rock House was torn down in 1926 and replaced by a new building, located farther south and out of the way of the roadway. This allowed a second road to be constructed from the Refectory to the Horseshoe Falls, along the west side of the International Railway Company tracks, thus creating a two-lane road with a boulevard between, along which the electric railway tracks ran. Two complete lines of cars could be parked along the length of the new road through the Park and still leave room for moving traffic. The Depression of the 1930's would reduce automobile traffic to such an extent that the 1920's road system would be adequate for many years to come.

Plans were made for the construction of a more suitable barrier along the top of the cliff and the Commissioners planned well - the parapet, also called a revetment, which they installed is the one still in use today. The parapet has a heavy base course of limestone with limestone pilasters placed at equidistant intervals to support the ornamental iron panels. They began construction of the parapet in the area between the Horseshoe Falls and the Refectory in 1904, completing and connecting sections as finances permitted. It was finished in 1923. Repairs and re-alignments have been made over the years due to rockfalls, notably the rockfall of 1917 at Table Rock and the blasting and scaling of the cliff at the same location in 1934-35. The rustic wooden shelters along the gorge bank called Rambler's Rest and Inspiration Point were in need of replacement by 1906 after 18 years of use. They were removed in 1907 and replaced with substantial open sided

structures made of boulder stone. Only one of these shelters, Rambler's Rest remains today.

In 1914, the wooden box, spring water reservoirs at Table Rock and the Refectory were replaced by larger concrete reservoirs, with gravel strainers. Greater care had to be taken with water coming from the springs because of the danger of pollution from the houses and industries located on the plateau above the Park. Water piped through the Park from the Town Pumping Station erected on Table Rock in 1889 was used for lawn watering purposes only. In 1909, the Town of Niagara Falls was allowed to bury a 30.5 cm (12 in.) water main in the Park, from Table Rock to Clifton Hill. The Commissioners arranged to tap this line to get an improved supply of water for the lawns.

It was not until 1921 that "sanitary" drinking fountains were installed in the Park. They were called sanitary because communal tin drinking cups were no longer used. The spring water system had to be abandoned because of possible pollution and filtered water from the Municipal Waterworks was used.

When you visit Queen Victoria Park today, it is

The boulevard leading to Table Rock, circa 1932.

F.H. Leslie

Rambler's Rest and the Promenade in Queen Victoria Park in the 1920's and the 1980's.

The Administration Building constructed 1926.

Canada Coach Lines buses at the Aero Car, October 27, 1940.

hard to believe that except for moonlight there was no night illumination of any sort when the Commissioners took over. This is in direct contrast to the extensive roadway and landscape illumination in operation in the Park today. Lighting was planned for 1905 but had to be postponed because of the prohibitive cost. In 1908 the Commissioners entered into an agreement with the International Railway Company, allowing an incandescent lighting system to be installed on the iron trolley poles running through the Park. Lights were installed in the area from the main entrance to Dufferin Islands. There were six 110 volt, sixteen candlepower lamps installed in a series on each pole, lit by direct current from the electric railway's voltage of from 600 to 660 volts. Power was supplied by the International Railway Company at a reasonable rate.

In 1916 the Carter Electric Company of Niagara Falls was engaged to remove the 1908 installations on the electric railway poles and replace them with two hundred, three-light Benjamin clusters which held six hundred Sunbeam tungsten lights of 400 watts each. The lights within the Park proper - from Mowat gate to the Horseshoe Falls - were covered with opaque globes, the remainder extending to Dufferin Islands were left bare.

In 1923 eighty-one light standards were erected along the roadway through the Park proper. They were in four main lines, two along either side of the main drive, and one along each of the front and rear footpaths. The whole northerly area of the Park was now well illuminated and the grounds were much safer for evening visitors. This system was extended to the Electrical Development Company Power-house (Toronto Powerhouse) in 1925 and by 1927 had reached the southern boundary of the Park at Dufferin Islands.

In the year 1926 an extensive building program was planned and for the most part completed. Besides building a new Table Rock House, and demolishing the old building, the Commission had the Refectory renovated and enlarged. A new Administration Building was constructed. Located at the base of the high bank where the Jolly Cut

(Robinson Street) enters the Park, it commands a fine view of the American Falls. The old Zimmerman Gate House, which served as the Park's first Administration Office, and later as a Police Office, was torn down.

In 1927 the Commissioners decided to adopt the name "The Niagara Parks Commission" instead of the "Queen Victoria Park Niagara Falls Park Commission". The new name reflected the broader scope of the Parks which now extended along the Niagara River from Lake Erie to Lake Ontario. Chairman P.W. Ellis who had served on the Commission since 1905 and who had succeeded John Langmuir as Chairman on May 12, 1915, died in the spring of 1929 after a short illness. He was replaced by R. Home Smith as Chairman. Chairman Smith served until 1933 when he was replaced on July 4 by Norman Somerville Q.C. Mr. Somerville's term lasted only until September 6, 1934 when a change in the Provincial Government occurred after the 1934 Provincial elections. A new Commission was appointed with the Honourable T.B. McQuesten as Chairman. Superintendent John H. Jackson retired and C. Ellison Kaumeyer was appointed to replace

The Clifton Hotel site, with the Lafayette Hotel still standing. Site of present day Oakes Garden Theatre. circa 1933.

Edwin H. Hodge.

The Memorial Arch and Clifton Gate House at the Canadian terminus of the Upper Steel Arch Bridge, 1937.

Dedication ceremonies for the Memorial Arch were held June 18, 1938 in Oakes Garden Theatre. Hon. T.B. McQuesten, Chairman of the Niagara Parks Commission is shown at the microphone. Honoured guests seated behind Mr. McQuesten include: second from the right, Sir William Mulock, Chief Justice of Ontario 1923-36; the Right Honourable William Lyon Mackenzie King, Prime Minister of Canada, who unveiled the Arch; Hon. C.D. Howe; William L. Houck M.L.A. for Niagara Falls Riding.

The Memorial Arch from the Rainbow Gardens circa 1947. The Arch became a traffic hazard and was removed after the 1967 tourist season.

him, but the position was no longer called Super-intendent, instead General Manager and Secretary to the Commission.

Beginning in 1927 sightseeing buses came into more general use and the Commission licensed those that operated within the Park. The Van Dyke Sightseeing Co. and the Buffalo, Niagara and Toronto Tour Company were the two main companies operating at that time. In 1933 the Commissioners granted the first exclusive privilege to carry tourists on sightseeing trips in the Niagara Parks to the Highway King Coach Lines. This Company sought to enlarge the potential market by allying itself with the Gray Line Sightseeing Companies Association Inc. One of the requirements of the Gray Line affiliation was that a competent conductor point out and describe points of interest during the tour. A "spiel" checked by a local historian, was used, giving tourists a much better interpretation of the points of interest than had hitherto been available from the random comments of individual sightseeing operators. From then on the Highway King Coach Lines and Gray Coach Lines had a virtual monopoly of sightseeing tours in the

Niagara Parks. In 1938 the Highway King Company became the Canada Coach Lines and the new Company signed an agreement with the Commission allowing it to continue operating in the Niagara Parks.

In 1934 Harry Oakes traded with the Commission two parcels of land, one of about 2.12 ha (5.25 acres) on the Niagara Boulevard above Chippawa, and the other the Clifton and Lafayette Hotel sites on River Road, accepting in exchange a parcel of land on the plateau above Queen Victoria Park adjacent to Clifton Hill. The Commissioners immediately began the development of the Clifton site "to improve the Falls View Bridge entrance to Ontario". A suitable design was accepted which would turn the site into an amphitheatre and ornamental gardens. Work began on Oakes Garden October 1, 1935.

Clifton Gate House, described as "a new entirely modern information booth", was built on the gorge bank just south of the Upper Steel Arch Bridge (known locally as the Falls View Bridge). The building was constructed "to provide a splendid view of the entire Cataract, and will handle souvenirs, be a source of accurate information and a call point for taxis when needed". The building was opened in the spring of 1937.[14]

The formal opening of Oakes Garden Theatre took place on September 18, 1937. To complement this new formal garden, River Road was widened and a Memorial Arch called Clifton Gate was constructed at the limits of the Queen Victoria Park next to the entrance to the Upper Steel Arch Bridge. The Annual Report of 1936-37 reported: "There is now a paved double highway of entry and another of exit. While there will continue to be a 'bottleneck' at the Upper Steel Arch Bridge during rush hours, the Commission cannot speed this up, there will be no congestion on Commission property". Before the Clifton Gate Memorial Arch was unveiled in June of 1938 by the Right Honourable W.L. Mackenzie King, Prime Minister of Canada, the Upper Bridge was destroyed as a result of an ice jam in January of 1938. The Parks Commission had succeeded in its objective of creating an improved entrance to Ontario at the Falls View Bridge, but the Bridge had disappeared.

While all this construction was going on, a time bomb was ticking away which would explode with disastrous financial consequences for the Commission. The International Railway Company had abandoned its franchise and stopped operating on September 11, 1932. Negotiations began immediately as to the amount of compensation to be paid to the I.R.C. by the Parks Commission, under the terms of the 1891 agreement. No settlement could be reached so the matter was referred to arbitration in 1933.

The Arbitrators met for 47 days in 1934 and awarded the Railway Company the sum of $179,104. with costs to paid by the Commission. The Company appealed this decision to the Supreme Court of Ontario. In 1937, the Appellate Division of the Supreme Court of Ontario refused the International Railway Company's appeal and reduced the amount to be paid by the Commission to $169,764. As Canada was still a "colony" of Great Britain, the International Railway Company had the option of appealing to the Privy Council in London, England. In 1937 the Privy Council overturned the earlier decisions and awarded the International Railway Company $1,057,456.

Winston Churchill with his daughter Mary during visit to Niagara Falls in 1943. Maxim T. Gray General Manager of the Niagara Parks Commission is to the left of Mary Churchill.

Edwin H. Hodge

The Commissioners were stunned but there was no higher Court of Appeal, they could do nothing but accept the result. This extraordinary financial burden placed upon it was made even heavier by the fact that the Commission had to pay the costs of the appeal, cross appeal and the final appeal. The Arbitrators and the Supreme Court of Ontario had based their award on the actual marketable value of the Railway Company's assets. The Parks Commission owned the right-of-way and there was no future market for the electric railway because of the increasing use of the automobile. The Judicial Committee of the Privy Council in England thought of compensation in terms of replacement value, while it ignored the fact that the railway had become unprofitable and had no future prospects, and that the equipment was obsolete.

The Commission was left with a total debt of $3,938,000. at the end of 1942. The Railway Company had paid only $400,000. over the 40 years of the franchise yet received $1,357,456. (the original award by the Privy Council plus $300,000. in interest). The Company left behind obsolete equipment and tracks which the Commission had to have removed and disposed of as scrap - for only $37,108.99. The whole affair cost the Commission almost $1,500,000. in the arbitration award, appeal costs and interest.

The final shock had been felt and in 1942 the Commissioners reported: "The effect of this case has been to cripple the Commission severely as far as capital expenditures are concerned. Coupled with the decrease in revenue because of war conditions ... it means curtailment of plans for expansion and instead devotion of much greater revenue to the payment of principle and interest upon the debt thus incurred".[15]

World War II began in 1939 and it was to have a great impact on the Parks Commission. After the outbreak of War the Commission co-operated with the Military authorities in every way possible. In order to protect the Ontario Powerhouse a barricade of barbed wire was erected by the Military authorities, on the main roadway in front of the Refectory, reaching to Table Rock House. The Parks Commission suffered financially because of this: "Table Rock House, which is our largest revenue producer, remained closed all winter".[16] After the invasion of Holland and Belgium in 1940, more barricades were erected in order to protect the Canadian Niagara Power Co. and Toronto Power Co. facilities, the Park was closed completely from the Refectory to Dufferin Islands and remained this way for the duration of the War. The Refectory was the closest point from which the Horseshoe Falls could be

Horse drawn surreys parked on Clifton Hill at Oakes Garden Theatre.

viewed and did well financially as it could be reached from behind the barricades.

In 1943 Winston Churchill, accompanied by his daughter Mary, paid a surprise visit to Niagara Falls after attending the Quebec City Conference. His visit brought a horde of newspaper reporters to the City. Many newspaper stories were written about his visit, but the story that brought the most attention and resulted in hundreds of columns of space was not about Churchill. Rather, it concerned the defacing of the parapet in Queen Victoria Park with lipstick. Visitors would write their names and addresses with lipstick, some with personal comment, on the cut stones of the parapet and on the stone face of Clifton Gate House. Names and addresses were taken from the lipstick roster, and letters were written to the people to notify them of the offence they committed. It was necessary to purchase an electric grinder, to grind down the surfaces defaced to a depth of 32 mm (⅛ in.) to remove the hideous red marks.

In the years 1941-44 there were several changes in the Parks Administration. C. Ellison Kaumeyer resigned as General Manager in 1941 to become General Manager of the Niagara Falls Bridge Commission. Maxim T. Gray O.L.S. of Fort Erie was appointed his successor. In 1944 after a change in the Provincial Government when the Conservatives returned to power, a whole new Commission was appointed and The Honourable Charles Daley, Minister of Labour for the Province of Ontario, was appointed Chairman.

Gasoline rationing and tire shortages became more severe as the War progressed, restricting pleasure travel. By 1944 automobile traffic in the Park had declined to such an extent that it almost reached the vanishing point. Immediately after the end of hostilities in 1945, the Commissioners began to provide for the return of the travelling public. The main tunnel at Table Rock was replaced by a new tunnel. Construction began on a new Greenhouse, which was officially opened on November 9, 1946. The parapet which ended almost on a line with the crest of the Horseshoe Falls was extended 134 m (440 ft.) south for the safety of visitors who frequented this area.

Since 1934 when the old souvenir store was removed from the top of the Clifton Incline, the Commission had operated a small refreshment stand in the former basement of the Incline building. Park information and post cards were dispensed from a tent located nearby. There was a need at this focal point at the foot of Clifton Hill for a new building which would combine the sale of refreshments, souvenirs, tickets for the Incline Railway and the Maid of the Mist, the distribution of Park literature and general information for Ontario visitors, and the provision of public lavatory facilities. Construction began in 1947 on the new building. It was built of sawn Queenston limestone and designed not to interfere with a clear view of the Falls from Oakes Garden Theatre. The building, named in honour of Her Royal Highness Princess Elizabeth, was officially

Princess Elizabeth Building 1956.

Niagara Parks Archives.

opened on July 24, 1948.

Work on the new Ontario Hydro Project began in 1951 and was carried on mainly outside the boundaries of Queen Victoria Park. Two causeways were built in 1953 across the waterways at Dufferin Islands to allow cement mixing trucks to reach the six locations where concrete was poured through 20 cm (8 in.) pipes to the twin tunnels that ran beneath Dufferin Islands.

After many years of planning the remedial work program began in 1954. The bed of the Niagara River was deepened at the flanks on both sides of the Horseshoe Falls, at Goat Island and at Table Rock. The flanks were dried to allow excavations to be made, the flow of water was diverted over the centre of the Horseshoe Falls changing the spray pattern. As a result the Table Rock area was in almost continual spray. This incessant spray from the Horseshoe Falls was credited with being responsible for a decrease in attendance at the Scenic Tunnels. The completion of the International Control Dam in the upper river beyond Dufferin Islands on September 28, 1957, resulted in a change in the flow of water over the Horseshoe Falls, alleviating the spray problem. There was a 22½% increase in Scenic Tunnel patronage after the opening of the Control Dam and the completion of the remedial work in 1958.

Traffic control and parking problems were a constant concern of the Commissioners in the 1950's moving them to state in 1958: "There is room for more people, but not for more automobiles which may be parked". Automobile manufacturers were aggravating the situation by designing and producing larger cars. The need for additional parking was so acute that in the mid 1950's on busy Sundays the Commission allowed parking on the turf between Table Rock House and the Canadian Niagara Powerhouse. There were 1500 parking spaces available within the Park, along the roadway between Clifton Hill and the Canadian Niagara Powerhouse.

In 1961 the Commissioners agreed to participate in the Greater Niagara Traffic Survey, on the assumption that the major traffic problems in the

A view from the crest of the Horseshoe Falls, with the Canadian flank of the Falls dried off to allow for the deepening of the channel. Table Rock House is on the left, the Ontario Power Generating Station is in the gorge below, circa 1955.

Ontario Hydro

Niagara Falls area were attributable directly to the attraction power of Queen Victoria Park and that the traffic congestion in the Park was basically caused by the deficiency of parking spaces. They did so also with the understanding that their participation would not indicate their acceptance of any recommendations made in regard to the Park. The General Manager was permitted to attend meetings of the Technical Co-ordinating Committee, to take part in this Study as an observer only.

The H.G. Acres Co. carried out this study and recommended that an interim solution for improving parking would be to have off-street parking lots established in Queen Victoria Park. The Commissioners realized that there was no room in the Park for additional parking lots, so they investigated where they could acquire land adjacent to the Park. In this way they would provide the needed parking spaces without encroaching on the grassy areas of the park. In 1963 a new parking area was built on top of the three large Ontario Hydro underground conduits. An area 366 m (1200 ft.) long by 21 m (70 ft.) wide was black topped. The new lot ran northerly past Table Rock House to the Canadian Niagara Power-house. This was soon extended to 533 m (1750 ft.) to reach the north side of Fraser Hill. The overflow parking previously allowed on the turf was dis-continued. During the early 1960's a privately operated parking area on the Sainovich property, the future site of the Skylon Tower, provided space for 600 cars. Despite the new parking areas available, the unsatisfied demand was estimated at 4000 spaces. In 1964, as a follow up to the Acres study, the Ontario Department of Highways commissioned the firm of DeLeuw Cather to undertake the functional planning study of the major highways and arterial roads in the Niagara Falls area, and to make a recommendation for future improvements.

In 1966 the Commission constructed the Horse-shoe Falls Incline Railway to connect the Table Rock area with Falls View on the upper bank. Immediately hundreds of parking spaces became available and tourists rode the incline down the bank to the Park and left their cars in the parking areas on the upper level. Besides the parking available at Falls View motels, the Seagram Tower (now called the Minolta Tower) owners guaranteed free parking space for 500 cars and the Commission's new parking lot, north of the Incline accommodated another 200 cars.

In an effort to co-ordinate and improve the operation of commercial sightseeing buses in the Park in 1966, the Commission did not renew its 1938 agreement with Canada Coach Lines. Instead an agreement was signed with Double Deck Bus Tours allowing them to conduct tours on Park property. Tourists using this service could get on and off at various points of interest - a service provided many years before by the electric railway. In 1971 in a further effort to reduce traffic congestion, four View-mobiles - trackless trains - were introduced to carry tourists in Queen Victoria Park. Each Viewmobile had a driver and a guide who gave a commentary as the trains toured the Park and the Dufferin Islands area. Two Viewmobiles were added in 1972 and three more in 1973.

The De Leuw Cather Report was published in late 1966. The report's recommendations were completely unacceptable to the Commissioners. Two new roads into the Park were recommended. Many trees would have to be cut down and the Rose Garden, which the report called a "Rose bed", would be destroyed. One recommendation was considered feasible - to have all traffic north and southbound past Table Rock House, run on the west side of the building. This would leave room for a pedestrian mall between the front of Table Rock House and the Horseshoe Falls. In 1972 roads in the Table Rock area were rerouted as recommended.

In 1967 the Commissioners decided to have their own traffic study made and on November 17 appointed Richard Strong Associates Ltd. of Toronto, Landscape Architects and Planning Con-sultants, to carry out a comprehensive planning study, which would include re-evaluation of all lands, future pedestrian and vehicular traffic needs and assessment of possible alternatives. Alterations would have to be compatible with the Commission's overall planning goals and objectives.

In January 1967 the Honourable James N. Allan was appointed Chairman of the Niagara Parks Commission. Following the February 10, 1967 Commission meeting, Mr. Daley and five Com-missioners resigned. Mr. Allan and the four remaining Commissioners carried on the business of the Com-mission until July 13. At that time, a new Com-mission was appointed under the provision of the Niagara Parks Act as amended by Bill 74. General Manager Maxim T. Gray retired on November 30, 1968 after 27 years of service. He was replaced on December 1, by Donald R. Wilson B.Sc.F., former Regional Director, Southern Region, for the Ontario Department of Lands and Forests.

Canada's Centennial was celebrated in 1967 and the Commission adopted as its Centennial Project, the improvement of Park lighting in the area from Table Rock House up to and around the Dufferin Islands. A special Centennial floral display bed, decorated with the Centennial logo, was installed at the Y intersection of the roads coming into the Park. Appropriate flags were flown from this site at all times during the year. Ontario Hydro removed the unsightly, black painted, steel plate overflow tank - the "temporary" tank of 1918 – from its location beside the Refectory. The Commissioners decided to remove the Memorial Arch, located opposite Oakes Garden Theatre at the Clifton Gate building, after Labour Day of 1967. When the Arch was built at this location it was to serve as the entrance to the Park from the terminus of the Upper Steel Arch Bridge. The Rainbow Bridge which replaced the Upper Bridge was in a different location. The position of the Arch no longer indicated the entrance to the Park, and it was a traffic hazard.

Since 1961 the Potvin Museum of animated wood carvings had occupied the Clifton Gate House, displaying the carvings in the basement in 1961 and then taking over the whole building in 1963. The Clifton Gate Souvenir Store was closed from 1963 to 1968. The Potvin Museum moved out of the building in early 1967 and Soundlight Productions were given permission to use the building for a multi-slide, audio visual presentation on the Battle of Lundy's Lane. Soundlight Productions moved out at the end of the 1967 season and beginning in 1968 the Clifton Gate House was once again operated as a souvenir store.

The Horseshoe Falls Incline. This funicular is able to transport 1600 persons an hour in its two plexiglass-topped cars which travel the 50m (165 ft.) embankment in 57 seconds. During the night of August 18, 1973 a serious and unexplained incident occurred when a bomb exploded in the works putting the funicular out of service until May 4, 1974.

A Viewmobile beside the Upper Cascades in Queen Victoria Park.

This fountain was part of the Zimmerman estate and was built around 1856. It was originally fed by spring water.

The fountain at night.

The Richard Strong Report was presented to the Commission in December, 1969. One of the report's recommendations was the construction of a major parking lot on the tract of land located just east of Dufferin Islands. In peak season tourists would park their cars and travel to the main Park area by means of a tractor train. The Commissioners approved the report in principle in 1969. In 1970 they began to implement the parking lot recommendation by purchasing the 57 ha (141 acres) parcel of land east of Dufferin Islands from Welland Securities. In 1972 an additional 4.9 ha (12 acres) adjacent to this property was expropriated and with other purchases of land, the total area in the proposed upper parking area became 71 ha (175 acres).

At the end of the 1972 season the picnic pavilions were removed from Queen Victoria Park. With so many picnic facilities available at other sites - King's Bridge Park, Queenston Heights and McFarland Point Park - it was no longer necessary to use Queen Victoria Park for group picnics. While no new parking spaces were created, the transfer of group picnics to other Parks made more parking space available for tourists.

In 1970 the Regional Municipality of Niagara formed the Technical Advisory Committee which included a representative from the Niagara Parks Commission. The TAC 4 Committee as it was called reviewed all the aspects of the 1966 De Leuw Cather report. However in 1976 the Ministry of Transportation and Communications (formerly the Department of Highways) for Ontario confirmed that revised traffic projections could not justify the major road changes suggested in the De Leuw Cather Report. Alternative solutions would have to be found. The Commission began work on its Master Plan and authorized the widening of the Parkway from Fraser Hill to the International Control Dam, opposite the proposed parking lot. On September 6, 1977 work began and approximately 1,465 m (4806 ft.) of

As early as 1967 the Parks Commissioners chose a site for a Memorial to King George VI. The site between the rose garden and the main Park roadway was chosen so that the Memorial could be easily seen by motorists as they drove through the Park. The Memorial which weighs 8.6 tonnes (18,900 lbs.) was sculpted by Elizabeth Wynn Wood. It is a carved stone figure of King George VI, made of Laurentian Rose Granite 3.15m (10 ft. 4 in.) high. It was officially unveiled on July 1, 1963.

roadway was widened. At Dufferin Islands one bridge was completely rebuilt and two were twinned.

Concurrent with the investigations being carried on by the TAC 4 Committee the NPC carried out preliminary investigations into the implementation of a people mover system. Discussions were held with staff from Disney World, with a review of all the transportation systems in use at this Florida attraction. Other transportation systems were also investigated. The result of these inquiries was a Parks' staff recommendation to the Commission that rubber-tired trains be used as people movers in Queen Victoria Park.

Concern was expressed by tourist operators in the Clifton Hill Area, regarding the possible impact of this system on their area. The Commission, acknowledging this concern in 1979, appointed the firm of Del Can to prepare a study, reviewing all the alternatives open to the Commission in this regard. Del Can proposed three alternative traffic circulation concepts as part of Phase I of their study. The Commissioners formally presented this information to a meeting of interested agencies, asking for comments. The City of Niagara Falls, after receiving comments on the proposals from the tourist industry and other interested groups, commissioned a further

Niagara Parks Archives

The Parks Commission in 1961 engaged John Wilson, a top-ranking specialist in the field, to treat the area of Queen Victoria Park extending from Clifton Hill to the Victoria Park Restaurant with landscape illumination. Five package unit transformers were installed requiring 3095m (10,155 ft.) of primary cable and 23,165m (76,000 ft.) of secondary cable, all of this placed underground. Four hundred and twenty-six specially designed lighting units were installed, some at ground level but mainly on trees. On June 2, 1961 formal ceremonies were held when the lights were turned on. The lighting of the upper foliage of the trees and the lawn areas, with the shadows created, greatly enhances this area of Queen Victoria Park.

Winter scenes at the Horseshoe Falls.

Niagara Parks Archives

The Horseshoe Falls, with Table Rock House and the South Building from the air, circa 1980.

Niagara Parks Archives

The Horseshoe Falls and Table Rock Observation Area.

The motel set for the movie "Niagara" filmed in Queen Victoria Park in 1952.

Christopher Reeve and Margot Kidder at the Horseshoe Falls during the filming of Superman II, 1979.

Niagara Falls has been the background for motion pictures ever since the advent of the motion picture. The earliest known movie film footage shot of the Falls was done in 1897 by a French film maker. The Edison Company made short films in 1901, the year of the Pan American Exposition, showing the Gorge Railway, a stunter going through the Whirlpool Rapids in a boat, people frolicking on the ice bridge, and general scenic views of both the American and the Canadian Falls.

In 1952 the first major movie production, called "Niagara", centered around Niagara Falls, was shot by Twentieth Century Fox, featuring Marilyn Monroe and Joseph Cotten in the lead roles. A movie set, consisting of a "Motel" which was only a facade, was built in Queen Victoria Park opposite the American Falls. It was used for the film and removed immediately after. For many years tourists enquired about the location of this motel.

Niagara Falls again became a part of a major feature film in 1979 when portions of Superman II, featuring Christopher Reeve and Margot Kidder, were filmed at Table Rock.

study and in July 1980, the firm of Lanmer-Fenco was retained to make a report on the problems advanced by the tourist industry.

The Commission, recognizing that co-operation with all affected parties was essential, participated in the City's study. All work on the Master Plan for Traffic Improvements in Queen Victoria Park was suspended while this study was being done.

For the Niagara Parks Commission 1980 was the most successful year ever financially. The availability of gasoline in the United States after a shortage there in 1979, and the high premium paid on United States currency, helped. A survey of licence plates in Queen Victoria Park indicated that the number of Canadian and American vehicles was almost equal. More Canadians were taking vacations in Canada because of the high discount on the Canadian dollar which they suffered in exchanging their money for United States currency. The Niagara Parks Commission as it always does, paid full exchange on United States currency in its retail, food and attractions operations. Business was up 21% over 1979.

The Lanmer-Fenco Report was completed at the end of 1981. In February 1982 the City of Niagara Falls submitted a formal response to the Commission on the major items of concern raised by Del Can's Progress Report Phase 1. The Commission modified its approach to ensure the Master Plan was developed as an interim stage of the City's overall Development Plan. The following considerations were confirmed prior to the commencement of Phase 2:

The retention of two-way traffic within Queen Victoria Park.

The retention of on-street parking on Falls Avenue and the Niagara Parkway, north of the Y-junction to the Rainbow Bridge.

The construction of a parking lot at the south end of Queen Victoria Park above Dufferin Islands, to

include 2300 parking spaces instead of 3500 as first planned and only 750 spaces in Phase 1, instead of 1500 planned. The people mover system would be put in operation in Phase 1, from this parking lot to the Rainbow Bridge.

In 1982, the Commission engaged the Urban Transportation and Development Corporation to report on the availability of Canadian-made people mover systems for use in Queen Victoria Park. Objections were still being made by the tourist industry with some members insisting on a fixed rail concept, either a raised mono-rail or a ground rail system, that would run in a loop and cover the Clifton Hill and Victoria Avenue tourist areas and double back along the plateau above the Park to the new south parking lot. In late 1983 the tourist industry made further submissions to the Commission asking them to delay their Master Plan. The Commissioners for their part felt that they had delayed long enough. Two reports, the Strong Report and the Del Can Report, had recommended the same form of people mover system. The tourist industry made a representation to the Provincial Government in an effort to get the Commission's project delayed. In September 1983 the Provincial Government upheld the Commission's decision.

Planning began immediately for the twelve stations required for the people mover system. The firms of Chapman-Murray Associates and Del Can Engineering were engaged to prepare plans and working drawings, and bids were received for the rubber-tired people movers. Ontario Bus Industry of Mississauga was the successful bidder. The company was to build a "futuristic" vehicle with a unique design, to be delivered by March 1985. The whole system was estimated to cost about $10,000,000 in Phase 1, and $16,000,000 to complete.

The Rapids View Parking Lot under construction, August 1984.

The rose garden in Queen Victoria Park.

The rock garden in Queen Victoria Park.

A massive display of daffodils in Queen Victoria Park.

Niagara Parks Archives

Niagara Parks Archives

Niagara Parks Archives

Tulips and magnolia blossoms in Queen Victoria Park.

A view of the flower bed in front of the Police Station, looking toward the American Falls, Queen Victoria Park.

An Autumn scene at Mirror Pond, Queen Victoria Park.

Dufferin Islands

The Dufferin Islands are quiet and secluded, away from the busy parkland, an embayment in the river, bordered by high glacial banks. The water flows gently over a series of small waterfalls, behind which are placid pools where swimmers, boaters, and fisherman share in the enjoyment of the water.

Less than 200 years ago the scene was entirely different. Then the river rushed around four very small islands at the head of the embayment and one large island in the centre of the embayment. The rushing water was from 1.1 to 1.7 m (3½ to 5½ ft.) deep and it tore at the base of the drift banks, making the embayment larger and larger. A saw and grist mill and an iron foundry were located side by side on the banks at the entrance to the islands. The sound of water wheels, wooden gears meshing, and the shearing of logs being sawn into lumber, rent the air. A haze of fumes came from the crude clay furnaces which were purifying bog iron, and from natural gas flares. These were our earliest industries. How did nature set the stage for all this? How were the islands created?

The strata of the various ocean sediments that lie under our region tilt southwest to the Canadian shore, sloping down 6 m in 1.6 km (20 ft. in one mile). As the Niagara River flows toward its plunge over the Falls, it hugs the Canadian west bank and erodes it easily. The rock beds of the first and second cascades in the Niagara River - which run under the Dufferin Islands - formed a flume for the deeper waters in this tilt, channelling the water toward the bank of glacial drift and sand, which was then gradually eroded in a great curve as the river struggled to get out again. It found an easy way out along the lower cascades rock ledge and the embayment now known as Dufferin Islands was formed.

In 1794 Governor Simcoe granted John MacGill a former adjutant in Simcoe's Queen's Rangers, and Benjamin Canby, a Quaker from Pennsylvania, a 999 year lease and permission to erect a saw and grist mill on the banks of the river at the Islands. They built their mills about .8 km (0.5 mi.) inside the curve on the north bank. A road was cut into the sloping bank, connecting with the Portage Road above. A small community of workers' houses sprang up along the Portage Road on the high bank above the mills. Governor Simcoe gave this community the name Bridgewater.

About 1799, Robert Randall, a native of Maryland, emigrated to Canada with the intention of establishing an iron works near the Falls of Niagara. Randall was refused permission to erect new mills and so he made a working agreement with Phelps and Ramsay who had purchased the lease and the Bridgewater Mills from Canby and MacGill in 1796.[1] He added an ironworks with clay furnaces to the saw and grist mills. Randall got his "iron" ore from the marshy banks of the Welland River. It was actually "limonite" a mineral described as "hydrated oxide of iron", often found in marshy or boggy areas. Using this material he claimed to be the first man to make wrought iron products in Upper Canada. Flour ground in Randall's mill was sold for export to Buffalo, New York. Flour ground in Burch's Mills

The Burning Spring, from a stereograph by George Barker, circa 1860.

Niagara Falls New York Public Library

When excavations were made in 1794 for the foundations of the Canby-McGill mills, a "spring" was discovered. Mrs. Simcoe who visited the site in 1792, described this spring in her diary as "emitting a gas or inflammable air which when confined to a pipe and a match applied to it, will boil a tea kettle in fifteen minutes." When this area was first settled, there was natural gas bubbling up through the water all along the shore as far as 1.5 km (a mile) upstream from the islands. This gas came from a layer of Queenston shale more than 183 m (60 ft.) down. What the excavators had done was to enlarge the opening of an existing vent, allowing for a more rapid emission of the natural gas.

The spring soon became a point of interest and some enterprising person saw an opportunity to make money from the spring. He built a wooden shelter over the spring and a barrel with a pipe protruding from the top was placed over the spring. A cork stopper was placed in the pipe, allowing the gas to build up in the barrel. When an audience had been assembled, the cork was removed, the gas was lit and "The Burning Spring" — Niagara Falls' first tourist attraction — was created. A small charge was made to see the spring. Early guide books listed the Burning Spring as a place that every tourist should visit, and for more than sixty years it was a point of interest at this site. When the Queen Victoria Park Commissioners took over control of the islands they did not continue operation of the Burning Spring attraction.

The entrance to the Clark Hill Islands with Sutherland Macklem's suspension bridge Pollux connecting the Islands with the Burning Spring, circa 1880. From a stereograph by George Barker.

Niagara Falls New York Public Library

located closer to the Falls was considered unsuitable for export as it was too moist, because of the continual dampness in the air there due to the spray from the Falls.[2]

Randall fell on hard times due to the failure of investments in the Montreal area. In 1801 the Bridgewater Mills property reverted to Phelps and Ramsay, who subsequently sold to James McCulloch, who later sold to Thomas Clark and Samuel Street. The mills and the houses at Bridgewater were burned on July 26, 1814, by the American forces who were returning to their camp above Chippawa, the day after the Battle of Lundy's Lane. The Bridgewater Mills were not rebuilt after the war.

In 1805 Thomas Clark built a house on the high bank overlooking the Islands. He called his house and estate Clark Hill . When Clark died in 1837, he had no direct heir and the greater part of his fortune went to his sisters in Scotland. Samuel Street then controlled the milling and allied businesses and he moved from his home on the lower level opposite the Mills, to Clark Hill. In 1844 when Samuel Street died, his 30 year old son Thomas Clark Street, known locally as T.C. Street, inherited the property. He immediately set about acquiring the Islands, which had already become known as the Clark Hill Islands. On May 16, 1849, he wrote to his friend, the Honourable Wm. H. Merritt, M.P.P. to ask if Merritt would: "Try what can be done for me, first in the way

of license of occupation." Street described the Islands as . . . "of no value to any person and have never been and cannot be put to any beneficial use. The Islands are a beautiful object in connection with my property and I am very anxious to acquire ownership to improve and beautify them as an appendage to my place. I have no other object or motive in making application except to improve the view from my grounds and have the property entirely under my control."[3] The next year, 1850, Street rebuilt Clark Hill incorporating part of the 1805 house in the new structure.[4]

The Islands, 4 ha (10 acres) in area, were valued at 12 pounds 10 shillings and James Fell, Deputy Provincial Surveyor, recommended that they should be sold to Street. Fell said in his report "It is my opinion that no one else would ever apply to buy it."[5] The Islands became Street's property on March 9, 1854.[6] He at once built a foot suspension bridge connecting the Islands with the bottom of a path leading down the bank from his house. He named the large Island Cynthia after one of Samuel Street's sisters. The Islands were now T.C. Street's private preserve.

T.C. Street never married and his mother and later his sister Caroline, the widow of Dr. T.C. Macklem of Chippawa, managed his household. Caroline had two sons and one of them, Sutherland Macklem inherited Clark Hill when T.C. Street died in 1872.

Niagara Falls New York Public Library.

The suspension bridge Pollux connecting the Clark Hill Islands with the Burning Spring, circa 1880. From a stereograph by George Barker.

Macklem continued his uncle's interest in the Cynthia Islands as they were now called. In 1877 he decided to open them to the public. He built two graceful suspension bridges connecting the largest island with the shore, to carry carriage and foot traffic. The bridges were named Castor and Pollux after the twin sons of Leda and Jupiter of Roman mythology. Carriages could now drive along Macklem's road from Table Rock to the Island, and cross the bridges to the Burning Spring. To recover the cost of his improvements, Macklem levied a toll for the use of the bridges.

The Queen Victoria Park Commissioners included the Cynthia Islands and the remainder of Macklem's property along the river in the boundaries of the proposed park. Sutherland Macklem who had inherited all of the land acquired by his uncle T.C. Street from Thomas Clark, now asked the Commissioners for $245,000 for his properties. The Commissioners offered only $26,175.[7] They reasoned that the 1.4 km (one mile) adjoining the river above the Islands, and the river front land south of Table Rock had been granted to Macklem's predecessors in 1816 as a political favour without payment, and that

Riverside Ramble along the bank at Dufferin Islands with Thomas Street's suspension foot bridge, built in 1854 spanning the stream, circa 1890.

Niagara Falls New York Public Library

Niagara Falls New York Public Library

On the promenade around the Dufferin Islands. The carriage and foot suspension bridge Pollux and the Niagara Falls Park and River Railway bridge in the background, circa 1896.

Cedar Island and the Cynthia Islands had been sold to him for a pittance. The matter went to arbitration. The Commissioners were outraged when Macklem was awarded $100,000.[8]

After the passage of the new Niagara Falls Park Act in 1887 the Park Commissioners took over the Islands. The operators of the Burning Spring attraction were dispossessed and the Spring was moved to the high bank above the Islands at the junction of the Portage Road and the Burning Spring Road. The Islands were named the Dufferin Islands in honour of Lord Dufferin, the Governor-General of Canada who had been instrumental in advancing the cause of a public park at Niagara Falls. The Burning Springs Road was graded, gravelled and drained. An iron railing was installed along the river side of the slope. A gate house and a gate named the Dufferin Gate were built at the bottom of the Burning Springs Hill at the southern entrance to the new Park.

The Dufferin Islands were a great favourite of Park Superintendent Wilson and over the years the attention he paid to this natural beauty spot led to many improvements. The water rushing around the embayment was cutting into the high bank, causing serious erosion. To solve this problem, Wilson had built all around the embayment, a wooden cribwork. When it was filled with stones and topped with fine gravel, this structure not only protected the bank from erosion but made a fine promenade which he

called the Riverside Ramble.[9]

Sutherland Macklem's suspension bridges were kept in repair and a network of walkways and planked bridges was built connecting the small islands. Cedar-work bowers were built at observation points on the small islands, allowing visitors to rest while they enjoyed a spectacular view of the rapids. These observation points were given names such as Cascade Point and Lover's Retreat. At first tolls were charged for entrance to the Islands but after pressure was exerted by the populace of the nearby Town of Clifton, the tolls were abandoned in 1892.

In 1894 the Niagara Park and River Railway built two iron bridges to carry their tracks across the arms of the embayment. Located beside the suspension bridges, they detracted from the beauty of the area. However, they were necessary to allow the electric railway to be extended to Chippawa and Slater's Dock, to meet the Buffalo steamers. In 1900 the suspension foot bridge built by Thomas Street in the 1850's was removed.

The development of water power resources of the river was to result in a complete change to the Islands. The Ontario Power Company chose to construct its gathering weir and forebay at the entrance to the Islands. Work was begun on the gathering weir in August 1900 and completed in November. A coffer dam was built, shutting off the flow of water to the Islands and laying bare the river

The Indian Spring at Dufferin Islands in the early 1900's.

Niagara Falls New York Public Library

The Lovers' Retreat, Dufferin Islands in the early 1900's.

Niagara Falls New York Public Library

Ontario Hydro Archives

1903. The south channel at Dufferin Islands dried off during construction of the gathering weir for the Ontario Power Company. Riverside Ramble is on the right.

1903. The cascades and islands created after the Ontario Power Company Intake structure was built at the entrance to Dufferin Islands. The Park Commissioners considered this arrangement to be too formal.

1920. New Islands were built and cascades were shortened by the Ontario Power Company. The Park Commissioners were now satisfied with the results.

The first swimming area in the north channel of Dufferin Islands.

F.H. Leslie

The dangerous swimming area used in the 1950's and 1960's.

Niagara Parks Archives

The Dufferin Islands swimming area today.

Niagara Parks Archives

bed from Dufferin Islands to the southern boundary of the Park.

When the Ontario Power Company was given the right to place its intake structure and forebay at the inlet to Dufferin Islands it carried with it the obligation to remodel the "elbow" and build cascades and islands, forming a series of pond areas. This would compensate for the reduced flow of water under the new conditions. This work, when completed had a formal appearance out of keeping with the surroundings.

The construction of the third water conduit line in 1918 provided a quantity of surplus excavation material which the Ontario Power Company placed along the edges of the water channel, against the high bank, forming an irregular shore line with widened areas for planting. At the same time new islands were formed and several cascades were shortened. Plantings were made on the new islands and on the bank to correspond with the natural growth on the

main islands. Where water formerly rushed in from the river, the flow was now regulated by stop logs placed at the Ontario Power Company forebay.

A bathing area was provided in 1907 at the lower end of the elbow, where the water flowed back into the river. Sand was spread on the rock river bed, making a soft bottom. In 1910 two bath houses with roofed observation decks on the second stories, were built. A Park policeman was present at all times to keep order. This area was used as a bathing area until 1940 when the bath houses were torn down. Access to the Dufferin Islands was completely shut off during the Second World War.

After the War, swimmers began to use the deeper area near the entrance to the Islands at the foot of the Burning Springs Hill. This was a popular spot, deep enough for shallow diving from the banks. Some of the more adventuresome and foolhardy swimmers took to diving into the not so deep water from the branches of nearby trees. Several serious accidents

Niagara Parks Archives

Paddle-boats at Dufferin Islands.

occurred. The area was fenced off and swimming in this area is now strictly prohibited.

In 1962 a new bathing area was built, in the centre of the Islands, lying between two of the little cascades. At the upstream end there is a shallow area roped off for small children. Two stone and timber buildings were erected to serve as combined change houses and washrooms. Lifeguards are on duty during the summer season and the area is a popular place for local bathers. It is an ideal spot for parents to bring their small children.

In 1920 Commission Chairman P.W. Ellis wrote to the *Toronto Mail,* describing improvements that the Commissioners planned for Queen Victoria Park and the Dufferin Islands "At Dufferin Islands the Commission is going to have a real gondola for visitors to glide over the waters, with a real Venetian to Pole it."[10] This gondola never materialized, but in 1973 fifteen paddle boats were provided for hire at the site of the old bathing area of 1907. They proved to be very popular. In 1976 the operation of these paddle boats was leased to a private concessionaire.[11]

The present Dufferin Islands area remains a favourite recreational area for local residents and visitors alike. Picnic tables, scenic paths laid out amongst the islands and an excellent swimming area for young and old are the main reasons for its continued popularity.

Niagara Parks Archives

Niagara Parks Archives

Niagara Parks Archives

Views of Dufferin Islands.

Oak Hall

On August 5, 1898 after Sutherland Macklem died, his heirs sold the Clark Hill property to James R. Smith, a wealthy lumber merchant from Tonawanda N.Y.. Smith's daughter, Grace, inherited the property from her father in 1904. She was the wife of Dr. Harry Y. Grant, a Buffalo oculist, and they took up residence in the old house. In 1916 the Grants sold the house and the adjoining land to Paul A. Schoellkopf, a member of the prominent Niagara Falls, New York family so long associated with the development of hydraulic power.

Harry Oakes, the mining millionaire, bought the estate from Schoellkopf on July 15, 1924. He hired the architectural firm of Findlay and Foulis, the same architects who designed the new Table Rock House, to design the 37 room Tudor-style baronial edifice that is present day Oak Hall. The reconstruction took four years and in 1928 the Oakes family moved in. The Oakes family lived in Oak Hall for six years until Harry Oakes, annoyed by the inroads that taxes were making on his income, wound up his affairs in Canada and moved his family to England. He left his properties in the Niagara area in the care of a holding company, Welland Securities. In 1935 he moved to Nassau in the Bahamas and it was while he was living there, in 1939, that he was created a baronet and became Sir Harry Oakes. On July 8, 1943 he died tragically in the Bahamas.

In 1943 Lady Eunice Oakes, Sir Harry's widow, deeded Oak Hall to the Government of Canada to be used as a convalescent hospital for the Royal Canadian Air Force. When there was no longer a need for convalescent facilities, the Federal Government deeded it back to Lady Oakes in 1952. Soon after, Sir Sidney Oakes, the eldest son and heir to his father's baronetcy, moved into the Hall with his wife, Lady Greta, and lived there for several years before returning to the Bahamas.

The Niagara Parks Commission purchased the estate on May 25, 1959. For the next few years the building was used only for public displays put on by the Niagara District Art Association. In 1964 the Commission furnished several rooms on the ground floor, with furniture which Sir Harry Oakes had purchased from the estate of Dr. Harry Y. Grant. The furniture included the historic dining chairs that were used at the dinner hosted by Dr. Grant at his estate Victoria Place, on October, 9, 1919, when Albert Edward, Prince of Wales was the honoured guest. Each chair used at this historic dinner has carved into the back, the name of the distinguished person who occupied it. At the same time the Commission acquired from Dr. Grant's estate the hand carved teakwood chairs that were used at the treaty signing that ended the Boxer Rebellion in China in 1901.

The terrace was covered with a colourful canvas canopy and furnished with tables and chairs, and "Tea on the Terrace" was instituted in 1964. Oak Hall was "open to view" and visitors were shown through the building for an admission fee of 50¢. A feature of the tour was the display of Niagara Falls

Oak Hall, now Administration Headquarters for the Niagara Parks.

art, oils, watercolours, lithographs and sketches on the subject of Niagara Falls. In 1966, to encourage larger attendance on the guided tours, the price of admission was reduced to 25¢.

The number of visitors to Oak Hall did not come up to expectations and a study was undertaken by a Commission committee to look into the reason for the limited popularity of the Oak Hall tour. The Committee found that while small sightseeing buses and cars entered the grounds, the percentage of visitors actually visiting the building was small. The visitors came into the grounds, looked around without getting out of their vehicles, and left. A Par Three Golf Course was chosen as a suitable use for the Oak Hall property adjoining the house. On June 17, 1966 a 9 hole golf course was opened. The combined rental shop and ticket office was located in the former three car garage at the west end of the building. In 1968 the "Tea on the Terrace" service was discontinued due to a lack of patronage. Oak Hall itself continued to be open to the public.

One of the recommendations of the Richard Strong Report presented to the Parks Commission in December 1968, was that Oak Hall be remodelled for use as an Administrative Headquarters. No

action was taken until the Fall of 1980 when the Commissioners allotted money for an architectural study, to consider the feasibility of converting Oak Hall to Administrative Offices. The feasibility report was presented to the Commissioners and it was decided to proceed. By October 1981 tenders had been received and a contractor chosen. The architects for the project were Chapman-Murray Associates. The renovations took a year to complete. The golf rentals shop and ticket office for the Par Three Golf Course were relocated to the gate house at the entrance to the grounds and the three car garage formerly used by the shop was converted to offices.

On October 24, 1982 the Administrative Offices were moved from the Administration building in Queen Victoria Park to Oak Hall. The Hall had been remodelled into 23 offices, meeting rooms and storage rooms, while still retaining the Great Hall reception area, the dining room and the living room in their original state. They are furnished with the historic chairs from the Prince of Wales' visit and the Boxer Rebellion Treaty signing. The Niagara Parks Collection of Niagara Falls art is also on display in these rooms. Of special interest is the living room which tradition says is lined with panelling Mr.

Niagara Parks Archives

The Interior of Oak Hall.

Niagara Parks Archives

The Living Room.

The Dining Room.

Niagara Parks Archives.

Niagara Parks Archives

The Great Hall Reception Room.

Schoellkopf acquired from Hampton Court, Henry VIII's Royal Palace on the Thames River. Visitors are welcome. After many years of investigation and study a use has been found for this attractive building which will assure its preservation. It will continue to be a familiar landmark in Niagara Falls for many years to come.

The Par Three Golf Course at Oak Hall.

Niagara Parks Archives.

The Hollow

The same conditions that resulted in the formation of the Dufferin Islands embayment prevailed in the area between Dufferin Islands and the Horseshoe Falls. Here the river overflowed its banks in high water periods and tore at the base of the high bank eroding and carrying off the glacial sand and gravel and leaving it spread out on the bed of the flooded area when it receded. Gradually the area was built up with this debris until there was a flat table land which was washed over only in periods of very high water level, that is, a flood-plain. By the time the early settlers arrived the area was usually high and dry.

It was in this area, which became known as "The Hollow" that John Burch built his saw and grist mills in 1786 near the present day site of the Toronto Power Generating Station. Burch's Mills made the first industrial use of the waters on the west bank of the Niagara River at the Falls. John Burch was a United Empire Loyalist who was granted land amounting to 230.7 ha (570 acres) on the river front between the head of the rapids and Chippawa. He asked Lieutenant Tinling, the Engineering Officer at Fort Niagara, for permission to build a saw and grist mill at the head of the rapids, adjoining his property. Tinling decided that a location lower down the river would be better suited for a mill and Burch was granted permission by Major Campbell, Commandant of Fort Niagara to build on the site Lieutenant Tinling recommended, on the river bank just below the islands.

Burch's Mills were unapproachable by water.

Settlers had to bring their grain and logs overland. Logs floated down the Welland River had to be hauled overland to the high bank behind the mill in winter, then rolled down the hill to the mill. This was a waste of labour and time. Although Burch had invested nearly all his money in his mills, he again sought permission to build at the head of the rapids, where the logs could be floated down the Niagara River to the mill. He was refused again, but not long after, in 1794 two other men, Benjamin Canby and John MacGill were given permission to build a saw and grist mill upstream of Burch's Mills. This was a great blow to Burch and his business suffered. John Burch died in 1797 and his mills were purchased by Samuel Street Jr. in 1798, and became known as Street's Mills.

The presence of an adequate supply of swiftly running water for water power soon attracted other industries to the area. A small hamlet which became known as "The Hollow" grew up in this lower level between the Mills and the high bank. An early traveller described the area: "As I approached the Falls, the banks of the river became higher, owing to its declivity in its bed, for the ground preserves its same level above and below the Falls. From the high bank on which I stood, I beheld at my feet a plot of cultivated ground, mills and houses - the Rapids - a mill race formed in the rapids."[2] Two roads led down into The Hollow, one from the south off Portage Road and the other from the north, providing access from two directions. Another writer in 1810 mentioned four or five buildings in The Hollow

Niagara — a view of the Flats and the Upper Cascades by John Vanderlyn, circa 1802.

New York State Parks, Senate House Historic Site, Kingston, New York.

including a mill and a tannery.[3] The tannery was established by John Hardy in 1808.

The American forces burnt Street's Mills and the other mills in The Hollow on July 26, 1814, after the Battle of Lundy's Lane, as they retired to their camp above Chippawa. After the war Street's Mills were rebuilt. The grist mill was enlarged and a fulling and cloth mill were added. A considerable village populated by the mill workers, grew up in The Hollow. Samuel Street built a house on the lower level, opposite the Mills and directly below Clark Hill which was located on the high bank above.

In 1826 Zeba Gay established a nail factory in The Hollow, where nails were cut from hoop iron. As many as 270 nails an hour could be cut from the hoop iron by one man. There was also a clock factory there, operated by a man named Utley, who made wooden clock cases into which he inserted wooden clock works imported from Pennsylvania.

The importance of Street's Mills is reflected in a statement made by William Hamilton Merritt in 1823. He said that they were the only Mills from Long Point (on Lake Erie) around to Dundas capable of doing a merchantable business.[4] An industrial survey made in 1847 states that 12,000 yards of woolens and satinets were turned out annually from these mills. The coming of steampowered mills greatly reduced the importance of Street's Mills. On September 30, 1874 the mills were destroyed by fire. *The Niagara Falls Gazette* reported: "The five-storey building known as Street's Mills burned to the ground. The building was occupied by Walker's grist Mill and Gillett's Woolen Factory."[5] By that time The Hollow had become known as "The Flats".

When the Queen Victoria Park Commissioners took over the area in 1888 only the ruins of Street's Mills remained. The area which was named "The Flats" remained undeveloped for many years except for the roadway which was widened to 5.5 m (18 ft). and a walkway laid along the base of the high bank and given the name Botanist's Ramble. Other paths were laid out along the river's edge, with shelters and bowers located at points giving a fine view of the Upper Cascade Rapids, which were called "White Horse" and "Tempest" rapids. The area was accessible only to those who paid the toll to cross the Cedar Island bridges. Roderick Cameron, the Park's chief gardener, occupied the former residence of Samuel Street. It was beside Cameron's house that a small conservatory was built in 1897 to house exotic plants and show off a modest display of winter blooming plants.

Beginning in 1902 and lasting for a period of almost twenty years, The Flats were torn up by the

Topography of Niagara, 1827, by George Catlin. This bird's-eye view of the Falls of Niagara and the surrounding area shows the Portage Road and the first road into the Park by way of the ravine. The Pavilion Hotel is shown on the high bank above the Horseshoe Falls, and details of the buildings in the Hollow, the Flats, are also depicted.

Hirschl & Adler Galleries.

construction of the Canadian Niagara and Electrical Development Company Powerhouses. As well, the three Ontario Power Company conduits were laid in the rock and soil of The Flats, close to the base of the high bank. The last conduit was laid in 1917-18, a "temporary" conduit made of wooden staves bound with iron. It remained uncovered in the area of The Flats until the 1950's when Ontario Hydro covered it with concrete. Only after this was it possible to cover the area with top soil and seed it. The area of The Flats is now occupied by the Greenhouse-Conservatory, the NPC Service Yards, the Canadian Niagara and the Electrical Development Company (Toronto Power Co.) Generating Stations. A large parking lot is laid out on top of the buried conduits from Fraser Hill to Table Rock. No trace remains of the former industrial activity which was so much a part of this area in the early 1800's.

View of the Falls of Niagara, from the bank near Birches' Mills. An aquatint, by George Heriot, coloured by hand.

Niagara Falls (undated). An oil painting on canvas by Robert Whale.

Picture Division, Public Archives Canada, Ottawa.

The Niagara Parks Collection

Cedar Island

A crescent shaped island in the river directly south of the crest of the Horseshoe Falls was known at various times as Swayze's Island, Long Island, Crescent Island and later Cedar Island. It was first occupied by Isaac Swayze who, in 1804, was granted a license to occupy it at pleasure, on condition that he would not erect any building other than one constructed of wood and that he would not assign his rights of occupation to anyone else.[1] Swayze made no effort to develop the 2 ha (5 acre) island and it remained in a wild state. In 1855 Thomas C. Street applied for control of the island. Street who already controlled the land along the river from Table Rock to the island was allowed to purchase it from the Crown for 12 pounds 10 shillings. He took possession on November 11, 1857.[2] The island had diminished in size due to the strength of the river current which was eroding the east side and its area was estimated to be slightly over 0.81 ha (2 acres).

Street immediately began to develop the island, first by erecting wooden bridges set on stone filled crib work, connecting the island with the mainland at its south end and at Table Rock. He then had a roadway laid to connect his mills on the Upper Rapids with the Table Rock area. He charged 10 cents per person for the use of the bridges. In 1859 or 1860 he had a 15 m (50 ft.) wooden tower built in a lattice work design and named it Street's Pagoda. It was supported by a two storey frame building at its base. The tower tapered to an observation platform at the top, reached by climbing seven flights of stairs. The Pagoda was never a paying proposition. Sutherland Macklem, T.C. Street's nephew and heir, continued to operate it after Street's death, as it was on the route from Table Rock to the Cynthia Islands, and the Burning Spring.

When the Queen Victoria Park Commissioners took over, they demolished the tower and converted the two-storey building at its base into a residence for William Whistler, one of the gate-keepers employed by the Park. The road through the island was widened to 5.5 m (18 ft.). The two Cedar Island bridges were found to be in a dangerous condition and were strengthened.

In 1904 the Canadian Niagara Power Company chose the mainland adjoining the west side of Cedar Island as the site for its new powerhouse. Cedar Island was fated to disappear during the construction of the powerhouse. The gap, where the water entered the channel around the island, became the powerhouse's water intake point, and the bed of the channel around the island was incorporated into the powerhouse's forebay. The rest of the channel was filled in, bridges were torn down and Cedar Island became part of the mainland. It remains only in pictures of the early days.

Street's Pagoda on Cedar Island, circa 1875.

Cedar Island and Street's Pagoda, circa 1879, from a stereograph by George Barker.

Table Rock House and Scenic Tunnel

When the Queen Victoria Park Commissioners took over Table Rock House they decided to continue the Behind the Sheet attraction as it was popular with tourists and would be a source of revenue for the Park. In 1887 the Commissioners decided that for the comfort and convenience of visitors "the toilsome descent and ascent by way of the circular stairway should be replaced with an hydraulic lift".[1] The Fensom Elevator Works of Toronto was chosen to install the lift at a cost of $7,300.[2]

The Annual Report of 1887 said "The Lift is sufficiently large to accommodate eight or ten visitors with their accompanying guides, and occupies but three fourths of a minute in the upward and downward journey. The car rises in an open wrought iron tower. The water required to work the lift is brought in large pipes from the river above the Falls, a distance of some 600 ft.. The pipes are laid in a channel blasted out of the compact limestone rock . . . Owing to the extraordinary accumulation of ice . . . it was found necessary to equip the iron tower in which the lift runs with wooden shutters, having glazed openings for the admission of light. These shutters will be removed in summer".[3] At the foot of the elevator a broad platform was constructed with a wooden walkway leading from it, winding around the large pieces of fallen rock to the river's edge close to the base of the Falls.

During the late winter and early spring of 1889 there was a series of major rock falls in the centre of the Horseshoe Falls which reduced the flow over the brink at the Canadian shore. This massive erosion plus general low water conditions in the Great Lakes "cut off most of the supply from the Sheet of Falling Water which has long been one of the chief delights of intelligent visitors to the Falls".[4] With little water falling over the Falls at the Canadian flank there was no longer an Under the Falls attraction.

The Commissioners decided to have a tunnel built through the rock to come out well behind the Horseshoe Falls at a point past Termination Rock. Here an observation portal would be cut, bringing visitors out behind the falling water. The bore of the tunnel was made through a layer of stratified blue clay which lay between two thick strata of limestone, leaving a strong ceiling and a smooth floor. The tunnel was 46 m (150 ft.) long and 2 m (7 ft.) high and 1.4 m (4½ ft.) wide. Visitors were guided through the tunnel passage by guides carrying lanterns. The new tunnel made operations in the winter possible and greatly increased the revenue from this attraction.[5]

When the Commissioners took over they did not allow photographers in the Park. Tourists did not have the opportunity of having their pictures taken while they were in water-proof dress ready to go Under the Falls as the attraction was known then. Instead Park employees offered to summon a photographer from outside the Park, who would then come by horse and carriage to Table Rock House to take the pictures. There was a long delay, and it was hot and uncomfortable waiting around in the water-proof clothing.[6] In response to public demand, the Commissioners reversed the decision and in 1889,

The dried off Canadian flank of the Horseshoe Falls, circa 1903.

Underwood and Underwood

for a $1,025. annual fee, they granted John Zybach, a Niagara Falls photographer, a three year lease for photographic privileges at Table Rock House. On June 6, 1893 the firm of Zybach and Brundage was granted an exclusive ten year lease with rights to the Hydraulic Lift, the "Under the Falls" attraction and the photographic business at Table Rock. The Commissioners had fresh in their minds the abuses inflicted on the unwary tourist by the private operators of Table Rock House during the days of the Front. Now, the Commissioners would be held responsible and criticized if the lessees did not treat the public in a fair and equitable manner.

Things did not always go smoothly. In the late summer of 1893 a complaint was lodged by the Commissioners of the New York State Reservation, that the name "Cave of the Winds" was being used to promote the area below Table Rock. The original Cave of the Winds was on the American side - it was the cavern behind the Bridal Veil Falls, the small falls to the right and forming part of the American Cataract. Clearly this was an attempt by the lessees at Table Rock to capitalize on the popularity of the American attraction. Chairman Langmuir, after an exchange of correspondence with the New York State Reservation over this matter, wrote Superintendent Wilson on November 1, 1893 and directed that the term "Cave of the Winds" be effaced from Table Rock.

From time to time the Superintendent had to deal

Entrance to the Scenic Tunnel circa 1900.

Niagara Falls New York Public Library

with complaints made by tourists against the lessees concerning merchandise which had been purchased but had not been forwarded as promised.[7] During 1901 complaints were made by visitors that the lessees, guides and assistants at the Under the Falls attraction were soliciting tips, telling visitors that it was the custom to give them. The Superintendent contacted Zybach and Co. demanding that this practice stop. He received in reply a memorandum signed by thirty-two of the Company's employees stating that they would not solicit tips from visitors.[8]

When the second ten year extension of the lease of the Table Rock concessions came up for renewal, the Commissioners regretted having included the provision for an extension. The Ontario Power Company wanted to take over the Hydraulic Lift and use it to transport their workers to the powerhouse construction site in the lower gorge below Table Rock. As part of the Pipe Line and Power House Agreement negotiated with the Commissioners in 1902, the Company agreed to extend the tunnel 244 m (800 ft.) behind the Horseshoe Falls and construct an elevator connecting with the new tunnel. They would also provide the electric power needed to operate the elevator for ten years. The new elevator and tunnel extension would be ready for the 1903 tourist season. In return the Ontario Power Company would take over the Hydraulic Lift.

The Commissioners were pleased with the new Refectory building which was being built as part of the same agreement and now that a new tunnel was to be built, they wanted to replace old Table Rock House with a new building on a different site. The lessees thought that Table Rock house was just fine, they didn't want a new building as they were sure that they would have to pay more rent. They refused to move and insisted that the terms of their lease be honoured. It would be twenty-three years before Table Rock House was replaced.

The Zybach and Co. lease expired on June 1, 1913 and they were allowed to continue to the end of the season. The Commission had plans for a new building but the beginning of World War I put off any thought of construction. New tenders were called for the Table Rock concessions and R.P. Slater was awarded a lease for one year only. The Slater lease was renewed in 1915 and again in 1916, with the provision that the Commission could take over at the end of any year. Business declined in 1915 due to a general reduction in wartime travel and an embargo on horse-drawn traffic crossing the Upper Steel Arch Bridge.

During 1916, to protect the power generating stations, the Military authorities barricaded Queen Victoria Park from the Refectory to Dufferin Islands. Table Rock House was closed and the Slater lease

Table Rock House area, with the Hydraulic Elevator, circa 1899.

terminated. The Commission purchased the Scenic Tunnel waterproof clothing and other equipment from R.P. Slater and prepared to take over the operation of this attaction themselves. In the winter of 1916-17 Table Rock House was used as a winter headquarters for the Military guard. The Commission was responsible for providing accommodation for the guard and during the winter bunk houses were built and guard houses were erected at the entrances to the Park. The guard moved out of Table Rock House in the spring of 1917 and the building was taken over by the Ontario Power Company to house their construction workers. When the Commissioners took back the building they found that a major renovation was required before the building could be opened for public use.

By 1924 the Horseshoe Falls had receded farther, so that the 1903 portal was exposed. A 55 m (180 ft.) extension was made to the tunnel. Table Rock House, in addition to being unsightly, occupied space in the Park where the land was narrowest, between the base of the high bank and the gorge. The increased use of the automobile in the 1920's made a wider road a necessity at this location. Table Rock House would have to be removed to make room for a wider road. An open competition was held in 1925 for the best design for a new Table Rock building. It was won by the architectural firm of Findlay and Foulis of Sault Ste. Marie. The new Table Rock House was built on a site south of the old building and closer to the Horseshoe Falls. It had space for a lunch counter, a souvenir sales room, lavatories and dressing rooms

Table Rock House, circa 1925. The elevator shaft added in 1903 is shown.

Saul Davis's Table Rock House in the 1920's.

le Rock House, Queen Victoria Park,
Niagara Falls Canada.

Table Rock House, circa 1927.

for those visiting the Scenic Tunnel. It also served as a station for the electric railway. Passengers were able to leave the electric cars on the west side of the new Table Rock House and immediately come under a protective overhang. Then they entered the building directly, avoiding the spray from the Horseshoe Falls. On completion of the new building the old Table Rock House was demolished.

Tourist business declined during the economic depression of the 1930's but Table Rock House and the Scenic Tunnel continued to draw visitors. In 1935 the roar of the Horseshoe Falls was broadcast worldwide during a Christmas radio broadcast, when a microphone was placed at the furthermost portal of the Scenic Tunnel to catch the sound of the falling water.

In 1939 when World War II began, barbed wire barricades were once again placed around the powerhouses in Queen Victoria Park. When Holland and Belgium were invaded in June 1940, the whole Park area from the Refectory to Dufferin Islands was barricaded and Table Rock House was closed. On September 29, 1944, the barricades were removed.

An inspection of the tunnel disclosed that it was not safe. There was only 1.7 m (5½ ft.) of rock left between the tunnel walls and the face of the gorge behind the Falls. A new tunnel was cut into the rock, approximately 18 m (60 ft.) back from the then main gallery of the old tunnel. The new tunnel was lined with concrete and lighted by electricity.

In 1951 an outdoor observation platform was built at the end of a branch of the old tunnel where a small outlook had been located. This new platform extended out from the edge of the cliff, allowing visitors a close-up view of the falling water. In 1954 during the Remedial Works program the flanks of the Horseshoe Falls were dried off and the bed of the river was deepened on both sides. This was to allow more water to flow over the flanks of the Falls and less in the centre, thus reducing the rate of erosion. While the flanks were dried off all the water ran towards the centre of the Horseshoe Falls and a new spray pattern emerged. Table Rock House and the viewing area in front of the building were almost continually in heavy spray. This resulted in a loss of revenue, as few tourists stayed around the area long.

The Scenic Tunnel Lookout, circa 1918.

The Observation Platform at the base of the Horseshoe Falls, 1984.

When the river bed was deepened and water once again flowed over the whole crest of the Falls, the spray pattern returned to normal.

In 1957, after the renovation of the former I.R.C. powerhouse the souvenir merchandise which had been stored on the second floor of Table Rock House, was moved to the renovated building which became the Merchandise Warehouse. This released a considerable amount of space in Table Rock House and a number of uses were proposed for it, including using it as additional selling space. In 1960 the area was leased to Paragon Holdings Ltd., to display replicas of the Royal Crown Jewels of Britain. The exhibition was planned as a permanent one. It opened on July 30, 1960 and attendance for the first year until October 31, was 33,850 people.

Extensive alterations were made to Table Rock House in 1963. Additions were made to both the north and south ends, and along the easterly side facing the Horseshoe Falls. Retail sales areas were doubled. The renovated building was ready for business in early 1964. At the same time, the main

Park road which ran between the building and the Falls, was widened by nearly 6 m (20 ft.) removing a bottleneck. The usable width of the roadway became 14 m (46 ft.) which provided diagonal parking space for an additional 60 cars. In 1969 an Observation Deck was opened on the upper balcony facing the Horseshoe Falls, to accommodate the people who were visiting the Crown Jewels Exhibit. In the first year of operation almost 60,000 people paid to enjoy the view from this location.

A recommendation of the De Leuw Cather report of 1966 was implemented when a major change in the roadway in the Table Rock area was undertaken. Work was begun in 1972 and completed in time for the 1973 season. The main roadway at the brink of the Horseshoe Falls was relocated to the west of Table Rock House, creating a totally pedestrian environment at the brink of the Falls. The change relieved congestion, and offered more people the opportunity to view the Falls.

In March 1973 Paragon Holdings Ltd., owners of the Crown Jewels exhibit, removed this display from

Table Rock House with 1963 additions.

Niagara Parks Archives

The South Building at Table Rock.

The view from the restaurant in the South building at Table Rock.

The picnic area at the South building, Table Rock.

the second floor of the building where it had been since 1960. Steadily declining attendance at the exhibit prompted the move. As fewer people climbed the stairs to the Observation Gallery now that the Crown Jewels exhibit was no longer there, the turnstiles were removed in 1974 and visitors were given free access to that area.

The facilities at Table Rock House were strained and stretched to the limit. In 1974 the building known as Table Rock South was built adjoining and upstream from the main building. It is connected to the Observation Deck of the main building by a walk which provides a breezeway underneath. From the semi-circular upstairs dining room of the new building diners get a panoramic view of the Horseshoe Falls and the Upper Cascades.

The lower floor contains a gift shop, snack bar and lavatories with special facilities for the handicapped. On the south side a pleasant, outdoor picnic patio adjoins where take-out food from the snack bar can be eaten in full view of the Upper Cascades. The area is frequented by gulls and terns which inhabit the river islands above the Falls, seeking to share the food of the picnickers.

How the Horseshoe Falls and the River have changed since the Queen Victoria Park opened on May 24, 1888 you can best understand when you realize that the pedestrian promenade in front of the buildings and the land on which Table Rock House stands were formerly part of the river bed. One hundred years ago all of these were covered by rushing water.

Refectory

The building now called the Victoria Park Restaurant was known for more than 65 years as the Refectory and it is by that name it will be remembered by many of the hundreds of thousands of visitors who have dined there over the years. The Refectory is located halfway between Table Rock and the American Falls on the site formerly occupied by Thomas Barnett's Museum, built in 1860, and later from 1889 to 1902, known as the Dufferin Cafe.

In 1902 the Dufferin Cafe stood on ground required by the Ontario Power Company for the underground distributor which would collect the water brought by the conduits from the Dufferin Islands Intake and distribute it to the penstocks supplying the generators in the powerhouse being built directly below the bank in front of the Cafe. As the Park Commissioners considered the building an eyesore, they were more than agreeable when the Ontario Power Company offered to pay $20,000 towards the cost of a new building and also to pay for the costs of demolishing the old Dufferin Cafe. The new Shelter and Refectory building, as it was called, was completed in 1904. The name Refectory in its original sense is a room in a monastery used for meals. The name was chosen for the new building because it was fashionable at the time to denote a place in a park where food and refreshment were sold as a Refectory.

In order to obtain full information about the public requirements for the proposed building, the Park Commissioners sent a representative committee, including the Superintendent, to Milwaukee, Minneapolis and Chicago, to inspect park buildings. Humboldt Park Refectory in West Chicago was thought to be the most suitable and its general plan was adapted to the special needs of Niagara Falls.

Originally modelled somewhat after a Swiss chalet, the Refectory has a distinctive green copper roof and walls of boulder stone. When the Electrical Development Company dried off 4.5 hectares (11 acres) of the river bed to construct their powerhouse and gathering weir, hundreds of granite boulders were left exposed on the river bed. These boulders which had lain under the rushing water for almost 12,000 years, were salvaged and used in the construction of the Refectory. Completion of the building was delayed until mid summer of 1904 because more boulders had to be found to complete the job.

The Refectory was designed for the convenience of the public, with spacious waiting rooms, dining rooms and wash rooms. The Zybach and Company lease which had expired on the old Cafe in 1903 was extended for ten years at an increased rental. John Zybach moved his photographic studio to the Refectory and with the approval of the Commissioners, Zybach and Company sublet the restaurant facilities at the Refectory to Samuel Barnett.

The picnic grounds were located beside the Refectory immediately to the north, and so the lower portion of the building was designed as a picnic shelter. It was open and outfitted with picnic tables

The Dufferin Cafe in Queen Victoria Park,

to accommodate picnickers in inclement weather. Hot and cold water were available. The building was 44 m (145 ft.) wide and 38 m (125 ft.) deep. A large verandah extended across the front of the building. Its most prominent feature was a large corner tower which was reached from the main hallway. It was a definite improvement over the former facilities.

The old Zimmerman lodge had become too small for the Park Administrative staff, and in 1907 the Park offices were moved to the Refectory. There a Board Room was provided for the Commissioners and a large storage safe was installed in the basement for the preservation of official papers and plans.

Zybach and Company lease expired at the end of 1913. The Commissioners advertised for new proposals and R.P. Slater was awarded a one year lease. Soon after World War I was declared in August of 1914, a barbed wire barricade was installed blocking access to the Park roadway in front of the Refectory, and up to Dufferin Islands. It was still possible for tourists to reach the Refectory dining room and it became more popular because diners could look out over the barbed wire barricades and see the Falls and the gorge.

Despite the War, renovations were carried out. The Balcony was enclosed, increasing the dining space; an excavation was made under the building for a new coal storage facility with a capacity of 68 tonnes (75 tons) of coal. The area was so designed that the sloping floor automatically fed the front of the bin. From there the coal was shovelled into the furnace. The Commissioners took over the operation of the Refectory Restaurant from the lessee in 1916. As an aid to the war effort a vegetable garden was planted and the Refectory staff grew vegetables for the restaurant - it wasn't a profitable venture, and was not planted again.

In 1920 there was high inflation and the *Niagara Falls Review* of August 20 charged: "Profiteering in the Park at the Refectory, an apple pie brings $2.00, beer costing 8¢ is sold for 35¢, two boiled eggs 40¢, and you can buy everything on Sunday. A 7 oz. glass of milk is 15¢, while the producer gets 11¢ a quart, distributor 4¢ and the Park the rest". The *Review* was soon able to report progress, prices were reduced and by September 20 the apple pies were cut in four pieces at 40¢, now $1.60 for a whole pie. The restaurant kitchen was improved, and gas for cooking

The Refectory, circa 1905.

F.H. Leslie.

The picnic shelter at the Refectory, circa 1905.

Zybach & Co.

The outdoor dining area of the Refectory Restaurant, circa 1905.

Zybach & Co.

Great Gorge Route cars stop in front of the Refectory to take on passengers, circa 1920's.

Dining on the outdoor patio, circa 1926.

The extended balcony with open air dining space, circa 1937.

The Victoria Park Gift Shop addition, circa 1951.

The Victoria Park Restaurant, circa 1982.

The Victoria Park Cafeteria, circa 1983.

Niagara Parks Archives.

The Victoria Park Restaurant, circa 1982.

was replaced by electricity. There was a bright side, a Refectory Orchestra became an added attraction but it did not play on Sunday. Dancing was so popular that in 1921 the verandah was enclosed to become the new dining room and the old dining room was made into a dance hall.

The Park Administrative offices moved out of the Refectory and into the new Administration building in 1926 and the Commissioners took the opportunity to redesign the whole Refectory. Considerable reconstruction was required as the existing foundations were not deep enough and some of the interior walls had settled. Interior changes included enlarged quarters for the Commissioners and more accommodation for the staff in a separate wing. A cold storage plant was installed on the ground floor. The front of the building was altered so that the restaurant was reached by two stairways, one on each side of the building with an open promenade at the top of the stairs extending across the front of the building. From there one could get a fine view of both Falls and the gorge.

By 1936 more space was required for dining and the dining room was enlarged. In 1938 the balcony was extended to provide open air dining space. Once again, during World War II, the area in front of the Refectory was barricaded. The restaurant was able to carry on business and it was 1944 before the barricades were removed. Again in 1948 the building

was extensively remodelled. The Commissioners' Quarters were enlarged to include a new Board Room and an attractive lounge. The main front wall of the dining room area was replaced with plate glass, giving diners inside a view of the Falls as they enjoyed their meals. The ground floor Cafeteria was remodelled at the same time and modern lavatory facilities were installed. The south side staircase was removed for the new Gift Shop. Work was completed in 1950.

The next alteration was in 1969 when the Gift Shop was enlarged and the Cafeteria remodelled to allow for an additional serving lane, which brought an increase in business because of the faster service made possible by the improvements. The dining room, now called the Victoria Park Dining Room, received a complete facelift. The original boulder stone walls were exposed and cleaned. Wooden beams and pillars were installed. A Bavarian style Patio Beer Garden was installed on the roof of the Gift Shop and provided light snacks and beer for refreshment. A new outside canvas canopy provided protection from rain and heavy spray.

In 1980 the Cafeteria underwent a major renovation. The new design has a Victorian theme with a fountain surrounded by plants and flowers as the focal point. The seating capacity of the Cafeteria was increased to 380.

King's Bridge Park

King's Bridge Park is located on one of the most historic sites within the Niagara Parks. In December 1678, La Salle's exploration party under Dominique LaMotte and including Father Louis Hennepin, spent a night camped near here at the mouth of the Chippawa River. Hennepin wrote: "On the 7th, we went in a Canou two Leagues up the River to look for a convenient Place for Building . . . We lay that night near a River which runs from the Westward, within a League above the great Falls of Niagara".[1] Francis Parkman, a recognized authority on Hennepin, interprets Hennepin's reference of "a River which runs from the Westward" as being the Chippawa.[2]

The French had a clearing, perhaps even a storehouse at this location at the mouth of the Chippawa in 1759 or earlier. They reached the place by boat, crossing from Fort du Portage (later Fort Schlosser) on the eastern bank of the river. They cut timber along the banks of the Chippawa to be used in shipbuilding on Navy Island.[3] Later the site of King's Bridge Park was part of the Crown Land Grant made to John Burch in 1796. By the terms of Jay's Treaty, signed by the British and the Americans after the end of the Revolutionary War, the Niagara River became the International Boundary. The British were required to give up their carrying place, or portage, on the east side of the river, and so had to establish a suitable portage on the west bank.[4]

Captain Gother Mann who commanded the Royal Engineers in Canada surveyed possible routes for a portage in 1788 for Lord Dorchester, Governor-in-Chief. He reported: "If . . . it should be thought expedient to carry on communication on this side of the River, then the landing place . . . must be opposite the present one. The situation above the Falls to be chosen ought I imagine to be Chippeway Creek; it is indeed nearer the Falls than Fort Schlosser and there is a very strong current which passes it, but there is no difficulty to get into the Creek. The Creek is about 80 yards across and has 7 or 8 feet depth of water; it would be necessary to have a bridge likewise a good road. The first would not cost a great deal and there is a good bottom and no current".[5]

In 1791 government wharves and docks, and blockhouses for troops were built at the "New Landing" at the mouth of Chippawa Creek. A wooden plank bridge, supported on pilings pounded into the soft bottom was built across the Creek.[6] As the bridge was paid for by the Crown, it was called the King's Bridge. The blockhouse was the first fortification at this place and was the beginning of Fort Chippawa, also known as Fort Welland and The Garrison.

When Lieutenant-Governor John Graves Simcoe came to Niagara to establish the first Government of Upper Canada, one of his first acts was to give English names to every county, township, townsite, river and lake within his jurisdiction. The Chippawa Creek became the Welland River. This led to confusion, even Mrs. Simcoe was confused. Writing in her diary she called the stream sometimes the Chippawa and sometimes the Welland.[7] Even today

Chippaway, taken from the Mouth of the Creek. A watercolour by Surgeon Edward Walsh, 1804. Fort Chippawa is on both sides of the Chippawa Creek (Welland River). The King's Bridge spans the Creek; soldiers' barracks and punishment stocks are on the left bank.

William L. Clements Library The University of Michigan

the stream is more often referred to locally as Chippawa Creek rather than the Welland River.

Erastus Granger, United States Indian Agent, made a survey of British fortifications on the west bank of the Niagara in 1807 at the request of Henry Dearborn, United States Secretary of War. He described Fort Chippawa as "merely a wooden block house, the pickets mostly rotted down, not capable of any defence".[8] During the War of 1812-14 the British forces retired to fortifications which they had set up at Fort Chippawa, after their defeat at the hands of the United States Army under General Winfield Scott at the Battle of Chippawa on July 5, 1814. To prevent the American forces from following them, they removed the plank decking from the King's Bridge. The British were forced to withdraw to Fort George the next day when Americans crossed the Chippawa at its junction with Lyon's Creek, 3.2 km (2 miles) to the west, outflanking the British position at Fort Chippawa.

Sometime between 1825 and 1829 the Welland Canal Company made the "Chippawa Cut" - they cut a channel which severed the point from the south bank of the river, creating an island.[9] The island and the area around the mouth of the Creek stayed much the same until 1917 when the Hydro Electric Power Commission began construction of the intake works for the Chippawa-Queenston Power Canal. The Creek was blocked off, and then excavated to a depth of 12.2 m (40 ft.) for a distance of 6.4 km (4 mi.), to the entrance of the Chippawa-Queenston Power Canal. The island was reduced in size, when most of the portion adjacent to the south bank was removed to create the entrance channel for the canal. The Hydro Electric Power Commission named the island Hogg Island, after Thomas Hogg, an engineer on the canal project and a native of Chippawa. During construction the original northern channel of the Creek was filled, so that what was left of the island then became part of the north shore.

The Niagara Parks Commission leased the 59 ha (146 acre) Hogg Island site from Ontario Hydro in 1937. The area remained undisturbed until the 1950's when Ontario Hydro began excavation of

F.H. Leslie

The south channel of Chippawa Creek (Welland River) leading into the Niagara River, 1915. This channel — the Chippawa Cut — was made in 1829 when the first Welland Canal had its southern terminus at Chippawa.

Niagara Parks Archives

The swimming area at King's Bridge Park.

the water intake structure and underground tunnels of the Sir Adam Beck Generating Station No. 2 project. Ontario Hydro covered the whole area of the "island" with rock debris from the excavation, then added a layer of earth fill. They left a small bay in the channel and is was used by local residents for swimming and bathing.

No further development took place until 1958, when the Parks Commission approved a plan for the development of a picnic park and swimming area on the site. Over the winter 7646 m³ (10,000 cu. yds.) of clean fill was spread over the area to increase the depth of the shallow topsoil. An entrance roadway and a parking lot were constructed and sand was dumped along the 91.4 m (300 ft.) shore line of the bay to create a sand bathing beach. An underground irrigation system was installed in 1961, making it possible to keep the turf covering the park area in a healthy condition. Public washrooms were installed in the waterworks building adjacent to the Park, which was formerly owned by the Village of Chippawa Public Utilities Commission.

In 1972 the picnic facilities were removed from Queen Victoria Park and provision was made at King's Bridge Park to accommodate the picnickers who would be visiting Queen Victoria Park. A covered picnic pavilion with a capacity of 500 people, a snack bar and public washrooms were built. At King's Bridge Park it is possible to picnic away from the traffic yet still within sound of the Falls. On the night of March 23, 1979 the pavilion and picnic tables stored inside were destroyed by a fire set by vandals. New picnic tables were provided for the 1979 season, but a new pavilion was not ready until the 1980 season.

King's Bridge Park, with its supervised swimming area, having lifeguards on duty from late June until after Labour Day, provides many happy hours of bathing and swimming recreation for thousands of visitors and Niagara area residents who regularly make use of its facilities. The swimming area freezes over in the winter and becomes a popular spot for ice fishing for smelt. The area has become important as a recreational area, enjoyed by young and old alike; its historic past is recalled only when one reads the marker which commemorates Fort Chippawa.

An air view of King's Bridge Park 1984. The Niagara River is on the right and the inlet for the Chippawa-Queenston Power Canal is at the left.

The Maid of the Mist

The Maid of the Mist boats have been an attraction at the Falls of Niagara for over one hundred and thirty seven years, since 1846 when the first Maid plied the waters of the Niagara River below the Falls. Christian Schultz who visited here in 1807 saw the possibility of navigating a boat in the river below the Falls: "Immediately below the Falls is a small space in the river, over which a boat might cross with the greatest safety . . . What first led me to this reflection was the manoeuvres of some wild ducks, which I observed swimming backwards and forwards in this space, and who carefully avoided every place which I should have thought dangerous for a boat. Could I have obtained a canoe or skiff, I should not have hesitated a moment about trying the experiment".[1]

What Schultz observed was that there was a current close to the Canada shore that went upstream. Another visitor perhaps best described how the row boats were propelled across the river:" . . . a back eddy enabled us to get up the stream towards the great falls without difficulty, and then thrusting forth into the stream, we were whirled downwards . . .while clouds of spray, driven by the wind from both falls, showered down on our waterproofs . . . Our surly Charon pulled right sturdily across this troubled tide, when much to our satisfaction, another eddy caught our boat, and took us up to a rough stage at the foot of a perpendicular cliff".[2] The row boat had landed safely on the American shore.

It was William Forsyth, the owner of the Pavilion Hotel on the Canada side, who first established a regular row boat ferry service across the lower river below the Falls in 1818. Working in co-operation with Parkhurst Whitney, the proprietor of the Eagle Tavern on the United States side, Forsyth operated for two years before he got into trouble with the Crown for encroaching on the Crown-owned Chain Reserve without permission. The ferry rights were subsequently awarded to Christopher Boughner, whose farm adjoined the gorge bank above the ferry. It was awarded to George Milmine for three years from 1822 to 1825, then the firm of Clark and Street was granted a 21 year lease on the ferry beginning on April 5, 1825.

A condition of the Clark and Street lease was that they build a carriage road down the side of the gorge to the ferry landing. The cobblestone ferry road was completed in 1827 at a cost of $5000 and for 65 years it was to be the only connection between the ferry landing and the upper bank. It is still in use today, having been widened in places, otherwise it remains the same route as when it was constructed in 1827. Clark and Street immediately sublet the ferry privilege and it was operated by a number of different individuals over the term of their 21 year lease.

The row boat ferries operated without competition until 1846 when the Niagara Falls Ferry Association received a charter from the State of New York, permitting it to operate a ferry across the Niagara River. The United States dock was located at the foot of a newly constructed carriage road which

The Maid of the Mist landing. A pencil sketch by Ferdinand Richardt, 1856.

terminated at the river's edge just south of the present Railway Arch Bridge. The carriage road was expected to accommodate the stage coaches and carriages which the Ferry Association thought would be making the crossing and connecting with other stage coaches on the Canada side.

In May 1846, the first Maid of the Mist was launched. It was a clumsy barge-like sidewheeler, powered by steam from a coal fired boiler, with two smoke stacks. The anticipated stage coach traffic did not materialize and with the opening of the Suspension Bridge over the gorge at the Whirlpool Rapids in 1848 the ferry lost business. The owners soon had the boat making sightseeing trips taking tourists up the river and close to the Horseshoe Falls. This odd-shaped craft operated on the river until 1854 and it was depicted in many of the paintings and sketches of the time.[3]

On July 14, 1854 a larger and more luxurious Maid of the Mist was launched at the United States dock site. She was a single stack, steam-driven paddle-wheel vessel over 22 m (72 ft.) in length. The

The Maid of the Mist, launched July 14, 1854. The boat was sold at auction and sailed through the Whirlpool Rapids by Captain Joel Robinson in 1861, so that it could be delivered at Queenston, enroute to its new owner in Montreal. A pencil sketch by Ferdinand Richardt, 1856.

beam was 5 m (17 ft.) and the boat had a 2.4 m (8 ft.) draught.[4] The boat was used primarily for sightseeing and India rubber oil skin coats and caps were provided to protect the passengers from the spray of the Falls. The vessel was under the command of Captain Joel Robinson.

F. H. Leslie

The Canadian dock of the Maid of the Mist Steamboat Company. The Upper Steel Arch Bridge is in the centre. Behind the bridge can be seen the industrial area of the Mill District in Niagara Falls, New York, circa 1912.

Niagara Parks Archives

The Maid of the Mist in front of the American Falls, circa 1950.

This second Maid of the Mist operated for six years. In 1857 the ferry and carriage fares were listed as follows:

Ferriage to the United States by row boat 18¾¢
Ferriage to the United States by steamer 25¢
Clifton House 64¢

During 1859 the Maid participated in one of Blondin's stunts and the next year, 1860, Farini made use of the Maid for one of his stunts. In September of 1860 the Maid carried the Prince of Wales, later Edward VII, on a trip to the Horseshoe Falls. It was at the end of this season that the Maid's owner, W.O. Buchanan, decided to sell the boat. Buchanan had financial problems and the prospects for future tourist business were clouded and uncertain because of the impending American Civil War. The boat was sold at private auction to a Montreal company. A condition of the sale was that the boat be delivered to Lake Ontario. Captain Joel Robinson piloted the Maid through the Whirlpool Rapids and the Lower Niagara River to Queenston on June 6, 1861.[5] The boat was delivered to her new owners, and renamed the Maid of Orleans. She served for years as a ferry between Quebec City and the Isle of Orleans.

The row boat ferries, which had not left the river during the Maid's six years of operation, now took over the ferrying and sightseeing trips, operating on the river until as late as 1893, charging 25¢ for the trip.[6]

In 1884, two Clifton businessmen, R.F. Carter and Frank LeBlond, formed the Maid of the Mist Steamboat Company and invested $10,000 in a new Maid of the Mist. The 21 m (70 ft.) boat was built of white oak, and had a glass enclosed wheel house. A second boat was built at the American landing and launched on July 16, 1892.[7] Also built of white oak it was a larger boat, 27 m (89 ft.) long with a 5.8 m (19 ft.) beam. The Maids were christened numbers I and II.

When the Company was formed, Carter and LeBlond applied to the Town of Niagara Falls for a licence of occupation, to enable them to establish a wharf and receive landing rights. On May 27, 1862 the Commissioner of Crown Lands for the Province of Ontario issued a licence of occupation to the Municipal Council of the Town of Niagara Falls for the Chain Reserve and the strip of land lying between the Reserve and the water's edge in front of the town. It was under this licence of occupation that the Town authorities sub-let the land for a wharf, on June 14, 1884 to Carter and LeBlond. An Order-in-Council passed by the Province of Ontario on July 15, 1887 vested in the Commissioners, for park purposes, all the lands below the high bank of the river and in the talus below - this included the Maid of the Mist landing.

The Town of Niagara Falls challenged the right of the Park Commissioners to take over jurisdiction of the land on which the Maid of the Mist Company had their wharf.[8] The matter was not settled until 1895 when the unanimous judgement of the Supreme Court of Ontario was rendered in favour of the Commissioners.[9] After this decision, the Maid of the Mist Company arrived at an agreement with the Park Commission under which they received wharf and landing rights beginning in 1898, at a rental of $300 a year.[10]

No accidents marred the safety record of these two boats. They carried hundreds of thousands of sightseers in the next 45 years, their powerful engines enabling them to go closer to the Horseshoe Falls than the two previous Maids. The great ice jam of 1938 which pushed the Honeymoon Bridge off its abutments, nearly destroyed the Maids as they lay in their winter berths, high up on the Canadian shore. The ice covered the landing area, pushed the caretaker's house off its foundations and came nearly to the deck level of the boats, but no serious damage was done.

On April 22, 1955, while the boats were being prepared for the coming season, one boat caught fire, and soon both boats were ablaze. The flames were fed by the many layers of paint which covered the woodwork, and they soon were in ruins. In less than a month a 12 m (40 ft.) yacht was built in Owen Sound and lowered into the Niagara Gorge and the river. Christened "The Little Maid" she helped fill the gap until a new, larger Maid of the Mist could be built.

The new, all-steel Maid of the Mist was built in four pieces in Owen Sound. The pieces were trucked to Niagara Falls and lowered over the bank. Welders worked around the clock to assemble the boat. This Maid was 20 m (66 ft.) long, with a 4.9 m (16 ft.) beam and powered by a 200 hp diesel engine. The boat was launched on July 28, 1955 and a sister ship was launched on June 12, 1956. These boats were licensed to carry 101 passengers and they were christened Maid of the Mist I and II, even though they were the fifth and sixth Maids of the Mist to sail the Niagara River, not counting the Little Maid. The Little Maid was removed from service in 1956 and sold.

In 1971 James V. Glynn purchased the assets of

Maid of the Mist in front of the American Falls.

Maid of the Mist Steamboat Company

Maid of the Mist V being towed through Queen Victoria Park, 1983.

Niagara Parks Archives

Maid of the Mist V sailing out of the horseshoe.

Maid of the Mist Steamboat Company

the Maid of the Mist Steamboat Company and became the sole owner. He immediately ordered a new boat. Maid of the Mist III was built in Wheatley, Ontario and sailed to Niagara Falls by way of Lake Erie and the Niagara River to Chippawa. Here the boat was hauled out of the water, put on a flat bed truck and driven to Queen Victoria Park. On June 13, 1972 the boat was lowered into the gorge and let down a ramp into the river. The 63.96 tonnes (65 ton), 19.8 m (65 ft.) long vessel was christened Maid of the Mist III. Powered by two 235 hp diesels, this boat is licensed to carry 150 passengers. Maid of the Mist IV, also constructed in Wheatley, was launched on June 15, 1976. A larger boat than Maid III, she is 21.9 m (72 ft.) long with a 7.3 m (24 ft.) beam, and is licensed to carry 200 passengers.

Thursday June 9, 1983 Maid of the Mist V was launched. Larger than any of her sister boats, this

Maid is licensed to carry 300 passengers. Over the winter of 1985-86 Maid III and IV were double-decked, increasing Maid III's passenger capacity to 210 and Maid IV's to 300.

Maid II, the boat which rescued Roger Woodward, was sold in October 1983 to the Pentecostal Church of Ontario for use as a missionary ship, to travel between outposts on the Amazon River.

Over the years the Maids have carried hundreds of thousands of sightseers into the turbulent waters at the base of the Horseshoe Falls. Queen Elizabeth II, Prince Philip, Nehru, Marilyn Monroe, and Soviet Premier Alexei N. Kosygin have made the trip. They looked just like other tourists when they were garbed in the Maid's head to toe waterproof clothing. To all who have taken it, the trip on the Maid of the Mist has given a never to be forgotten view of the cataracts of Niagara.

Maid of the Mist Incline

In 1894 the Niagara Park and River Railway built an electrically powered incline railway down the bank at the foot of the Ferry Road for the convenience of those using the Maid of the Mist boats. The Maid of the Mist Company built a new dock at the foot of the incline. The incline station at the top housed the machinery, a ticket office and a souvenir store. The whole concession was leased to the Clifton Hotel in 1895. The Clifton Incline as it was officially called became the property of the International Railway Company in 1901 when the Niagara Park and River Railway was purchased by the I.R.C. and became the Park and River Division of the I.R.C.

On September 12, 1932 the I.R.C. surrendered its

The top of the bank at the road leading to the ferry landing, circa 1840.

The ticket office, souvenir store and upper station of the Maid of the Mist Incline - then called the Clifton Incline, circa 1898.

Niagara Parks Archives

franchise for the electric railway. The incline and the equipment became the property of the Parks Commission. In 1937 the obsolete and unsightly building housing the souvenir store and ticket office was removed and from that time until 1976 the incline operations were carried on from what had formerly been the basement of the old building.

The 1894 Clifton Incline Railway was slow and carried only 12 passengers per car each way. The increased popularity of the Maid of the Mist boat rides made it imperative that a new incline be built. Work began on October 18, 1976 and the new incline

was ready for the opening of the Maid of the Mist season on May 21, 1977. Designed and installed by Von Roll of Switzerland, the incline railway has two cars on a common rail with a fail-safe centre by-pass directing each car automatically to its branch. The actual length of the incline is 96.9 m (318 ft.) with an effective length of 92.4 m (303 ft.). The cars carry 24 passengers each and take 45 seconds to travel the 50 m (165 ft.) 31° grade. In 1983 side entrance doors were installed on the cars allowing passengers to embark and disembark more quickly. In 1973 the incline was renamed, the Maid of the Mist Incline.

Maid of the Mist dock at the foot of the Incline Railway, circa 1900.

The new Maid of the Mist Incline, with the cars just about to enter the fail-safe centre by-pass, circa 1978.

The Clifton Incline as seen from the upper loading platform, circa 1946.

The International Railway Company souvenir store and ticket office for the Incline Railway, 1932.

The Maid of the Mist ticket office at the top of the Incline Railway, 1984.

Maid of the Mist - Roger Woodward

On July 9, 1960 Maid of the Mist II participated in the most spectacular event in the history of the Maids. On the 2:30 p.m. trip, the boat carrying 60 passengers was in command of Captain Clifford Keech, a veteran of some 23 years on the river. About to make his turn away from the Horseshoe, Keech spotted a bright orange object. It was a lifejacket and there was a small boy in it, floating in the turbulent water.

The boy was Roger Woodward, a 7 year old, who with his 17 year old sister Deanne had gone for a boat ride in the Upper River with Jim Honeycutt, a family friend. Unfamiliar with the river, Honeycutt had piloted his motorboat past the "point of no return", the International Control Dam on the Upper River. Unaware of the danger, Honeycutt came within sight of tourists on Goat Island, only half a mile away from the brink of the Horseshoe Falls. Suddenly, realizing his perilous position he vainly tried to turn the boat away from the approaching rapids. The motor failed, the boat entered the rapids and capsized. Roger and Honeycutt were tossed into the water. Deanne was trapped beneath the boat, she fought to free herself and by good fortune drifted close to the bank at Terrapin Point. Two men, out of the hundreds watching, took action. John R. Hayes, a truck driver and auxiliary policeman, from Union, New Jersey, climbed the guard rail, stretched out one arm, while grasping the rail with the other and caught Deanne's arm. Hayes was in trouble and found it difficult to

hold on. John Quattrochi of Pennsgrove, New Jersey came along, climbed the railing, and grabbed Deanne's other arm. Then the two men pulled her to safety.

Honeycutt, without a lifejacket, went over the Horseshoe Falls and was killed. Roger rode the crest, buoyed by the lifejacket and fell into the turbulent water below. Captain Keech on seeing the boy in the water, manoeuvred his boat so that his crew could pick up the boy as he drifted past on the starboard side. First Mate Murray Hartlin and Deckhand Jack Hopkins flung a life perserver on a rope to the boy. Twice it landed 1.5 m (5 ft.) away from Roger. The third toss fell within an arm's length and he grabbed for it and mounted it. He was pulled out of the water and was landed safely on the Maid's deck.

Captain Lawrence McGinn, the President of the Canadian Maid of the Mist Steamboat Company, arrived alongside in the Company launch. He headed closer to the Horseshoe to check out a red object. It turned out to be the gas tank from Honeycutt's boat. There was no sign of Honeycutt.

In the 114 years since the first Maid of the Mist steamed up the angry waters of the Niagara River on the way to the Horseshoe, nothing so spectacular had ever occurred. Looking back, some may say that it was luck or fate, some that it was the hand of God. Interpret it as you will, it stands out as the Maid of the Mist's finest hour.

Ralph Grant

Roger Woodward astride a Maid of the Mist life preserver.

Niagara Parks Archives

Mr. and Mrs. Roger Woodward when they visited Niagara Falls in 1981 on the anniversary of his fortunate escape from death.

Maid of the Mist Steamboat Company

Jack Hopkins, a deck hand on the Maid of the Mist, extending a hand to Roger Woodward.

Illumination

It was not until 1860 that advances in the science of artificial lighting permitted man to give serious thought to lighting the Falls of Niagara at night. Before that time, the only way the Falls could be seen at night was with the assistance of Mother Nature.

George Ticknor, who visited Niagara Falls in 1845 and again in 1852, left this record of an experience he had while staying on the Canada side: "The finest thing we have seen yet - and one of the grandest I ever saw - was a thunderstorm among the waters, as it seemed to be, the other night, which lighted up the two Cascades - with a most magnificent effect. They had a spectral look, as they came out of the darkness and were again swallowed up in it, that defies all description and all imagination." Later in his stay, while he was on the U.S. side, he went for a nighttime ride in a row boat in the river below the Falls and he recounts this experience as he was passing in front of the American Falls: "The moon was nearly full . . . and began to illumine the edge of the waters above us, as they plunged down, there was a quivering mass of molten solvent, that ran along the whole flow of the waters as they rushed over, that was a thing of unconceivable brilliancy."[1]

In the summer of 1860 a Mr. Blackwell from England conceived the idea of lighting up the Falls of Niagara in honour of the upcoming visit of the Prince of Wales. It was the first planned illumination of the Falls. Using about 200 Bengal lights, he arranged them 50 to 60 in a row under the cliff on the Canadian side facing the American Falls, another 50 or 60

under Table Rock and the rest were installed behind the sheet of water of the Horseshoe Falls.

At 10 o'clock on September 14, with the Prince of Wales watching, the lights were lit. Nicholas A. Woods, *The Times* special correspondent from London, reported: "The first view which the Prince got of the cataract was on the evening of his arrival, when he saw them as no man has ever seen them before, and as they will probably never be seen again. He saw the Falls of Niagara illuminated!"[2] Woods continued his description: "In an instant the whole mass of water, glowing vivid and as if incandescent in the intense light, seemed turned to molten silver. From behind the Falls, the light shone with such dazzling brilliancy that the waters immediately before it looked like a sheet of crystal glass, a cascade of diamonds, every bead and stream in which leapt and sparkled and spread a glare over the whole scene, like a river of phosphorous."[3]

Although the effort was a success it was not repeated. Later in 1860, some "white calcium torpedo lights" were used in the gorge, according to George Holley, a long time Niagara Falls New York resident and engineer.[4] It was not until 1879 that the Falls were again illuminated by man. This illumination was on the occasion of another Royal visit, that of the the Princess Louise and her husband the Marquis of Lorne, Governor-General of Canada. This time the lighting was by electricity!

The Brush Electric Company of Cleveland Ohio was the first to light the Falls electrically over 100 years ago. Using arc lights, it set the pattern for lighting the Falls that remains in use today. The Brush system used an arc light, a technique not satisfactory for home lighting. Although it was a system not seen in Niagara Falls before, it was one that would prove to be very popular. To generate the electricity required to light the arc lights, a water wheel was located in the rapids along the bank above the American Falls. It was connected to a dynamo, which was wrapped with 680 kg (1500 lbs.) of copper wire. When revolving at 760 revolutions a minute, it was capable of supplying 36 hp of electricity to 16 "burners" or light bulbs. The revolutions, just as they are today, were made by the water as it flowed against the water wheel. Each lamp produced light equal to 2000 candlepower, a total of 32,000 candlepower.[5]

The system was officially inaugurated on July 4, 1897. The *Niagara Falls Gazette* reported: "The Park was crowded with visitors and citizens, and a very satisfactory exhibition of the new lights was given."[6] Twelve of the lights lit up Prospect Park

beside the American Falls, where, for the first time, a night rainbow was visible.[7] One would assume that if the lights were successful, more lights would be installed. But even though the press reported glowing success, the Brush arc lights were not seen again after that one season.

In 1892 Frank LeBlond, one of the owners of the Maid of the Mist, ordered a 4,000 candlepower searchlight to be shone on the American Falls from the Maid of the Mist Landing, on the Canadian side. He planned to use gelatin plates in front of the light to give the effect of various colours. There appears to have been no problem with this plan and it certainly worked to light the American Falls.

During the Pan-American Exposition which was held in Buffalo in 1901, the Falls were lighted with searchlights in an attempt to attract attention away from the Exposition at night. One of the searchlights used in this illumination was mounted beside the Michigan Central Railway station at Falls View. Power for this searchlight came from a wire connected with the International Railway Company electric

Buffalo and Erie County Historical Society

Beginning in 1901, the International Railway Company ran night illumination trips on the Great Gorge Route, using a special search-light car to light up the Whirlpool Rapids.

The 1907 illumination battery set up along the Ontario Power Company access road below the gorge bank, opposite the American Falls.

street car line located directly below.[8] It is only a coincidence that their Royal Highnesses the Duke and Duchess of Cornwall and York, later King George V and Queen Mary, visited Niagara Falls during the time of this display.

With greater quantities of electric power available, it is not surprising that in 1907 bigger plans were on the drawing boards for lighting Niagara Falls. The impetus for all this planning was the desire to bring visitors to Niagara Falls and to keep them here longer. To support this idea, Mayor Anthony C. Douglas, of Niagara Falls, New York, put up $5,000 of his own money to finance the scheme. Searchlights designed by W. D'Arcy Ryan of the General Electric Company of Schenectady, New York were mounted on the roadway north of the Ontario Power Company Powerhouse below the cliff on the Canadian side. There were 36 projectors beamed at the American Falls, and they were rated at 1,115,000,000 candlepower. Coloured gelatin film was placed across the front of the light to project a coloured light on the American Falls. Mr. J.J. Pretty of Niagara Falls, Ontario, who is 92 years old as this is written in 1983, remembers working on these lights. He was responsible for one light and was paid 50 cents a night to stand in the spray beside the light, ready to change the coloured gelatin sheets on command, in order to change the colour projected on the American Falls.[9]

On October 5, the experiment was over, the lights had been on for a month. Mayor Douglas got his money back from grateful Niagara Falls businessmen because they too had profited by the lighting experiment. The lights were not projected on Sundays except on one occasion. This was the visit of His Royal Highness the Duke of Cornwall. Evidently there was a special showing for him after October 5, according to a letter Superintendent Wilson wrote to Premier Oliver Mowat: "On Sunday, October 9, His Royal Highness the Duke of Cornwall viewed the illumination searchlights on the Falls."[10] Once again Royalty was associated with the illumination of the Falls.

It was on the visit of His Royal Highness the Prince of Wales on October 18, 1919 that the Horseshoe Falls were illuminated. No details of the installation are given but the event is reported by Superintendent John H. Jackson in the 1919 Annual Report of the Queen Victoria Park Commission. It can be assumed that the light projectors were installed on the roof of the Ontario Power Plant, below the bank at Table Rock, for on August 9, 1920, the following item appeared in the Toronto *Mail and Empire* when P.W. Ellis, Commission Chairman,

wrote: "I wish to express the keen appreciation of the Park Commissioners for the co-operation afforded by Sir Adam Beck in arranging for the full illumination of the Horseshoe Falls. As a result of this action by the Chairman of the Hydro Electric Power Commission, the whole Canadian Cataract is nightly flooded with light from the powerhouse at the bottom of the gorge and from Table Rock House. The work of illumination is so cleverly carried out that the source of light is not discernible."[11]

After this success if seemed that a permanent installation of lights would be provided to light the Falls on a regular schedule. In 1912 a Bill was passed in the New York Legislature appropriating $50,000. for such a project on condition that the Province of Ontario would support it with a similar amount of money. The Provincial Legislature rejected the offer and the project was dropped.[12] Another proposal was put forward to buy the 48 projectors, 91 cm (36 in.) in diameter, designed by D'Arcy Ryan of General Electric, and used to light the Panama-Pacific Exposition held in San Fransisco in 1915. Although $25,000 was put into the fund by the City of Niagara Falls, New York, the Park Commissioners declined the offer to participate as it was felt that illuminating the Canadian Cataract would not be in keeping with the war situation at the time.[13]

In the early 1920's a group called the "Generators", made up of members of the Niagara Falls, New York Chamber of Commerce, met to discuss the advantages of lighting the Falls. Working with the city governments on both sides of the river and with others interested in the project, this group raised $58,000. to install 24 arc lights 91 cm (36 in.) in diameter. But equally as important they managed to get commitments from both city governments to maintain the lights. This plan would not only light the Great Falls - this plan would keep them lighted!

The Niagara Falls Illumination Board, formed February 24, 1925, was composed of ten members: six from Niagara Falls, New York, two from Niagara Falls, Ontario and two from the Queen Victoria Niagara Falls Park Commission. It was not until 1938 that the Hydro Electric Power Commission, which was supplying the power free of charge, was given representation, with two members appointed to the Board. The Board operated on a budget of $28,000. and was responsible for the operation and maintenance of the illumination system.

The new lights were installed on the roof of one of the Ontario Power Company surge tanks located south of the Refectory in Queen Victoria Park. This location made it possible for the lights to illuminate the

The illumination battery of lights, circa 1937.

American Falls almost head on and still be close enough and powerful enough to penetrate most of the spray from the Horseshoe Falls. On May 25, 1925 the lights were turned on for the first time. Thousands of people packed the Parks on both sides of the river to see the spectacle.

A "Festival of Lights" was planned to coincide with the dedication of the Illumination of the Falls. On June 8, 1925 a parade was held in Niagara Falls, New York with organizations from both sides of the border participating. The dedication of the Illumination took place on the International line in the centre of the Upper Steel Arch Bridge. A serious incident occurred during the dedication ceremonies when the bridge swayed so much under the weight of the people assembled for the ceremony that, according to Mayor Harry P. Stephens of Niagara Falls, Ontario, "It seemed like we were on a boat." The official parties, led by a band and followed by interested spectators, started from each side of the

bridge, to meet in the centre for the ceremony. When the Canadian party, led by the Shredded Wheat Company Band, had gone about 30.5 m (100 ft.) onto the bridge it began to sway. The band and the crowd were ordered not to march in step. Still the swaying continued. Two members of the band became so frightened that they ran back toward the Canadian shore.

After the formal ceremony the official party continued toward the Canadian shore. The crowd followed. Later, when the signal was given to begin the Illumination, the crowd again poured onto the bridge to view the spectacle. The swaying began again, worse than ever. At the end of one swing a grating sound was heard. There were some moments of panic which ended only when bridge officials hurried people off the bridge.

When the lights were turned on the Falls were seen in brilliant white and a rainbow of colours. A display of fireworks, set off from Luna Island on the

On July 4, 1928, Sky View Lines, flying a Ford Tri-Motor aeroplane from their landing field south of Chippawa on the Niagara River Boulevard, inaugurated sightseeing flights at night over Niagara Falls to view the illumination. The Niagara Falls Gazette reported: "The big plane piloted by Major Leach, took off in the dark and in a few moments was over the Falls . . . the mighty Horseshoe clothed in rainbow shades . . . seemed only a few feet away. The American Falls were resplendent in white lights and all the time a white searchlight played on the big plane, which had all the appearance of a mighty silver fish and the moon looked on". Fifty people made the trip that night, among the earliest tourists to see the illuminated Falls from the air.

U.S. side, added to the festivities. The lights, twenty-four of them, operated that summer by a crew of three men for each light, generated 1,320,000,000 candlepower. When autumn came the crews were reduced as all the lights could not be used in inclement weather. From then on, with only a few interruptions due to wartime and other power shortages, the Falls were illuminated.

In January 1938, a sudden ice jam filled the lower river flooding the Ontario Power Generating Station, putting the generators out of service, thus cutting off the source of power for the illumination battery. The lights were off until the Generating Station was put back in service. Often during World War II, the lights were not turned on in order to conserve power for war production purposes. During the summer of 1942, for a very brief time, they were turned on again, then they were turned off again until October 1944 when,

with victory close, the Falls were illuminated on a regular schedule. After the war there were times when the lights were off because there was a shortage of electric power. The construction of new electric generating facilities could not keep pace with the housing and industrial construction boom. Sometimes, as in 1942, the lights were on only during the busy weekend tourist periods. It was not until January 9, 1950 that the Illumination Board was able to have enough electricity guaranteed to operate the lights again on a regular schedule.

In 1951 a new agreement was approved between the participating parties in the Illumination Board. Niagara Falls, New York was to pay 50% of the costs; Niagara Falls, Ontario 6.87%; the Niagara Parks Commission 25.55% and Ontario Hydro 17.58%. In 1953 the Niagara Frontier State Parks Commission was officially recognized by having

Niagara Parks Archives

The illumination battery of Xenon lights installed in 1974.

two members of their Commission appointed to the Illumination Board. At this point the Niagara Frontier State Parks Commission did not become financially involved. The Niagara Parks Commission has supported the Illumination Board financially since 1927 when they gave a grant towards both the construction and the maintenance costs.[14] The grants have increased over the years, with reductions during the war years when the lighting program was curtailed.

On June 20, 1958 a new installation of 20 great carbon arc lights from Canadian General Electric Ltd. and Amalgamated Electric Ltd. of England was inaugurated. These new lights emitted 4,200,000,000 candlepower and cost $153,000. Mr. Stephenson who designed the lights for the English Company had never seen the Cataracts until he came here to install the lighting, planned to illuminate not only both Falls, but also the edge of Goat Island and the Upper Rapids. Ten of the lights were projected on the Horseshoe Falls, three on the Upper Rapids, two on Goat Island and five on the American Falls. His system included white lights, along with fifteen possible colours. When the switch was turned on, the Falls were then lighted with ten times the former brilliance using the same amount of electricity.

By now the Illumination Board had an operating budget of $28,000. Millions of visitors were coming

to see the Falls every year and a large percentage of these were staying over just to see the lights. This resulted in an increase in business for hotels, motels, restaurants and other attractions, on both sides of the border. These people stayed longer than they might otherwise. In 1970, green only was used for one night on October 14 in honour of the visiting Irish Consul-General.

In June 1969, the lights shone on a new site - the "turned off" American Falls. The lights shone nightly on the silent gorge wall where water should have been falling. The American Falls had been dewatered to enable engineers to study the rock formation and make recommendations which might lead to the preservation of the Falls. The Horseshoe Falls, of course, remained lighted. By the American Thanksgiving Day holiday in November of 1969, water was once again flowing over the American Falls.

In mid 1974 further improvements were made to the illumination system by the introduction of a Xenon system which permitted the lights to shine brighter. By the summer of 1981, still newer Xenon lighting developments improved the efficiency of the lights even more. The 18 Xenon gas spotlights in present use in the main illumination battery are 76 cm (30 in.) in diameter, each produces 250,000,000

The illumination of the American Falls and the Horseshoe Falls. Oakes Garden Theatre is in the foreground.

Winter illumination of the Horseshoe Falls

Wayne Farrar

The Horseshoe Falls illuminated.

candlepower. Colours used besides white, are red, amber, green, and blue. A lone operator programs the night's spectacle and then changes the colours by operating switches to slide predetermined combinations of coloured film into place. In the late 1970's a battery of four Xenon lights was installed on the lower river bank to shine directly on the American Falls. They are operated by remote control from the main illumination battery. As well, another isolated battery of two lights was installed in 1979 just south of the Canadian Niagara Power Company intake. These lights are directed to shine on the plume of spray from the Horseshoe Falls.

It has taken years of continually developing technology, years of planning, hundreds of hours of meetings and thousands of dollars to illuminate the

Falls of Niagara as we see them today. Over the years visitors have been asked to give their opinion of the illumination spectacle. Prince and Princess Taksonatsu of Japan visited Niagara Falls in 1931 and the Prince was asked how he liked the illumination: "I thought it would be greater. There was a feeling in the Royal Party that the illumination of the Falls which we saw was somewhat gaudy. We are much impressed with the sublimity of this waterfall but to light it in striking colours is like gilding the lily." In contrast, most visitors who see Niagara Falls illuminated would agree with the Niagara Parks brochure distributed in 1946 which said it this way: "To see the Falls of Niagara at Night is to be Wide Awake in the Land of Dreams."

On the night of December 10, 1978 a special illumination display was held to commemorate the 300th anniversary of Father Louis Hennepin's visit to the Falls of Niagara. Original plans called for the projection of pictures of Hennepin onto the Horseshoe Falls, but weather conditions prevented this and they were projected onto the gorge wall at Goat Island instead.

Ice Bridge

The phenomenon of the ice bridge occurs a number of times during the winter, depending on the severity of the weather. A December cold spell, extending into January, will produce from 15 cm to 38 cm (6 to 15 inches) of ice in the shallow water along Lake Erie's shore. A mild spell, followed by a strong southwest wind breaks up this Lake Erie ice and sends the ice mass down the Niagara River in ice floes of varying size. The floes are broken into smaller pieces by the rapids as they move towards the Falls.

The mixture of ice and slush drops over the Horseshoe Falls, and when it reaches the Maid of the Mist eddy downstream, just past the American Falls, it is forced by the river current to the Canadian shore, where it jams. As the river brings more ice and slush against it, the whole mass heaves and humps under the pressure of the following ice. When the wet ice is forced up out of the water it freezes in an agglomerate mass, growing into a structure of considerable size and length. In 1938 under ideal conditions for ice formation, followed by a thaw and an 80 km (50 mi.) an hour southwest wind lasting more than 10 hours, the river was filled with ice from the base of the Falls to Niagara-on-the-Lake 19 km (12 mi.) away and toppled the Upper Steel Arch Bridge.

When the wind subsides, the water level is lowered, leaving the ice mass looking not unlike a glacier, suspended above the water, a true ice bridge, which spans the river from shore to shore. Some ice bridges are 12 m (40 ft.) thick with more or less flat surfaces and only a few crevasses. Others spawned under more severe conditions have jagged furrows and crevasses 30.5 m (100 ft.) or more in height and depth.[1]

The earliest known reference to the ice bridge was made by the Duke de La Rochefoucault Liancourt, who wrote in 1796: "Enormous flakes of ice rush constantly down this cataract, when the thaw sets in, without being entirely dashed to pieces on the rocks; and thus frequently piled in huge masses, up to half its height."[2] While the ice bridge was a popular winter attraction for tourists who would walk and slide on the ice bridge, from the 1880's until 1912, the first reference made in literature to travel on the ice bridge was made in 1843: "Here, last year, joined together in great quantities was formed a thick high ice bridge completely across the river, safe for passengers for some time; and in the middle of it a Yankee speculator had erected a shanty for refreshments."[3]

William Dean Howells writing in 1860, described the activity on the ice bridge: "The name ice-bridge deceived me, but the ice-bridge did not finally disappoint me. It is not a bridge at all. It is the channel of the river blocked as far as the eye can see down the gorge with huge squares and oblays of ice, or of frozen snow . . . This was curiously heightened by some people on sleds among the crowds, making their way through the ice packs from shore to shore . . . It is best to look down upon it all from the cliffs, when at times the effect was more than arctic, it was lunar, -

An ice bridge of the late 1890's with huts placed along the path.

Niagara Parks Archives

you could fancy yourself upon the face of a dead world, with these small black figures of people crawling over it like flies."[4]

The 1880's saw the beginning of the railway excursion boom and it did not take the railways long to realize that the ice bridge had great potential, and that they could run special Sunday excursions, from the larger cities in the Eastern United States, for a trip to see the winter spectacle. 1888 was a banner year for the winter tourist. The ice mountain which formed each year in front of the American Falls was described as "a grand sight and sightseers can gain easy access to it without much difficulty. The mountain slopes towards the river, the surface is smooth and the walking is good, and it can be said that this formation has not occurred in 20 years."[5] The *Niagara Falls Gazette* even ran a weekly column entitled "Ice Bridge Notes" reporting special happenings that occured on the ice bridge the past weekend. One "note" told of the Salvation Army holding a Sunday Service at the bottom of the ice mountain.[6]

The *Niagara Falls Gazette* sent a reporter out to see what the fuss was all about and he had this to say: "On the mountain were a number of young ladies and gentlemen enjoying the sport of coasting. No sleigh or boards were needed. Crawling up the steep side to its top was a hazardous trip, but it was accomplished and the trip down was an exciting one. Sitting down, one had hardly the time to say 'Jack Robinson' before you found yourself at the bottom.

"After tiring of this sport, the scribe continued on his mission: On striking the bridge, the first booth, or rather teepee, was one operated by James Cailan, dispensing souvenirs only, but he has a rare collection and attired as he is on such a gala occasion he attracts many to his teepee and few go away without purchasing some of his wares. Just beyond the deep cut in the bridge which is appropriately called Chilcoot Pass, one finds the booth run by the firm of Sheldon and Brown. Hot coffee is served here and some of the best views of the ice bridge and scenery about it that have ever been taken are for sale.

"Continuing, the next place visited was the Gorge

A Saloon on the ice bridge in the 1890's.

A photographer's shanty on the ice bridge in the 1890's.

Hotel, run by James Markham and George Kingsley. Gold letters over the door informed strangers of the name and fame of the place. But to get a proper idea you have to try a little of Seagram's and Walker's Club Canadian Rye. They also sell photographs of the bridge.

"James LeBlond struck about the middle of the ice bridge when he placed his shanty which he calls the Clifton House, on its present site. Eatables and drinkables of all kinds are sold here, and a good warm 'hot dog' will go along with a rye chaser.

"At the Klondike Hotel, farther along the bridge they also have some of the hard stuff. Chasers are out of the question for by the time the visitor arrives at this place, he is well chilled and thinks of getting nothing but the 'warm stuff'. Alongside the Klondike stands a tent, inside of which is Fred Clark, who displays photographs for sale and incidentally he warms up the people as he has a stove going at all times.

"From the top of a large mound just beyond,

M. Davis greets you with a smile and asks you to have your picture taken right on the bridge with the falls as a background. He has all the necessary apparatus on hand and as soon as you are seated on a cake of ice and are told to look pretty, he squeezes the rubber and it is all over. He soon emerges from his shanty, to which he has taken the negatives, to hand you your likeness, for which he charges you a reasonable sum. All receiving a sample of his work are satisfied and as you are then on the Canadian side of the river there are no other places along the route to welcome you, you turn and retrace your steps across the ice."[7]

The Park authorities on both sides of the river condoned travel on the ice bridge, as it was good for business. The January 9, 1899 edition of the *Niagara Falls Gazette* carried this article which gives some indication of how the New York State Reservation felt about the ice bridge: "The Upper River is full of floes which are coming down from the Lake and there is every possibility of a good ice

The ice bridge of 1956, the last major ice bridge prior to the installation of the ice boom.

Niagara Parks Archives

bridge. Such an attraction . . .would bring thousands of visitors to the City. The water wheel which runs the incline railway is being repaired and the cars are not running at present. The work is being hurried however, in anticipation of an ice bridge, and if it remains the public will not be forced to any inconvenience on getting down to it."

This ice bridge was formed on January 9, 1899 and it broke up suddenly on January 16. A new and much larger ice bridge formed on January 22, with the ice rising so high in the river, and along the river bank that a ridge of ice almost took out the abutments of the new Upper Steel Arch Bridge.[8] It was a Sunday when the new ice bridge was formed overnight and people got out on the bridge on Sunday while it was still forming. There were from fifty to one hundred persons on the ice bridge when the whole mass broke loose from the shore and started to drift down the river. All but three persons quickly reached the shore and safety. Soon only one young man was left on the ice bridge and he was fortunate as the portion he was on passed under the arch of the Upper Steel Arch Bridge close to the Canadian shore and he was able to climb to the highest point on the ice and pull himself up on the girders of the bridge as the ice passed beneath. From here he was able to reach the Canadian shore.[9]

This brush with tragedy did not dampen the enthusiasm of those who wanted the thrill of crossing the ice-choked river. Long lasting ice bridges stay in the river well into spring. In 1835, according to a diary kept by a C.H. Witmer, the ice bridge lasted until May 4. Mr. Witmer crossed to the American side on May 2 to purchase some clover seed and returned the next day.[10] The ice bridge of 1888 went out on April 5. The second ice bridge of 1891 lasted until April 1. The ice bridge of 1909 has rarely been surpassed. On April 9 of that year a spectacular ice jam flooded the Ontario Powerhouse putting it out of service, plunging Niagara Falls, Ontario and several other cities into darkness on Friday night. Workmen were not able to complete a line to connect the City's distribution system with the Toronto Power Company's lines until Sunday.[11]

The ice bridge fun continued for many years until 1912 when the ice bridge broke up and went down the river, carrying three tourists to their deaths. Authorities on both sides of the river decreed that from that time on, crossing the river on the ice bridge would be prohibited. The ice bridge formed that year on January 15 and from January 20 to February 4 crowds of visitors crossed over it. It was considered perfectly safe. With good weather, the Sunday crowd was alway large and Sunday, February 4 was an ideal winter day for sightseeing. Large numbers of excursionists came by train to view the Falls and hundreds of local people were prepared to visit the ice bridge, when the news came that the ice bridge had broken loose and was carrying three people downriver.

The word spread and thousands of people on both sides of the river arrived at the gorge to witness the incident. Valiant attempts were made to rescue the victims, by firemen, police and railway workers from both sides of the river, who lowered ropes down to the river from the Cantilever Railway Bridge. Even though the ropes were caught, the force of the current made it impossible for the ropes to be tied securely around the waists of the victims and they were pulled out of their hands. Mr. and Mrs. Eldridge Stanton, a honeymoon couple from Toronto and Burrel Hecock of Cleveland were drowned when the ice floes carrying them went to pieces in the Whirlpool Rapids. One man, Ignatius Roth, who was a companion of Hecock's was one of those led to safety and rescued by William Red Hill.[12]

Hill went to the hotel where Roth and Hecock had been registered and got Roth's address and wrote to him. Roth's reply was as follows:

Cleveland, Ohio
February 20, 1912

Wm. Hill
144 Stanley Street
Niagara Falls
So. Ontario

Dear Friend: -

I received your letter of the 9th inst. I hope that you will pardon me for not answering sooner.

I wish to state that I have fully recovered from the shock and am now in perfect health.

Through your letter and also through a Buffalo paper, I noted that you were confined to your bed from the effects of the ducking received in your efforts to save my life.

I did not know until I received your letter and the paper you sent with it, who my real benefactor was.

I am thankful for your great kindness, and I hope God will reward you in a way worthy of your noble deed.

I received a letter from Mr. Charles Black, a member of the Royal Canadian Humane Association, requesting my declaration and signature in order that he might obtain a medal for your bravery.

Mr. and Mrs. Eldridge Stanton with their arms clasped around each other as they rode to their death in the Whirlpool Rapids, February 4, 1912.

Buffalo and Erie County Historical Society

I am going to fill out the blank sent me with the hope that you will obtain a medal. I hope that this letter will reach you in good health and with many thanks from a loving and thankful friend.

> Ignatius Roth
> 2114 Fulton Road,
> Cleveland, Ohio.

Hill was subsequently awarded a Carnegie Life Saving Medal for his work in rescuing people from the February 4, 1912 ice bridge.

Hecock could have saved himself, but heroically lost his life in a vain attempt to save Mrs. Stanton. Had the accident happened an hour or two later the loss of life would have been appalling, for the crowds were just arriving and were just moving down the inclines for the purpose of venturing out on the bridge.[14] In 1917, after this appalling disaster, the Park Commissioners erected a memorial tablet at the end of the parapet, near the present Princess Elizabeth Building,

to commemorate the heroism of Burrel Hecock in sacrificing his life in an attempt to rescue others.

By the mid 1930's people were again crossing on the ice bridge and in 1936 the Commission found it necessary once again to forbid the practice of crossing the ice bridge. It was a spectacular ice jam on the night of Tuesday, January 25, 1938 which led to the destruction of the Upper Steel Arch Bridge. By Wednesday morning the river was full of ice and more was coming down from the lake. A pressure ridge of ice on the American side pushed against the bottom girders of the Upper Steel Arch Bridge, eventually snapping the girders at the abutments. The bridge fell into the river at about 4:10 p.m. on the afternoon of January 27. This spectacular ice jam which also flooded the Ontario Powerhouse, putting it out of service for months, was to last until April 13, when a large portion on the Canadian shore broke away, carrying a huge section of the fallen bridge downstream almost a mile before it sank in one of the deepest sections of the river.[15]

The American Falls in winter.

The Ice Bridge, looking toward the American Falls.

New York Power Authority

The ice boom has been installed across the upper end of the Niagara River every winter since its inception in 1964. It is owned and operated jointly by Ontario Hydro and the New York Power Authority under an Order of Approval from the International Joint Commission.

The boom is a series of floating timbers or logs, each 9.1 m (30 ft.) long. There are 22 cable spans that make up the boom and each span has 13 timbers individually chained to it. Each span is anchored to the lake bottom at 122 m (400 ft.) intervals by 6.4 cm (2½ in.) steel cables.

Lake Erie freezes over almost every year creating a 25,900 km² (10,000 mi.²) potential supply of ice for the 60 km² (23 mi.²) Niagara River. Due to the very small size of the Niagara River relative to the size of Lake Erie, less than two per cent of the ice cover on Lake Erie can leave the lake by way of the Niagara River. The rest melts. This makes the ice boom invaluable since even a small percentage of the ice on Lake Erie can totally clog the Niagara River.

In the twenty years that the boom has been in operation, there have been no ice jams as severe as those which occurred in the days before the boom. Ice jams such as those that caused the collapse of the Honeymoon Bridge, or twice flooded the Ontario Power Company Generating Station with ice, or destroyed buildings and property along the shore of the lower Niagara River, or caused flooding on the upper Niagara River, are a thing of the past.

Ice bridges are still a part of Niagara's winter scene, although they are less spectacular than those of the early days. An ice boom which is spread across the entrance to the Niagara River at Lake Erie each winter, prevents large onrushes of ice which formed the ice bridges of former days. The huge ice jams frequent in early years, today could clog the water intakes to the powerhouses, interfere with the generation of electric power and damage the generating station in the lower river below the Falls. The less spectacular ice bridges of the present day are still dangerous. It is illegal to venture upon the ice bridge from either the Canadian or the American side of the river, a law strictly enforced. From safe viewpoints visitors today continue to marvel at this winter spectacle at Niagara.

Stunters

The era of the Niagara stunters began in 1859 when Jean François Gravelet, also known as Blondin, made the first tight rope walk across the Niagara Gorge. The *Daily Globe* of Toronto reported the event in its July first edition: "The daring feat of walking across the Niagara Gorge on the tight rope was accomplished by M. Blondin yesterday afternoon at five o'clock, in the presence of over 10,000 spectators, who cheered lustily when the agile little Frenchman reached the Canada side of the river . . . a collection was made for Blondin at various hotels on the Canadian side. About three hundred dollars was contributed by the hotel-keepers on the American side; and it is generally believed that taking all things into consideration, Blondin would have a moderate surplus after paying all expenses". Actually a collection was made by volunteers who passed the hat amongst the spectators and almost two thousand dollars was received, barely enough to pay for the cost of the rope Blondin strung across the gorge.

Blondin performed on the rope throughout the summer, carrying out a variety of stunts. He carried his manager, Harry Colcord, on his back as he crossed the gorge; he crossed pushing a wheel barrow; he made a night crossing with coloured lanterns fastened to the ends of his balancing pole; with baskets on his feet; blindfolded and enveloped in a sack with only his hands and feet free. His most spectacular stunt was to carry a cook stove made of Russian sheet iron, with a skillet, ladle, sundry dishes, and a pair of bellows fastened to the stove. He set the stove down in the centre of his rope, lit a fire and when smoke billowed from the two foot high smoke stack, he prepared an omelette. When the omelette was cooked he cut it into small pieces and lowered it in a dish to the deck of the Maid of the Mist waiting in the river below, where it was served to some of the many passengers on board.

William Hunt, a resident of Port Hope, Ontario, was among the spectators for one of Blondin's performances. He felt that the adulation being heaped on Bondin was excessive and he vowed to return himself the next summer, to set up a rope across the gorge and to duplicate and even surpass Blondin's feats. In 1860 he returned to Niagara Falls and set up his tight rope across the Niagara Gorge in a position close to the location of the present day Rainbow Bridge. Hunt adopted the stage name of Farini and advertised his first walk extensively. He was an astute businessman and on his first crossing he collected over $12,000 from admissions, railway and steamboat commissions and donations from grateful hotel-keepers whose business increased because of the advance publicity given the event. A rivalry developed between Farini and Blondin.

Blondin prepared for the 1860 season by setting up his rope over the Whirlpool Rapids, just downriver from the Railway Suspension Bridge. Performances were held every two weeks throughout the summer. Blondin would advertise the stunt for his coming performance and Farini would immediately counter with his advertising in an attempt to lure people away

Blondin on the rope, 1859. From a glass stereograph by O.B. Evans.

This stereograph view by Platt D. Babbitt shows Blondin carrying his manager Harry Colcord on his back as he crossed the gorge on his rope, August 19, 1859. Blondin, unable to recruit a volunteer, persuaded Colcord to accompany him. A crowd, estimated at almost fifty thousand witnessed the successful crossing.

Farini's Broadside advertising his Washing Machine stunt, September 5, 1860.

SIG. FARINI
THE INEXHAUSTIBLE!
FARINI THE COMICAL
SIGNOR FARINI WILL ON
ON WEDNESDAY,
SEPT. 5, 1860, AT 4 O'CLOCK, P. M.
AT
NIAGARA FALLS,
Introduce himself in his Wonderful and Laughable Character of
BIDDY O'FLAHERTY
THE IRISH WASHERWAOMN,
BY CARRYING OUT UPON HIS CABLE A NEW
PATENT WASHING MACHINE!
Standing over Six feet high and weighing nearly 100 pounds, when he will
Draw up Water from the River AND DO HIS OWN WASHING
Hanging his clothes out to dry upon his Guys, where he can leave them out all night without fear of having them stolen. If any one doubts the being washed clean, they can go and examine them.

FARINI'S CABLE IS WITHIN A FEW RODS OF THE FALLS
AND CLOSE TO THE FERRY.
TICKETS OF ADMISSION, - - - 25 CENTS.
Reserved Seats, Twenty-Five Cents Extra.
FRANK SOPER, Agent.

NIAGARA FALLS, Sept. 1st, 1860.   Gazette Print, Niagara Falls, N. Y.

Buffalo and Erie County Historical Society

from Blondin's performance. Blondin advertised that he would carry a cook stove on his back out to the centre of the rope, where he would place the stove on the rope and cook an omelette. Farini countered by carrying a washing machine on his back to the centre of his rope, where he set the machine down, drew a pail of water from the river and proceeded to wash a number of handkerchiefs belonging to several ladies in the audience. He then hung the washing out to dry on the supporting rope guys.

The August fifteenth edition of the *Niagara Falls Gazette* reported on Blondin's difficulty in attracting a crowd: "Mons. Blondin performed yesterday according to announcement at Niagara City. He would have had a large crowd but for the attraction of Farini's walk. Heretofore a large portion of Mons. Blondin's audience has been drawn from our hotels and from our village, but on this occasion there was

no disposition to pass by Farini to see Blondin. Before the performance Mons. Blondin rode up to the Clifton House with his stove and fixtures, but of the great crowd on that side few or none followed to the bridge." Blondin was planning to perform again one of his 1859 stunts. The crowd had seen the cook stove stunt before. They wanted something new and so stayed to watch Farini.

In September of 1860, Albert Edward, Prince of Wales, visited Niagara Falls for three days. Both Farini and Blondin planned special acts in honour of the visiting Prince. Blondin planned to carry his assistant, Romain Mouton, on his back across the Whirlpool Rapids Gorge. Farini planned even more sensational acts. First he would cross with a man on his back. Then on another trip across he planned to drop from his rope 30.5 m (100 ft.) into the river and then to be picked up by the Maid of the Mist

The Niagara Falls Gazette reported Farini's September 5, 1860 Washing Machine stunt. "He strapped an Empire Washing Machine to his back and walked slowly to the desired place in the centre of the rope. He secured his balancing pole and machine on the cable. He then drew water from the river, nearly 200 feet below, in primitive style with a pail and cord. Several ladies, desiring to patronize him in his character as a washerwoman, had given him their handkerchiefs to wash. Before long his washing was done, the handkerchiefs wrung out and hung up to dry on the uprights and crossbars of the machine. With the washing flapping in the wind, he readjusted his load and returned."

Niagara Falls New York Public Library

Maria Spelterina, the only woman to cross the Niagara Gorge on a rope, is shown crossing in 1876, with peach baskets on her feet.

steamboat waiting in the river below. Farini describes the difficulty he had in arranging for the Prince to view his performance. In his hand-written autobiography he wrote: "I did not appear again until the visit of the Prince of Wales. The opposition having a strong programme under his immediate patronage, I without asking permission advertised the same and also announced my intention of dropping from the rope into the water. In the meantime one of my friends calling on the Committee arranged that His Royal Highness should stop on the road from Mr. Zimmerman's . . . and witness my performance. The opposition had the advantage of having the Mayor of the Town on the Committee but my programme was more sensational."[1]

On September 8, 1860 the Prince of Wales saw the performance of Farini, as he was enroute to watch Blondin's scheduled act. The newspapermen following the Prince reported his encounter with Blondin, where he offered to carry the Prince over the gorge. The Prince declined and is reported to have given Blondin the gift of a sum of money in recognition of Blondin's skills in performing on the rope. Blondin is remembered in history as the first funambulist at Niagara Falls and because of the patronage of the Prince of Wales, he received the most publicity.

After the 1859 and 1860 performances of Blondin and Farini there was a lull until 1865 when Harry Leslie, billed as "The American Blondin", crossed the Whirlpool Rapids gorge on a rope. In 1869

Samuel Dixon in 1891 crossing the Gorge on Stephen Peer's wire cable, the first stunt carried out after the Queen Victoria Niagara Falls Park Commissioners took over jurisdiction of the Canadian side of the Niagara Gorge.

Andrew Jenkins crossed at the same site, riding a velocipede. In 1873 Bellini set up his rope near the Upper Suspension Bridge and in 1876 Maria Spelterina, the only woman to cross the Niagara gorge on a tightrope, carried out a series of performances from a rope strung across the river,

upriver from the Railway Suspension Bridge. On June 25, 1887, Stephen Peer, a local resident, was killed when he fell from his wire during an attempted night walk.

After the Queen Victoria Park Commissioners took over jurisdiction of the Chain Reserve along the

Niagara River gorge on July 5, 1887, they decided to prohibit rope and wire walkers from anchoring their ropes and wires on the gorge wall, as they did not want a repetition of the Peer tragedy.

Samuel Dixon, a Toronto photographer, was the first to challenge the Commission's ruling when he announced a planned wire walk over the Niagara Gorge, to take place on September 6, 1891. Dixon planned to use Stephen Peer's 2.22 cm (⅞ in.) steel cable which was still in place and attached to what was now Commission land between the Railway Suspension Bridge and the Cantilever Railway Bridge. The Commissioners refused to grant Dixon permission for the proposed walk. Chairman Gzowski, unaware that Dixon planned to use Stephen Peer's wire that was already attached, sent Thomas Young of the Ontario Police to prevent anchorage of the cable needed for Dixon's stunt. When Young inspected the proposed anchorage site, he found that a cable was already in place. On July 9, 1891, the Council of the Town of Niagara Falls sent the Park Commission a strongly worded resolution asking

Clifford Calverley hanging from the cable during one of his crossings in 1892.

Captain Matthew Webb who lost his life in attempting to swim the Whirlpool Rapids, July 24, 1883.

William J. Kendall, the Boston policeman who went through the Whirlpool Rapids wearing only a life preserver, September 1886.

them to relent and let the performance go on. The Commissioners had the legal right to order the removal of Peer's wire and anchors, but they did not want to antagonize the Town Council and the citizens who were anticipating the event. Therefore Chairman Gzowski wrote the Town Clerk on July 13, saying that the Commissioners would not interfere with the stunt. He also said the Commission wanted it understood that any responsibiltiy for accidents to persons or property in connection with the stunt was to lie with the Town Council.[2]

Dixon's walk took place on September 6, 1891. Attired in terra cotta coloured tights and black silk trunks and wearing his "lucky" Civil War cap, he made a number of crossings, performing various stunts on the wire. On October 12, 1892, Clifford Calverley, a Toronto steeplejack and painter, crossed several times at about the same location as Dixon on a 1.9 cm (¾ in.) steel cable. On one of his crossings he established the unequalled record for a crossing time when he made the trip in 6 minutes 32⅝ seconds. He returned in 1893 and on July 4 and July 13 he crossed on a wire strung across the Whirlpool Rapids. In 1896, James Hardy, at 21 years the youngest person to cross the gorge on a wire, made a series of crossings. His performances brought the age of the funambulist to an end.

Beginning in 1883 when Captain Matthew Webb lost his life in an attempt to swim the Whirlpool Rapids, the Rapids were challenged by a wide variety

Charles Percy standing beside the lifeboat in which he made three successful trips through the Whirlpool Rapids. The first trip was on August 28, 1887; on September 25, he was accompanied by William Dittrick.

of daredevils. They rode the turbulent water in wooden barrels, in life-boats and even with no other protection than a life preserver. While these stunters risked their lives *in* the river, (See section on Whirpool Rapids) the rope and wire walkers, risked theirs *above* it. When it seemed there were no other challenges to be met, the era of the "Over the Horseshoe Falls" stunters began.

This new group used barrels and balls made of rubber and metal for their stunts. While the Park Commissioners had jurisdiction over the upper Niagara River Boulevard and the banks of the river from which the barrels had to be launched, there were not enough Park Police to prevent the stunts from taking place. It is almost certain that the stunters did not have official permission for their stunts, but it is not so certain that the Commissioners in the first third of this century didn't turn a blind eye to their antics, as the publicity for these stunts brought crowds to Niagara Falls to see the events, and they were good for business.

The first barrel trip over the Falls was made by

Annie Edson Taylor, a school teacher from Bay City Michigan, on Oct. 24, 1901. Annie's barrel was curiously constructed, tapered almost to a point at the bottom and bound with metal hoops. It was padded with pillows and had a 45.4 kg (100 lb.) anvil in its bottom to keep it upright as it floated downriver. It had an air supply, "enough to last her a week",[3] forced into the barrel with a common bicycle pump after the barrel's lid was closed. To ensure that the barrel would float down the river and over the Horseshoe Falls, it had to be set adrift in the Canadian current. It would have been impossible for Canadian authorities to stop her trip even if they had wanted to, because Annie's handlers towed the barrel from Grass Island on the United States side and into the Canadian current where it was set adrift at 4:05 p.m. The barrel tipped slightly forward as it went over the brink of the Horseshoe Falls and disappeared behind the curtain of falling water. Seventeen minutes later it floated out from behind the Falls and was stranded on the rocks close to the location of the present day Table Rock Observation Platform. The barrel was opened and Annie Taylor emerged, delirious and with a slight cut on her jaw. She made the trip in an attempt to achieve fame and fortune but achieved neither in her lifetime. She died in the poorhouse twenty years later.

Bobby Leach, a native of Cornwall, England began his career as a daredevil on July 1, 1906. Supported only by a frail parachute he survived a drop into the the Niagara River from the Upper Steel Arch Bridge. In June 1907, Leach was a spectator at Madison Square Gardens in New York City when Captain Paul Donaldson, diving from a platform 46.9m (154 ft.) high into a tank of water only 1.52m (5 ft.) deep, was killed. Leach immediately offered to replace the dead man in the stunt. The programme was continued and Leach made a successful dive. He returned to the Niagara area with his reputation as a daredevil firmly established.

In 1908 he announced his intention to go over the Horseshoe Falls in a rubber ball but the trip didn't

Annie Taylor after she had been taken out of her barrel. She was the first person to go over the Horseshoe Falls in a barrel.

Niagara Falls New York Public Library

From a post card which Annie Taylor sold as a souvenir of her trip over the Horseshoe Falls. She achieved fame, but not fortune. She died in the poorhouse twenty years after the trip.

materialize because he couldn't make arrangements with the railway companies for financial backing. Instead he made a trip in a barrel through the Whirlpool Rapids in 1909. In 1911 he again planned a trip over the Falls in a cylindrical steel barrel. On July 25, 1911 Leach made the plunge over the Horseshoe Falls and lived. His barrel was badly dented, he suffered a fractured jaw and two broken knee caps and spent twenty three weeks in hospital recuperating. In an attempt to capitalize on his fame in the area he went into the restaurant business in Niagara Falls, Ontario.

It was not until 1925 that he returned to the limelight. At that time he attempted to swim the Niagara River below the Falls. He had to abandon the attempt due to an unusual circumstance. His false teeth slipped out of his mouth when he had gone half way across and in grabbing for them he swallowed so much water that he was unable to continue. His next feat was successful, another parachute drop, this time from an aeroplane over Falls View. Soon afterwards he left on a vaudeville tour of Australia and New Zealand. In New Zealand he slipped on an orange peel while out walking, injured his leg and was hospitalized. Complications led to the amputation of one of his legs, gangrene set in, and he died there on April 29, 1926, at the age of 64.

Charles Stephens, a barber from Bristol, England, was the next to challenge the Horseshoe Falls. His previous experience as a daredevil was in jumping with a parachute from an aeroplane and putting his head in the mouths of lions. For the trip over the Falls on July 11, 1920, he used a hooped oaken barrel. Stephens was concerned that he would land on his head, so he had himself strapped in the barrel with a heavy anvil tied to his feet. Annie Taylor also used an

Niagara Falls New York Public Library

Bobby Leach posing beside the barrel he used for his trip over the Horseshoe Falls, July 25, 1911.

Helen Hodge

Jean Lussier's rubber ball on the crest of the Horseshoe Falls, July 4, 1928. From a photograph by Edwin H. Hodge.

Edwin H. Hodge

Jean Lussier is shown at the right after his trip over the Horseshoe Falls, July 4, 1928. William Red Hill who assisted Lussier is shown at centre. The man on the left is unidentified.

anvil for ballast but she had better luck. Stephens' barrel broke into pieces when it hit the water at the bottom of the Falls, the anvil sank, taking Stephens along with it to the bottom of the river. Only pieces of the wrecked barrel, along with a man's arm with a strap attached to it, were found after this unsuccessful trip.

On July 4, 1928, Jean Lussier a machinist from Niagara Falls, New York, made a successful trip over the Horseshoe Falls in a 1.8m (6 ft.) rubber ball which he designed and built himself. The ball had a framework of steel bands covered with automobile tire material and was lined with interconnecting rubber compartments filled with oxygen under 15.9 kg (35 lbs.) pressure. The ball floated on the surface of the water and was out of sight for only 65 seconds after going over the Falls. Lussier survived the trip, suffering only a bump on his forehead.

George Stathakis, a Greek cook from Buffalo, lost his life in an unsuccessful trip over the Horseshoe Falls on July 4, 1930. His heavy oak barrel dropped behind the curtain of falling water and spun around in the backwash of the Falls until the next morning. When the barrel was pulled ashore and opened,

Stathakis was dead, suffocated. His pet turtle, taken along for good luck, survived.

Major (his given name, not a military rank) Lloyd Hill attemped a trip over the Falls in 1950, but was taken out of his steel barrel when it grounded on the Canadian Niagara Power Company's weir in the upper river above the Falls. His handlers were prepared to push him back into the current but thought better of it when the Niagara Parks Police who had arrived on the scene, cautioned them that they would be held personally responsible if Hill lost his life.

William Red Hill Jr., a brother of Major Hill, lost his life on August 5, 1951 when he attempted a trip over the Horseshoe Falls in "The Thing", a strange contraption made of thirteen inflated inner tubes, tied together with canvas webbing and fish nets. Thousands of spectators had assembled along the river banks to see the spectacle and watched in horror as a twisted tangle of inner tubes and a red air mattress were all that emerged from the base of the Falls.

On July 15, 1961 the most mystifying trip over the Falls occurred. At 10:56 a.m. several calls were received by the Niagara Parks Police reporting

Maid of the Mist Steamboat Company

A Canadian Customs official left and Captain L. McGinn of the Maid of the Mist Company looking into the rubber covered steel ball after its plunge over the Horseshoe Falls. Nathan Boya was inside. Corporal Sawada of the Niagara Parks Police is at the top right.

Niagara Falls Evening Review

In 1971 Nathan Boya, shown in the centre, renews his friendship with Corporal Sawada of the Niagara Parks Police, right. On the left is Joe Collins, a sightseeing driver.

a dark "ball" in the river above the Horseshoe Falls. Corporal Alex Sawada was sent to investigate. Niagara Parks Police Chief Rehfeld telephoned Captain Lawrence McGinn at the Maid of the Mist Dock and told him about the ball and that Corporal Sawada was on his way to investigate. With Corporal Sawada, Captain McGinn of the Maid of the Mist Company took the Company launch out on the river where the ball, having gone over the Falls, was already floating in the turbulent water at the base of the Horseshoe.

By the time they reached the ball it was already out in the river current and floating downriver. They drew up alongside and debated as to whether anyone was really inside. The top was already open and a head popped out. William FitzGerald, known by the pseudonymn Nathan Boya, was the stunter. He describes what happened next. "Corporal Sawada first asked me if I were O.K Then he said, 'Grab hold of the boat'. The second I touched the boat, he added, 'You are under arrest' ". In describing his

trip Boya says:"The cover was not completely off but banged loose in a kind of waffle pattern. It was ripped out of my hands after the Plunge-O-Sphere went over the Falls and began righting itself."

Boya was helped out of the ball and into the launch which then proceeded to the Maid of the Mist dock, with the ball being towed behind. The party was met by a Canadian Customs official who impounded the ball. Boya was questioned by both Canadian Immigration and Customs officials and then due to his complaint of a possible chest injury, he was taken to the Greater Niagara General Hospital for observation. The following Monday he appeared in court, paid the fine assessed which was $100.00 and $13.00 in courts costs, and returned to New York City, giving no explanation for his stunt.

Shunning publicity, he made trips to Niagara Falls in 1970 and 1971. On the 1971 visit, he renewed his acquaintanceship with Corporal Sawada. Prior to another visit in 1983, he leased his ball to Ralph Grant, the operator of the Great Gorge Trip

Great Gorge Trip

The Niagara Daredevil Gallery of stunters' barrels and balls at the Whirlpool Rapids Great Gorge Trip.

and Daredevil Gallery. The ball was lowered over the gorge bank and placed in the Daredevil Gallery of stunters' barrels, boats and balls, which are displayed on the lower level of the Great Gorge Trip attraction.

William FitzGerald has remained a mysterious figure. He would say only that his reason for going over the Falls was "very, very personal". Known to be living in the New York City area, he has an earned doctorate in Sociology. In addition, he has two years of post doctoral training as a Medical Behavioural Scientist and as a Faculty Fellow at one of the medical schools in New York City. Dr. FitzGerald reports: "While at medical school I inadvertently discovered a new method of controlling labile hypertension through the use of exercise. My paper delineating my program was published in a very prestigious international medical journal in 1981. I have recently completed a further paper which will be published soon, dealing with a radically new and comprehensive theory on the cause of High Blood Pressure itself".[4] These are the credentials of the first man to be charged and fined under the Niagara Parks Act for going over the Horseshoe Falls in a ball.

Since 1961, a number of would-be stunters have gained fleeting fame when newspapers and T.V. news bureaus have given space and coverage to their grandiose schemes. The stunts proposed included jumping over the gorge in front of the Horseshoe Falls in a steam-powered snowmobile and in a rocket-powered automobile. One trip over the Horseshoe Falls in a converted steel propane tank was aborted when the device grounded on a shoal above the Falls. A helicopter rescue unit plucked the stranded stunter from his dangerous perch. He was fined $100 in a United States Court. The rescue cost Canadian taxpayers $1500 and endangered the lives of the Canadian Armed Forces Helicopter Rescue Unit.

In 1974 and 1975 there was a renewed interest in wire and tight rope walking when requests were made for permission to make wire walks over the Niagara Gorge to celebrate the United States Bicentennial in 1976. Two funambulists, Henry Rechatin and Phillipe Petit, spent some time in the area publicizing the events while permission was being considered by the Niagara Parks Commission and the Niagara Frontier State Park Authority for the walks. By June of 1975 it was apparent that neither organization would sanction the stunts. Phillipe Petit accepted the refusal and left Niagara Falls; Rechatin persisted. On June 4, 1975 he made an unauthorized wire walk over the Whirlpool on the cables of the Aero Car; and with his wife and a driver assistant he also rode the Aero Car cables using a motorcycle specially adapted to the wire. Rechatin performed stunts on a steel frame specially constructed above the motorcycle; his wife Janyck, made the trip upside down, hanging by her foot from another frame underneath the motorcycle. The event was covered by the media who had been alerted about the early morning event. The Niagara Parks Police arrived at the scene soon after the event began but made no attempt to stop the stunt. Rechatin was not charged. He left the area and returned to France soon after.

On July 2, 1984, Karel Soucek, a professional stuntman from Hamilton, Ontario, became the first Canadian to go over the Horseshoe Falls in a barrel and live. His barrel was put in the water about 200 m (656 ft.) above the Falls. In less than twenty seconds it had plunged over the Falls but it was trapped for forty-five minutes in the eddy below, before being rescued. On July 11, Soucek appeared in court and was fined $500 for performing an illegal act on Niagara Parks property.

Karel Soucek was fatally injured while performing a stunt in the Astrodome at Houston, Texas, on January 19, 1985. He was dropped in a wooden barrel 55 m (180 ft.) from the top of the Astrodome and was supposed to land in a 3 m (10 ft.) deep pool of water. The barrel struck the rim of the pool and Mr. Soucek suffered multiple injuries on impact. He died the next day in a Houston hospital. Mr. Soucek was buried in Drummond Hill Cemetery in Niagara Falls, Ontario. on February 1, 1985.

Karel Soucek claimed to be "The Last of the Niagara Daredevils", but on August 18, 1985, Steven Trotter, a twenty-two year old part time bartender from Barrington, Rhode Island, became the sixth and youngest person to survive a barrel plunge over the Horseshoe Falls. Trotter made the trip in what he called a "rig". It was made from two plastic Greek pickle barrels, surrounded by huge helium filled inner tubes. The barrels were fused together and protected at the ends by fibre glass caps that had been moulded from egg-shaped supermarket panty hose displays.

Trotter's rig was placed in the river above the Falls off Goat Island on the American side. After his plunge he was rescued by employees of the Maid of the Mist Company and taken, with his rig to the company's Canadian dock. Trotter was fined $503 in a Canadian court for stunting, and he was subsequently fined $5,000 by an American court for violating a United States Federal Law - "causing a vessel to be brought into a safety zone".

Before the year was over another daredevil would challenge the Horseshoe Falls. On July 28, Dave Munday, a 46 year old diesel mechanic from Caistor Centre, Ontario, inside his aluminum capped plastic barrel, was dropped into the river just upstream from the International Control Dam.

The Niagara Parks Police were expecting him, tipped off by a telephone call from someone who knew of the planned stunt and feared that Munday would be killed. The Police had the operators of the Control Dam close the gates after Munday went through, shutting off the flow of water. By the time he reached the river above the Falls, the water level had dropped and the barrel was trapped behind the Canadian Niagara Power Company gathering weir. Munday was forced to abandon the attempt to go over the Falls.

He was fined $503 and put on probation for two years, violation of his probation would make him liable to thirty days in jail and a fine of $1,000. However, Munday said that he would risk going to jail simply because he wanted to go over the Horseshoe Falls - "It is something I've wanted to do".

Throughout the rest of the summer and on into the fall Dave Munday and his crew played a "cat and mouse" game with the Niagara Parks Police. Munday was determined to go over the Horseshoe Falls before the end of October when the water level would be lowered because the power companies would be taking additional water out of the river beginning November 1, for electric power generation.

On Saturday, October 5, a rainy day, Dave Munday in his barrel, was dropped into the river, a few thousand feet above the Horseshoe Falls. In less than a minute it was all over and the barrel floated in the river eddy below the Falls. Dave Munday made his successful trip over the Horseshoe Falls. He was fined $1503 in Provincial Court - $1000 for violating his probation and $503 for performing a stunt.

The Niagara Parks Commission continues to refuse permission to use Park land and water areas for stunts, even though requests are still being made. It is their belief that to grant such permission would jeopardize the lives of others who might be required to assist in the rescue of these stunters.

Power

The first step taken by the Park Commissioners toward solving the impoverished financial conditions of the Park was the granting of a franchise to the Niagara Park and River Railway in 1891. But the second step, the granting of franchises for the development of hydro electric power from the waters of the Niagara River within the boundaries of the Park, was more important.

The first use of the power of the Niagara River at the Falls is believed to have been made about 1757-58 by a Frenchman, Chabert Joncaire Jr., who built a short narrow loop canal on the river bank a short distance above the American Falls. Using a wooden overshot water wheel, under a head of about 1.8 m (6 ft.), he cut logs. In 1760 John Stedman settled on the bank of the river at the American Falls. He repaired the mill which had been abandoned and put it in operation again.[1]

John Burch, a United Empire Loyalist, was granted permission to build a water-powered saw and grist mill on the British west bank of the Niagara River, just above the Falls, near the present site of the Toronto Power Company Powerhouse. Another saw and grist mill was built in 1794 by Benjamin Canby and John McGill at what is now Dufferin Islands. In 1889 no fewer than five companies had been granted franchises to develop hydro electric power on the American side. As Canada possessed equal rights with the United States in the use of Niagara's waters, public opinion on the Canadian side demanded that Canadians should have an equal share in the

benefits to be received from the development of electric power from the waters of the Niagara River.

As early as 1889 negotiations began between the Queen Victoria Niagara Falls Park Commissioners and a group of American capitalists who would later form the Canadian Niagara Power Company, to generate electric power from the Niagara River waters. They withdrew their application within a year when they could not arrange financing. They were succeeded by a group of English financiers associated with the electrical transmission pioneer S.Z. de Ferranti. This group was granted an option for one year upon payment of $10,000, which was renewed for a second year upon payment of an additional $10,000. Their option expired on March 1, 1892 and was not renewed.

The Park Commissioners then signed an agreement with a group incorporated as the Canadian Niagara Power Company.[2] Its principals were the same men who organized the Niagara Falls Power Company on the U.S. side. They were granted monopoly rights to use the water from the Niagara River within the boundaries of Queen Victoria Park to generate electric power, on condition that they had their generating station in operation by May 1, 1897 and that they would have 10,000 hp ready for use by November 1, 1898. This franchise lapsed by default when the plant was not completed in time, according to the agreement.

In 1899 the Park Commission renewed the franchise with the Canadian Niagara Power Company,

Niagara Parks Archives

Niagara Falls Park and River Railway Company Powerhouse.

    Built in 1893 the Powerhouse of the Niagara Falls Park and River Railway was a unique generating station. Not only was it the first hydraulic power station to provide revenue to the Queen Victoria Niagara Falls Park Commission, it also produced direct current for the railway, park lighting for Queen Victoria Park and alternating current for local industries. The first Carborundum manufactured in Canada was produced in this powerhouse in 1893, as reported by the July 1893 edition of the **Canadian Engineer:** *"The Carborundum Company of Niagara Falls has commenced the manufacture of its product in Canada under a patent which it holds. It has just built a new factory at Niagara Falls, Ontario but the electrical apparatus not having arrived in time for the plant to be utilized in accordance with the patent provision, in order to maintain its rights, the Company with considerable enterprise, erected a furnace in the Powerhouse of the Niagara Falls Park and River Railway Company and there made the first Carborundum produced in the Dominion."*

    In this 1930 view there is shown between the Powerhouse and Table Rock House an open-sided car of the Great Gorge Route. This railline was operated by current from this Powerhouse. Since 1902 both the Railway and the Powerhouse were owned by the International Railway Company.

The Ontario Power Company Headworks at Dufferin Islands, 1912. On the left the Gate House leading to the underground conduits; centre, the Forebay; right the Screen House.

The Powerhouse of the Electrical Development Company of Ontario, operated by the Toronto Power Company.

The Toronto Powerhouse, a view from the north side. From a post card by Valentine & Sons.

without the monopoly provision previously granted. Construction resumed on the powerhouse, which was being built on the mainland behind Cedar Island. The forebay of the powerhouse was a portion of the river channel which ran around the Island and the entrance to the forebay from the river was formed by enlarging the inlet, called the Gap, south of Cedar Island. The tail race water flows through a low level outlet tunnel, cut through solid rock, and lined with concrete and brick. It exits into the lower Niagara River just below the Horseshoe Falls.

The Canadian Niagara Power Company was authorized to install 10 generators of 10,000 hp each and 1 spare generator, for a total capacity of 100,000 hp. With ground rent and the tariff agreed upon, based on the horsepower developed, the Queen Victoria Park Commissioners would receive $67,600 per annum. The Canadian Niagara plant went into operation on January 1, 1905 and the first 10,000 hp was delivered to the Niagara Falls Power Company on the United States side. The Canadian Niagara Plant is still in operation today, as part of the Niagara Mohawk (United States) power group. It provides domestic power to Canadian customers along its transmission line which runs inland, west of the upper Niagara River Parkway to Fort Erie and Buffalo. The Canadian Niagara Power Company building, with its green tile roof and rusticated masonry of grey cut stone is located just south of the Horseshoe Falls.

Two other franchises were granted, one to the Ontario Power Company in 1902 and the other to the Electrical Development Company in 1903 to build along the river bank south of the Canadian Niagara facilities. Some criticism was made of the "undue defacement of the Park and the water views" caused by the power plants. It was pointed out by the Commissioners that the greater part of the building of the plants would take place above the Horseshoe Falls and out of the main area of the Park. Two of the plants were located in the area known as The Flats or The Hollow which was often flooded in the early days when the river ran high due to the effects of a strong southwest wind pushing water out of Lake Erie and down the river to the Falls. This area of the Park contained playing fields and a gravel pit where the Park maintenance department obtained gravel for the Park roads and paths.

The Canadian side was ideally suited for the establishment of the power plants, having a plentiful supply of water along the bank. The rock strata in the river bed tilts southwest toward the Canadian shore 6 m (20 ft.) in 1.6 km (1 mi.) and this tilt brings the river water towards the Canadian shore.

The Ontario Power Company, composed of American investors, was granted its franchise on April 11, 1900. The Company had two options open to take water from the river. One was to bring water from the Welland River at Chippawa by way of an open cut canal to the Powerhouse north of the Horseshoe Falls (opposite the present day Victoria Park Restaurant). It chose to exercise its second option, to gather water from the river at the entrance to Dufferin Islands. The right to conduct an open cut canal through the Park was cancelled and instead the stipulation was made that all water required by the Company should be conveyed under the surface of the Park in conduits or pipes, and that no part of the Park surface should be occupied by a canal or forebay.[3]

The Ontario Power Company gathering weir was constructed in the river above Dufferin Islands. From here the water passes through a screen house which keeps logs and ice from entering the forebay. The forebay and the screen house are in a French neo-classic design, and are located at the northern end of Dufferin Islands. From the forebay the water passes into the three conduits, one steel, one reinforced concrete and one made of wooden staves, bound with iron hoops and covered with concrete, which run for over 1.8 km (6000 ft.) underground through the Park to the Ontario Powerhouse below the Falls.

Additions made to the Powerhouse in 1910 and 1918 brought the installed capacity up to 125,000 hp. A unique feature of this plant is that the turbine runners and generator rotors are on one great horizontal shaft. Changes in the Park resulting from the construction of this Powerhouse and the conduits involving The Hollow and Dufferin Islands, Table Rock House and the Scenic Tunnel, and the Refectory (now called the Victoria Park Restaurant), are dealt with in other sections of this book.

On January 29, 1903, the Commissioners entered into an agreement with a syndicate of Canadian investors, William Mackenzie, Henry M. Pellatt and Frederick Nicholls, later to be known as the Electrical Development Company. The agreement allowed the Company to develop 125,000 hp using the water from the Niagara River above the Falls, on terms similar to those of the other companies.[4] The design for an Italian Renaissance style building was approved by the Park Commissioners. The Power-house, built of Indiana Limestone, is located above the Horseshoe Falls about midway between the Ontario Power Company screenhouse at Dufferin Islands and the Canadian Niagara Powerhouse.

A novel and practical feature of this plant is that the powerhouse is constructed on what was previously the river bed.[5] The area reclaimed contained the most turbulent rapids of the Upper Cascades, known as the Tempest and the Whitehorse Rapids. Here it was found that the depth of the river varied from 2.4 m to 7.3 m (8 to 24 ft.). The wheel pit is about 122 m (400 ft.) long and 6.7 m (22 ft.) wide with vertical turbines. Alternate turbines discharged into one of two tail race tunnels which ran parallel to the wheel pit. About 46 m (150 ft.) beyond the wheel pit the tunnels unite to form one 610 m (2000 ft.) long tail race tunnel 4 m (13 ft.) in diameter which discharges into the river under the Horseshoe Falls. The Powerhouse had a total capacity of 137,500 hp with 11 generators of 12,500 hp capacity each, one generator was considered as a spare.

The work both underground and above ground proceeded rapidly. The Powerhouse cornerstone was laid in 1906. Power was first delivered from this plant on November 21, 1906. There were two stages in the construction; approximately half of the project was completed in 1907, but the Company's financial difficulties and its early political struggles against the emerging movement for public control of hydro-

Number 2 conduit of the Ontario Power Company completed July 1910. This conduit is buried along with conduits Numbers 1 and 3, beneath the parking lot which runs from Table Rock, south behind the Canadian Niagara Power Company Powerhouse to the foot of Fraser Hill.

An inspection party, travelling by automobile in Number 2 conduit, July 1910.

Concreting the top of shell of Number 2 Surge Tank of the Ontario Power Company, October 1911.

The Ontario Power Company Surge Tanks at the end of Number 1 and 2 conduits in Queen Victoria Park, 1920.

electric power development in Ontario, postponed further development until 1911. In 1908 the Powerhouse became known as the Toronto Powerhouse, named for the Toronto Power Company Ltd., which controlled the plant by lease beginning in March 1908. The plant was completed in 1913. In 1922 the Toronto Power Company was taken over by the Provincially owned Hydro Electric Power Commission of Ontario.

The station produced 25 HZ (25 cycle) electricity, now used only in older steel making processes and in electro-chemical equipment. More efficient use of the same water could be made at the Sir Adam Beck Generating Stations at Queenston, so Ontario Hydro closed the Toronto Powerhouse in 1974. For a time in 1982 it was operated by the Sir Sandford Fleming Foundation as a Museum celebrating the development of hydraulic water power. The Museum was called The Engineerium and at the request of the Foundation the name of the building reverted to the old name - The Electrical Development Company Powerhouse.

For twenty years from 1892 until 1912, the area extending from south of Murray Street at the Refectory to the Dufferin Islands was torn up and disfigured for much of the time by powerhouse construction. A compensating factor was the boost the construction gave to the local economy. The total value of the power companies' investment was $1,500,000 and the power produced would benefit the general economy of both Canada and the United States. For the Park Commission, there were annual rentals of nearly $60,000, plus the "horsepower" fees, which when the stations reached full capacity, would yield more than $200,000 a year.

While all of this powerhouse construction was in progress at Niagara Falls, public pressure was being exerted on the Provincial Government by those municipalities which were buying power from the private companies. The movement for public ownership of electric power generated in Ontario seems to have started in 1902. Local businessmen attending a series of Board of Trade meetings in Berlin - now Kitchener, Ontario - pressed for some guaranteed low cost electric power from Niagara Falls to the communities in southern Ontario from Brantford to London. The cause was taken up by an influential group of Mayors in 1903, amongst its members was Adam Beck, Mayor of London, Ontario and a Conservative member in the Legislature.

The movement gathered momentum but the Liberal Government took no action and was defeated by the Conservatives in the election of 1906. The Conservatives campaigned on the issue that the water power at Niagara Falls belonged to the people. Adam Beck who had been in the forefront, championing the cause of public power, was re-elected member for London. Premier Whitney appointed Beck Minister without Portfolio in his cabinet. Unofficially, and in fact, he was Minister of Power. On May 10, 1906 the Legislature passed a Bill entitled "An Act to Provide for the Transmission of Electric Power to the Municipalities". The Bill, given Royal Assent on May 14, 1906, created the Hydro Electric Power Commission of Ontario, the forerunner of today's Ontario Hydro. The first Hydro Commission was appointed on June 7, 1905, with Adam Beck as Chairman.

While the movement for public power was gathering strength, the three generating plants at Niagara Falls were in operation. Two of the plants were developing horsepower in excess of the terms of their franchises. The Canadian Niagara Power Company reached this stage in 1906 and the Electrical Development Company in 1907, where

payments had to be made on their water rental contracts with the Commission. In 1908 the Ontario Power Company reached the same stage.[6]

The Park Commissioners insisted that the companies were obligated to pay rentals based on the peak capacities of their generating stations, which were achieved by utilizing the amount of water rented to them. The companies argued for rates at so much per horsepower per year, as determined by the average power generated during the 24 hour day. Negotiations failed and the Park Commission went to the courts for a decision.

In 1912 the Privy Council in London settled the Park Commissioners' claim against the Canadian Niagara Power Company by passing judgement for payment for excess power to be paid on a peak basis. The Electrical Development Company and the Ontario Power Company, now took the attitude that the judgement suit against the Canadian Niagara Power Company was not applicable to their agreements, and made no effort to settle with the Commission. Further negotiations dragged on for years, while the two companies tendered payment on the basis of average horsepower generated and the money offered was received by the Park Commissioners without prejudice.[7]

In 1908 the H.E.P.C. had contracted with the Ontario Power Company to supply electricity and transmission lines were built to Toronto and south-western Ontario. Niagara Falls power lit the streets of Berlin (now Kitchener) on October 11, 1910. It reached the other municipalities soon after. In August, 1917, the Ontario Power Company was acquired by the H.E.P.C. without a settlement being made on the rental issue. The Park Commissioners refrained from further litigation in the belief that under the new management of the Hydro Electric Power Commission the settlement of past rental would be undertaken without delay. It was 1925 before the standard of a "minute peak"[8] was adopted and the arrears in rental were paid.

The Toronto Power Company had strenuously objected to the concept of public power and had led an unsuccessful press campaign against public power legislation. It persisted in its objection, refusing to pay any rentals based on peak load. As well it refused to sell electricity from its station to the H.E.P.C. and payment was made in 1925 to the Park Commission on "minute peak" basis, along with the payment made on the Ontario Power Company account. The Canadian Niagara Power Company had paid the rentals required by the Privy Council judgement and it remains a privately-owned power plant to this

Ontario Hydro Archives

June 1922. An aerial view of the Toronto Powerhouse and the scow in the upper rapids. This view shows the "temporary" uncovered conduit Number 3, built to carry water from the Dufferin Islands Headworks of the Ontario Power Company to the Powerhouse below the Falls. The former Park Greenhouse is in the centre.

day. The Ontario Power Company and the Toronto Power Company fought the issue to the last and eventually were absorbed into the H.E.P.C.

On New Year's Day in 1917 Ontario's electors voted on a scheme to establish a hydro generating station at Queenston "which would be larger than any ever contemplated anywhere in the world".[9] The power generating scheme received overwhelming approval. This power project had been under consideration since 1914 and the success of the vote was due mainly to the urging of one man, Adam Beck.

The H.E.P.C. purchased the Ontario Power Plant to alleviate a wartime power shortage. Only half of the output of the plant was available for Ontario's needs as the H.E.P.C. had to fulfill the contract made by the Ontario Power Company with United States suppliers, to provide 60,000 hp to the United States. The agreement ran for 50 years and was not due to terminate until 1950. To provide more power at the newly aquired Powerhouse an expansion was undertaken and the third conduit allowed under the franchise was constructed to bring more water from the Dufferin Islands intake to the power plant.

The third pipe line, 4 m (13½ ft.) in diameter, was built of wooden staves wound with iron hoops, and was left uncovered along its length except for a few hundred feet at either end. It was considered a temporary pipe line because it was felt that the 35,000 hp that the additional water produced would be needed only to assist in wartime manufacturing. A temporary steel plate surge tank was built at the end of the conduit, just north of the Refectory, on the old picnic grounds. It was intended that the tank and the conduit would be removed and the surface of the Park restored within five years of March 1, 1918. The conduit is still in place, but it was cemented over in the 1950's and it, along with the other two conduits laid previously, are now covered with earth, black topped and serve as parking lots in the area at Table Rock and behind the Canadian Niagara Powerhouse. The "temporary" steel surge tank was removed in 1961. Its function was the same as the other tanks still in the Park, south of the Victoria Park Restaurant, one of which has the Illumination battery on top. All three were overflow tanks, ready to receive the water from the pipe lines should an emergency require that the generators be turned off and the water shut off.

Construction began on the new Queenston Power-house in May 1917. The project, known as the Queenston-Chippawa Development was planned to use the greatest amount of the total fall of the Niagara River, or the maximum head possible for the generation of power. Of the total fall of 100 m (327 ft.) between Lake Erie and Lake Ontario, about 3 m (10 ft.) occurs in the upper Niagara River between Lake Erie and the beginning of the Cascades above Dufferin Islands. Another 1.5 m (5 ft.) occurs between Queenston and the mouth of the Niagara River at Niagara-on-the-Lake. The remaining 95 m (312 ft.) are made up of the Upper Cascades, the Horseshoe Falls, the Whirlpool and the Niagara Glen Rapids.[10]

The effective head of the new plant, to be built on Park Commission land at Queenston was 90 m (294 ft.), considerably more than the maximum height of 55 m (180 ft.) available in the vicinity of the Horseshoe Falls, where the three operating power-houses were located. 28.3 litres (1 cu. ft.) of water used in the new Queenston powerhouse would produce 30 hp compared to only 16 hp it would produce in the existing powerhouses at the Falls.

The intake structure was built at the mouth of the Welland River at Chippawa. The Welland was deepened and its flow reversed so that water is taken from the Niagara River, then through 6 .4 km (4 mi.) of this deepened channel, then by way of a 13.7 km (8½ mi.) open cut canal to the powerhouse at the edge of the cliff south of Queenston Heights. The power-house has 10 generating units. At peak construction 10,000 workers were employed with a semi-monthly payroll of $750,000 all of which had to be paid in cash.

On December 28, 1921, the first generators went into service. The hopes of those who sponsored the venture were more than fulfilled when the generators produced as much as 60,000 hp each instead of the 55,000 hp anticipated.

The establishment of a publicly owned electric utility had many implications for the Park Commission. Not only was the intake structure and the Queenston powerhouse built on Park lands, but the question of what compensation would be paid by the H.E.P.C. for the use of water from the Niagara River for power generation, had to be answered. On September 20, 1918, a preliminary agreement was entered into between the Park Commissioners and the H.E.P.C. reserving all the Commission's rights as riparian owners of land in the Niagara River until further negotiations could take place. This confirmed the right of the Park Commission to compensation for the diversion of the waters of the Niagara River by way of the intake and power canal, at the mouth of the Welland River.

Compensation for water diversion was slow in coming, agreement had to be reached on the basis for calculating the price to be paid for water used. There were also the outstanding claims of the Park Commission for excess rents against the Ontario Power Company and the Toronto Power Company, acquired by the H.E.P.C. in 1917 and 1922.

In 1928 a settlement was made, the H.E.P.C. paid $545,997.33 on the basis of the Ontario Power Company and the Toronto Power Company use of the Niagara River water and $1,455,122.93 in full settlement of all rentals owing on the Queenston-Chippawa development up to October 31, 1928.

The $545,997.33 went into the Niagara Parks Commission account, while the $1,455,122.93, although appearing on the books of the Niagara Parks Commission, was paid directly to the Treasurer of Ontario.

A power shortage developed after World War II when the construction of new housing and new industrial facilities in Ontario placed an ever increasing demand on the existing generating facilities. A new agreement between the Canadian and the United States Governments provided for the increased diversion of water from the Niagara River for power generating purposes. Ontario Hydro, as the Hydro Electric Power Commission of Ontario was now known, undertook their largest development to date, a development which would triple the power output of their original plant at Queenston, renamed the Sir Adam Beck Generating Station No. 1.

Work began in 1950 with much of the construction carried out on Park property. This included the Powerhouse at Queenston, the intake structure at Chippawa, temporary roads and causeways to the shafts excavated to provide access to the twin tunnels being bored to carry water to the new plant, and access holes bored at intervals to facilitate the pouring of concrete for the tunnel linings. The Parkway was temporarily diverted at the intake structure site and at the powerhouse site. In addition, an access road was built down the side of the gorge, from a point just north of the Niagara Glen picnic area on Wintergreen Flats to the site of the Power-house at the river's edge, to facilitate the delivery of materials. This road destroyed the virgin wooded talus in the area from the Glen to the new power plant, and encroached on the dry gorge area of the Glen. Planting and reseeding, along with the appearance of some natural growth, is now covering

Preparation of the site for the Ontario Power Generating Station, 1904. The Refectory is on the right, the Hydraulic Elevator and Table Rock House are on the left. The large rocks at the river's edge in front of the elevator are the remains of Table Rock. The last big pieces fell from Table Rock in 1850.

Sir Adam Beck Generating Stations Numbers 1 and 2 from the air. The Pump Storage Reservoir is at the right.

Ontario Hydro Archives

The Ontario Power Generating Station as seen from the American side in the 1950's. The Illumination battery is on the surge tank in the centre. Also shown is the Victoria Park Restaurant. Partly hidden in the trees on the right is the former "temporary" black, painted, steel surge tank, erected during the First World War. It remained in place for almost fifty years, and was removed in 1961.

the banks of this road with greenery.

The water from the upper Niagara River at Chippawa is diverted to the new power plant through two 13.7 m (45 ft.) inside diameter concrete lined tunnels which run as deep as 100 m (330 ft.) below ground level under the City of Niagara Falls. Water enters the tunnels through two 152 m (500 ft.) long gathering tubes, looking like huge mouth organs, which are submerged off shore. Two massive tunnel portal gates are kept in constant readiness to be dropped to close off the tunnels and stop the flow of water should an emergency occur at the power plants.

The tunnels carry 54 million litres (12,000,000 Imperial gallons) of water a minute to the forebay of the powerhouses. The Sir Adam Beck Generating Stations No. 1 and No. 2 share a common forebay. From here the water passes through 16 generating units of Sir Adam Beck Generating Station No. 2, to produce 1,828,000 hp. Construction began in 1950

and was completed in 1958. Power production began on August 30, 1954 when H.R.H. the Duchess of Kent officially opened the plant, placing the first three generating units in production.[11]

Water rental fees are a steady source of income. From the $67,000 received by the Park Commission in 1905 for ground rent and water rental fees from the Canadian Niagara Power Company, water rental fees have risen to the $3,125,046 paid by Ontario Hydro and the Canadian Niagara Power Company in 1983. Water rental fees allow the Commission to plan capital improvements and to keep up with the ever increasing cost of Parks maintenance. Thanks to the steady income provided by the water rentals, residents and tourists can visit Queen Victoria Park and the Falls, or picnic along the upper and lower river, Queenston Heights, McFarland Point Park, or King's Bridge Park, without paying any admission charges.

The Scow

The dumping scow marooned in the Upper Rapids has been a point of interest since August 1918 when, with two men on board, it broke loose from its towing tug and drifted off down the river toward the Falls. Gustav F. Lofberg and James H. Harris, employees of the Great Lakes Dredge and Dock Company, who were on the scow, resigned themselves as they started through the rapids and prepared for the plunge over the Falls.

Lofberg prepared by tying himself to the scow in order to go over the Falls with it. Harris wanted to be free of the scow if it went over, so he tied a line about his waist and made the other end fast to a barrel. He believed that the barrel would carry him free of the scow and that he might have a chance to grasp hold of a rock as he was borne toward the cataract. Fortunately they had the presence of mind also to open the bottom dumping doors and the scow grounded on a shoal about 767 m (2500 ft.) from the brink of the Horseshoe Falls, and opposite the Toronto Powerhouse.

A crowd of men, employees of the nearby Toronto Power Company and Canadian Niagara Power Company, soon gathered. Police and firemen arrived from both sides of the border, all assembled to attempt to rescue the stranded men. By means of a life-saving gun brought up from the United States Coast Guard Station at Youngstown, New York, a line was shot out from the roof of the Toronto Powerhouse to the stranded men and they soon fastened the end of the line to the scow. The other end

on the Toronto Powerhouse roof was drawn taut and tied securely.

It was dark by the time a breeches-buoy was sent out on the line, and it jammed - the line was fouled. William Red Hill of Niagara Falls, Ontario, volunteered to untangle the lines. He was told that the line was probably safe, but it had not been tried out under a weight. His only answer was that he was willing to take the risk.

Hill made his first trip out in the breeches-buoy shortly after 3 o'clock in the morning. Working by the light from powerful searchlights which were directed towards the line and the scow, Hill unfouled the ropes and the block and tackle, removing the obstruction that prevented the buoy from reaching the stranded men. At 8:30 a.m. he went out again, this time he travelled to within 39.6 m (130 ft.) of the scow where he was able to talk to Lofberg and Harris. He discovered that one of the small coils of rope on the scow was wound around the big rope from the breeches-buoy, preventing the buoy from getting closer to the scow. Hill shouted directions to Lofberg and Harris but they were so weak that they had difficulty in untangling the ropes on the scow. The task was finally completed and with all lines free and clear, Hill returned to the roof of the Powerhouse. Charles Possett and Thomas Darrington, boss riggers from the Toronto Power Company, worked the lines while Hill made his trips.

Harris, who was weak from hunger and exposure, was the first off the scow, followed by Lofberg. A

Gustav F. Lofberg and James H. Harris marooned on the scow, August 7, 1918.

James H. Harris on the breeches-buoy, on his way to the roof of the Powerhouse.

Gustav Lofberg hanging low over the rapids on the breeches-buoy, on his way to the Powerhouse roof.

An aerial view of the upper rapids and the rusting scow taken in the 1970's. Oak Hall, now the Niagara Parks Administration building, is visible at the top left. The Niagara Parks Greenhouse is to the right of the Toronto Power House and behind the Greenhouse are the Service Yards.

cheer went up from the assembled crowd of rescuers and onlookers when both men were safely landed. It was nearly 10 a.m. when Lofberg was landed on the Powerhouse roof. Nineteen hours had passed since the scow had broken loose. William Red Hill was awarded a Carnegie Life Saving Medal for his part in the rescue.

The scow which for many years seemed impervious to the ravages of time, has over the past five years shown signs of deterioration. The left front, on the riverside, has a huge piece gouged out. The scow will eventually break up and the rusty pieces will disappear in the River.

The Horseshoe Falls Recession - Diversion - Remedial

All Cataracts are doomed to die as they run out of levels to erode between Lakes. Every horseshoe-shaped falls is prone to concentrate in the centre and become a smaller stream in a narrow gorge.[1] The last century has been an interesting point in geological time as the Horseshoe Falls is making a right hand turn, cutting across the pre-glacial Falls-Chippewa Valley. It is this turning plus the massive diversion of water from the Upper River for generation of electric power, which led to the need for the remedial work which has been done over the years, to space out the flow of water over the Falls.

Up until the time of Father Hennepin's visit in 1678 the western branch of the Cataracts was eroding in a straight line. It was not until 1721 that the designation "horseshoe-shaped" was given to this Falls. François Xavier de Charlevoix, a Jesuit, wrote: "As to its figure, it was in the shape of a horse-shoe, and is about 400 paces in circumference; it is divided in the middle by a very narrow island, half a quarter of a league long."[2]

Our earliest accurate picture of Niagara Falls was made in 1827 by Captain Basil Hall, of the British Army. He used a Camera Lucida, an instrument similar to a periscope, which was projected out of the top of a tent-like enclosure and directed towards the subject to be reproduced. A reduced image of the subject was projected onto a sheet of white drawing paper. Hall then carefully and painstakingly drew a sketch of Niagara Falls by tracing over the projected image. His accurate sketch has enabled geologists to determine the rate and amount of recession during the past 155 years.[3]

The most dramatic change in the contour of the Falls occurred in 1889. On January 10, a strong south west gale drove a flood of water out of Lake Erie, downriver and over the Horseshoe Falls. The additional weight of this flood on the lip of the cataract caused huge pieces to break off the lip. After the gale had subsided and the water level in Lake Erie had returned to normal, it was found that the depth of water going over the flanks of the Horseshoe at Table Rock had dropped by 38 cm (15 in.).[4] This rockfall at the apex of the Horseshoe changed the direction of the flow; after that most of the water flowed over the centre of the Horseshoe.[5]

The *Toronto Empire* reported in its January 15, 1889 issue: "The contour now resembles the extra-ordinary view of a double horseshoe, the smaller one caused by the recent displacement of rock, being located in advance and to the right of the centre of the Great Horseshoe. Visitors familiar with the shape of the Canadian Falls during recent years will be able to appreciate the change at a glance."[6]

The drying off of the flanks of the Horseshoe caused by the sudden erosion and general low water conditions in the Great Lakes during 1899, took away the sheet of water from the Behind the Sheet attraction and a tunnel had to be built to take people farther behind the Falls in order to see the sheet of water.

"On Friday evening January 8, 1891 at 9 p.m. a

The Horseshoe Falls from Falls View Station showing the notched centre which resulted from the large rock falls from the crest in 1889.

large mass of rock fell in the centre of the cataract, and on Saturday night at 10 p.m. another large mass broke away", reported the *Niagara Falls Gazette.* "Table Rock House was jarred to such a degree that the doors were thrown open and the residents who had retired, jumped out of their beds greatly excited. The vibrations of the building resembled the severe shocks of earthquakes. The effect . . . on the contour is quite marked - the change being from that of an angle at the vortex to the original horseshoe shape."[7]

The lowering of the flow over the flanks at Table Rock affected more than the Behind the Sheet attraction. There was often an insufficient supply of water for the Niagara Falls Park and River Railway Powerhouse and the Town of Niagara Falls Municipal Waterworks. In 1895 the Town authorities constructed a vertical concrete structure which they toppled into the river at the Niagara Falls Park and River Railway Powerhouse intake from which they drew the Town's water. This "weir" provided some temporary relief, diverting water toward the intake

entrance and raising the level of the water entering both the Niagara Falls Park and River Railway Powerhouse and the Municipal Waterworks. While nature was making drastic changes in the direction of the flow of the River, man came along with his grandiose plans for the development of hydro electric power from the Niagara River water.

By 1905 no fewer than nine franchises had been granted by the New York State Legislature permitting the diversion of water from the Niagara River above the Falls for electric power generation. There were practically no limitations on the amount of water allowed to be diverted. Fortunately only three of the franchises had been taken up, in the other six, construction had not begun.[8]

Besides the five Canadian Charters already in operation, Niagara Falls Park and River Railway Powerhouse, Town of Niagara Falls Waterworks, Canadian Niagara Power Co., Ontario Power Co., and the Electrical Development Co., the Dominion Government had granted three other charters which were undeveloped - none was in any way limited in the quantity of water that might be taken for electric power development purposes. Overwhelmed and in awe of the vast size of the construction projects, the boldness of the engineering plans, and the great economic boost which the availability of cheap electricity would give, the public at first offered little or no opposition to the power projects.

Suddenly it became apparent that if all of the franchises granted on both sides of the river up until 1906 were taken up, not only would the Niagara River be drained but the water in Lake Erie would have to be drawn upon. There began public agitation to have the scenic grandeur of the Falls preserved, while at the same time using the maximum amount of water for power generation. Reacting to this public pressure the Canadian and United States Governments passed the matter over to the International Waterways Commission which was formed in 1902.[9] On May 3, 1905 the Commission recommended that the diversion for power purposes on the Niagara River at the Falls be limited to 523.6 m^3/sec. (18,500 cfs) on the American side, and 1018.8 m^3/sec. (36,000 cfs) on the Canadian side. The Burton Act of 1906 which followed this recommendation was passed by the United States Congress cutting the American allotment to 441.5 m^3/sec. (15,600 cfs) leaving the Canadian share at 1018.8 m^3/sec. (36,000 cfs).[10]

In 1905 negotiations began between the United States and Great Britain with the object of arranging a treaty dealing with the waters along the International Boundary between the United States and Canada.[11] The Boundary Waters Treaty was signed on January 11, 1909 and ratified in 1910. The International Niagara Board of Control was established, with one member from Canada and one from the United States, to regulate the water permitted for power development under the Boundary Waters Treaty. Water diversion for electric power generation was limited to 566 m^3/sec. (20,000 cfs) for the United States and 1018.8 m^3/sec. (36,000 cfs) for Canada.[12] This treaty brought about a practical compromise between the requirements of power generation and the preservation of the scenic beauty of the Horseshoe Falls.

The advantage to Canada over the United States in the amounts of water to be diverted was more apparent than real. The water to be diverted was to service those powerhouses on both sides of the

The dried off flank of the Horseshoe Falls at Table Rock in the early 1900's.

Ontario Archives

river which were already in operation, or under construction. No new franchises were contemplated. The Canadian "advantage" disappears when it is realized that 160,000 hp of electricity generated by 339.6 m³/sec. (12,000 cfs) of the Canadian water diversion, was being exported to the United States and 283 m³/sec. (10,000 cfs) was being diverted out of Lake Michgan for the Chicago Sewage Canal.

The erosion and recession of the crest line of the Horseshoe Falls was taking place in the centre. As more and more water flowed over the centre, the flow over the flanks of the Falls dried off. At times it was almost reduced to a trickle. In 1906 the Commissioners decided to fill in the exposed flanks of the river bed near Table Rock. Material excavated from the Canadian Niagara Power Company tunnel was placed along the Canadian shore filling in the unsightly river bed. Almost 122 m (400 ft.) of the crest line of the Horseshoe Falls was filled in, adding to the Park area and affording views of the Falls hitherto unobtainable.

In 1918 representatives of the City of Niagara Falls Waterworks and the International Railway Company advised the Commissioners that the City of Niagara Falls had at times been entirely without water for domestic purposes. The Railway Company reported that it had been unable to generate power to operate its electric cars at times, due to an inadequate supply of water.[13] Low water conditions in 1923 caused by power diversion and natural causes, exposed the Great Falls Portal of the Scenic Tunnel. The rock bed of the river was lowered, partially restoring the flow of water over the flanks and the operation of the Scenic Tunnel improved.

The International Board of Control was enlarged to four, one additional member from each country, to become a Special International Niagara Board to study the problem. On December 17, 1927 their recommendations included remedial work in the form of submerged weirs to take water from the deep current near the axis of the Horseshoe Falls and thus ensured that both the Canadian and American flanks would be covered at all times.[14] The Parks Commissioners had proposed that islands be built in the Upper Rapids to divert the flow and spread the water over both flanks.[15]

A Convention and Protocol, allowing for a further 283 m³/sec. (10,000 cfs) to be diverted by both sides,

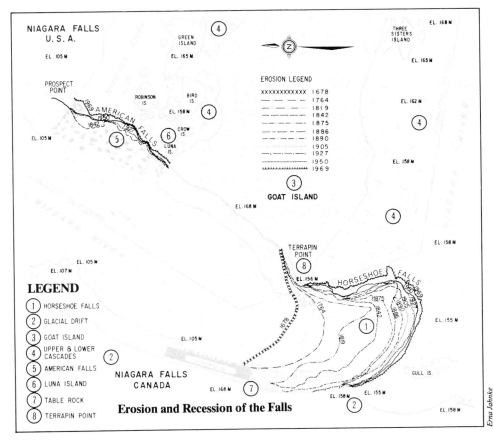

Erosion and Recession of the Falls

LEGEND
1. HORSESHOE FALLS
2. GLACIAL DRIFT
3. GOAT ISLAND
4. UPPER & LOWER CASCADES
5. AMERICAN FALLS
6. LUNA ISLAND
7. TABLE ROCK
8. TERRAPIN POINT

EROSION LEGEND
XXXXXXXXXXXX 1678
———————— 1764
————·—— 1819
——————— 1842
——————— 1875
——·——·— 1886
——·——·—— 1890
············· 1905
—·—·—·—·— 1927
——————— 1950
⊥⊥⊥⊥⊥⊥⊥⊥⊥ 1969

and for the remedial work recommended by the International Board of Control, to be carried out, was passed by the Canadian Government in 1929, but the United States Senate in 1931 rejected the plan because they felt that the power development and scenic preservation should be considered separately. The door was left open for further negotiations but no international action was taken unitl 1941.[16]

Computations made over a period of 63 years from 1842 to 1905-06 placed the mean rate of recession of the Horseshoe Falls at 1.16 m (3.8 ft.) a year. From 1906 when large quantities of water began to be diverted for electric power generation, until 1927, the rate of recession decreased to .70 m (2.3 ft.) a year.

In the 1927 study it was also found that at times the quantity of water flowing over the American Falls fell to as little as 198.1 m^3/sec. (7,000 cfs), resulting in the rock structure showing through the veil of falling water - a condition which disappears when the volume is increased to about 254.7 m^3/sec. (9,000 cfs). To assure that a minimum flow over the American Falls would be sufficient to retain its full beauty, it was proposed that a submerged weir be constructed in the smooth water above the Upper Rapids, thereby raising the level of the Grass Island Pool. The Grass Island Pool, or the Chippawa-Grass Island Pool, is that portion of the Niagara River below Navy Island, extending from shore to shore and down to the limits of the Upper Rapids. The water is held back naturally in this pool by a ridge of rock which runs just below the surface from the Canadian shore to Goat Island.

The urgent need for additional power to supply World War II industries led to an agreement in 1941 which authorized the construction of a submerged weir. This not only diverted more water over the American Falls and the Goat Island flank of the Horseshoe Falls but allowed for the diversion of additional water for the generation of power to the maximum capacity of the existing power plants on both sides of the border, 919.8m^3/sec. (32,500 cfs) for the United States and 1415m^3/sec. (50,000 cfs) for Canada.[17]

The submerged Grass Island Weir is 443 m (1455 ft.) long. It is composed of rock fill made up of very large blocks of limestone with no bonding material, with a top width of about 12 m (40 ft.) and ranges in height from .6 m (2 ft.) at its mid-river terminus to 3 m (10 ft.) at the Canadian shore. Work was begun in March 1942. To place the stone in the river a cableway was strung between two 47.2 m (155 ft.) steel towers, one on the United States side of the

boundary - on an artifical island 0.8 km (0.5 mi.) out in the river - and the other on the bank just above Dufferin Islands at the start of the rapids. The artificial island was constructed by building a rock fill causeway extending 671 m (2,200 ft.) upstream from Goat Island. When the weir was completed the towers and the causeway were removed while the artificial island remained. It is called Tower Island. The underwater weir raised the level of Grass Island Pool .30 m (1 ft.). The weir served its purpose until 1953 when the International Control Dam was built some 76 m (250 ft.) downstream. [18]

The higher water level in the Grass Island Pool allowed the H.E.P.C. to divert an additional 169.8 m^3/sec. (6,000 cfs) to produce 60,000 hp additional for wartime production. The United States benefitted by 212.3m^3/sec. (7,500 cfs). The greater amount available for the U.S. was accounted for by the fact that Canada was nearer complete utilization of the previous maximum diversion allowed.

A post-war power shortage focused international attention on the two-fold problem of additional water diversion for power and the preservation of the Cataracts. Negotiations begun in 1949 and completed in 1950, resulted in the Niagara Diversion Treaty of 1950 whereby an International Joint Commission was appointed as trustee to preserve and enhance the beauty of the Falls and River. In addition, and most important to the power interests of both countries, water diversion limits were raised, allowing both countries to take more water from the Niagara River for electric power generation.

Out of an average flow of slightly more than 5660 m^3/sec. (200,000 cfs) which enters the Niagara River from Lake Erie, 2830m^3/sec. (100,000 cfs) of water must be allowed to flow over the Falls in daylight hours during the tourist season - from April 1 to October 31. During night hours and during the off-season months when scenic considerations are considered to be less important, the flow may be reduced to 1415 m^3/sec. (50,000 cfs). All water in excess of these amounts may be used for generation of power. By the terms of this agreement the diversion is divided almost equally between Canada and the United States. Canada is allowed 141.5 m^3/sec. (5,000 cfs) more because of Canadian water diverted into the Great Lakes system from the Hudson Bay drainage area. [19] With a supply of water guaranteed for additional power generation, Ontario Hydro proceeded with the construction of the Sir Adam Beck Generating Station #2 and the Power Authority of the State of New York built the Robert Moses

An aerial view of the remedial work in progress at the Canadian flank of the Horseshoe Falls in 1953.

The deepened channel at the Canadian flank of the Horseshoe Falls with winter diversion conditions resulting in low water levels, circa 1960.

New York Power Authority

In 1969 the United States Army Corps of Engineers carried out a study of the rock formation at the crest of the American Falls. A coffer dam, constructed of rock and fill, was built extending from the mainland to the head of Goat Island, cutting off the flow of water to the Falls. The dam was completed and the Falls were shut off on June 12, and remained dry while the inspection was being carried out. The coffer dam was removed beginning on November 25 and by midnight on November 26, the Falls were in full flow again. In 1974, seven years of study and deliberation came to an end when several possibilities were proposed which involved either cosmetic changes to the Falls — the removal of the huge piles of talus from in front of the Falls — or leaving the Falls to erode naturally. The growing environmental movements of the late 1960's and early 1970's influenced the decision to allow nature to take its course. The Falls were left to erode naturally.

The International Control Dam, built in 1953 to control the flow of water over the Horseshoe and American Falls, while at the same time raising the level of the Grass Island Pool area to provide sufficient water for the tunnels leading to the power generating stations at Queenston.

Ontario Hydro Archives

Generating Station.

The Niagara Diversion Treaty prescribed a four year target for the completion of the remedial project. This would include the construction of the International Control Dam and the remedial work to be carried out to spread out the flow of water over the Horseshoe Falls. Work began on the International Control Dam in 1953. The river at the dam site was dried off with a cofferdam and the dam structure was built on the dried off river bed. The dam was 472 m (1550 ft.) long and was composed of 13 movable sluice gates, each equipped with a control gate. In 1957 the dam was extended to 671 m (2200 ft.) when 5 more gates were added. The gates serve a dual purpose. Water can be held back to increase the depth of water in the Grass Island Pool thereby providing more water to go through the upstream tunnel intakes of both the Sir Adam Beck and Robert Moses generating stations. At the same time, water can be passed through specific gates to direct it towards the flanks of the Horseshoe Falls, or over the American Falls.

In 1896 low water on the flanks of the Horseshoe Falls at Table Rock hindered the operation of the Hydraulic Elevator and exposed the tunnel portal at the Behind the Sheet attraction. John Zybach, lessee, asked the Park Commissioners to "depress the river bed (at Table Rock) to put more water over the flanks of the Horseshoe Falls and the 'Sheet of Water' ".[20] The Annual Report of 1920 recorded "the top of the Horseshoe Falls at the Canadian shore line was lowered to allow water to pass over the brink. During dry spells visitors had been attracted to the edge of the Falls by a dry river bed. This will be impossible now."[21]

In 1953, as part of the overall remedial program which included the building of the International Control Dam, 18,360 m³ (24,000 cu. yds.) of rock were excavated from the Goat Island flank and 48,960 m³ (64,000 cu. yds.) from the Table Rock flank of the Horseshoe Falls. This deepened the river bed and allowed water to flow over the flanks, presenting a more even flow over the whole crest of the Falls.[22]

Also included was a landfill addition to Goat Island which provided a large observation area extending to the crestline of the Horseshoe Falls at Terrapin Point. During 1969 a crack was noticed in the rock formation at the Point and the area was closed to visitors. Subsequent investigation revealed a serious fault. It was felt that Nature would eventually take its course and the rock ledge would fall.

The Niagara Frontier Parks and Recreation Commission became impatient and in 1983 hired an engineering firm to blast off the unstable rocky promontory. Nearly 3500 sticks of dynamite were used. The construction company drilled 87 holes, some up to 39.6 m (130 ft.) deep, into the rock to hold the dynamite. The blast was set off at noon after a number of half hour delays - the original blast time was to be 8:30 a.m. A series of explosive charges ignited milliseconds apart broke off 22,675 tonnes (25,000 tons) of rock in a clean cut. The resulting surface was scaled then 231 steel rods were horizontally and vertically placed, and fastened with 2.5 cm (1 in.) bolts in the cliff side, securing what was left of the promontory.[23] The Terrapin Point viewing area which had been closed since 1969 was re-opened to the public in mid September 1983.

Whirlpool Rapids

The Whirlpool Rapids were inaccessible to travellers in the early days. The earliest record of anyone having seen them from the Canadian side was left by Richard Bonnycastle, writing in 1841: "I attempted to make a road from the Clifton Hotel toward the Whirlpool, but found many conflicting interests, that I had not the success which a longer residence might have afforded me. At the present the road is somewhat difficult to follow along the top of the high, rocky precipitous wall which hems the stream; but an active adventuresome person may achieve it, and well he is repaid. A succession of magnificient rapids, caverns and precipices are presented to his view . . . The road is a military reservation and should be opened."[1]

The river bank below the Chain Reserve along the Whirlpool Rapids was leased to John Drew on October 31, 1876, by the Ontario Government at an annual rental of $50. He later sub-leased this river bank property to Dr. W.H. Ferguson M.P. who developed the tourist potential of the rapids.[2] He built a steam powered incline railway which operated on wooden rails, to take visitors down the talus slope to the river's edge where a stone pathway was laid out running along the edge of the rapids. Here visitors were able to get a close-up view of the tumbling water as it rushed through the narrow gorge.[3]

In 1888 Dr. Ferguson sold the incline railway to the Whirlpool Rapids Company, an association of American businessmen headed by J.T. Brundage. The new company improved the incline railway, replacing the wooden rails with iron "T" rails imported from Pittsburgh and installing new cars which operated by water power. The cars had water ballast tanks behind the seats. Each car could carry twelve passengers and 12,700 kg (28,000 lbs.) of water. Only an additional 22.7 kg (50 lbs.) of water in the tanks of the upper car were needed to change the balance with the lower car. Therefore the amount of water required to operate the cars depended on the number and weight of the passengers.

When the passengers were seated, the tanks of the car at the top of the incline were filled with enough water from a nearby spring, to conterbalance the lower car. After an additional 22.7 kg (50 lbs.) of water were added, the brake was released and the loaded car went down the incline, simultaneously drawing the lighter - by 22.7 kg (50 lbs.) - car to the top of the incline. The brake was reset, the passengers got off, the discharge pipe was opened and the lower car's ballast tanks emptied. With empty tanks the lower car was ready for the next ascent.[4]

J.T. Brundage who controlled the cab business on both sides of the river had been dispossessed when the Queen Victoria Park Commissioners expropriated his livery stable and land within the new Park's boundaries. Brundage lost his share of the lucrative commissions previously paid to his cab drivers who took their fares to Barnett's Museum, Saul Davis' Table Rock House and Sutherland Macklem's Islands. The Queen Victoria Park Commissioners did not pay commissions and they also restricted the

The Whirlpool Rapids Incline, 1914.

F.H. Leslie

The Whirlpool Rapids from the air.

Niagara Parks Archives

operation of cabs in the Park by not allowing them to be driven into the Park empty.

Brundage now set about to retaliate for the expropriation of his property and the loss of income from his commissions. He had his drivers intercept potential visitors to the new Queen Victoria Park and bring them instead to his Whirlpool Rapids Park. Then the drivers prevailed on their fares to cross the Railway Suspension Bridge to visit the Park on the American side, and the Cave of the Winds - a tourist attraction in which Brundage also had a financial interest. Brundage also put salesmen on the excursion trains to sell "coupon books" and other package deals for his Whirlpool Rapids Park and for attractions on the American side. This effectively diverted many of the potential visitors to the Queen Victoria Park. By the time Brundage and his drivers were through with the tourists, they were tired and had spent all their money. Not many tourists who passed through Brundage's hands visited Queen Victoria Park.

The competition hurt the Park. Superintendent Wilson wrote to Chairman Gzowski on June 13, 1888: "We have an application for the use of the grounds for a large excursion party and Mr. Langmuir authorized me to give them a 5¢ rate over Cedar Island. They were however captured by the Whirlpool people who cut their rate for their elevator to 10¢."[5] Admission to the Queen Victoria Park hydraulic elevator cost 25¢. Superintendent Wilson, frustrated and unable to counter this competition, called them "the Whirlpool gang".[6]

In his letter to the Chairman he also pinpointed what he thought was part of the problem: "The tolls to the Island are giving great offence . . . and the newspapers are howling loudly for their abolishment."[7] The problem was not solved until 1893 when the Park Commissioners accepted the bid of the firm of Zybach and Brundage for a ten year lease to operate the hydraulic elevator and the Behind the Sheet attraction. By having a share in this lease at Table Rock, Brundage now allied his interests with those of the Queen Victoria Park Commissioners.

The Niagara Park and River Railway purchased the assets of the Whirlpool Rapids Park from Brundage and his partners in 1892, for $15,000.[8] AEmilius Irving, the Commission's solicitor, described the Whirlpool Rapids Company operations in his *Draft Report on the Additions to the Queen Victoria Park* in 1887: "connected therewith is a curiosity store built on the top of the bank, a tramway or elevator down the bank to the water's edge. Also built on top of the bank is a large unsightly shed for hack

carriages to drive under and a fence that prevents the public from looking down on the river below".[9]

The Railway Company cleaned up the property and changed the operation of the incline cars to electricity. No structural changes were made in the building. The souvenir store, the carriage shed and the high fence remained. Only necessary repairs were made to the buildings during the Railway Company's ownership. In 1932 when the International Railway surrendered its franchise and ceased to operate, the Whirlpool Rapids Incline and buildings on the upper bank became the property of the Niagara Parks Commission.[10]

The Whirlpool Rapids have been the scene of a variety of stunts and antics. The first to use the Whirlpool Rapids as the backdrop for his stunts was Blondin, the most famous of the Niagara funambulists. He chose the gorge at the Whirlpool Rapids for his 1860 summer appearances. With his tight rope stretched across the gorge just 116m (380 ft.) north of the site of the present Whirlpool Rapids Bridge and directly over the Whirlpool Rapids, he put on weekly performances.

On one occasion he took out a cookstove, set it on the rope in the middle of the gorge, cooked and ate an omelette. It was here that on September 8, 1860, His Royal Highness the Prince of Wales, later King Edward VII, watched Blondin carry Romain Mouton on his back, as he crossed the Whirlpool Rapids on the tight rope. The Prince refused an offer to make a trip on Blondin's back, but was so impressed that he is reported to have given Blondin a gift of 60 guineas.

It was on June 6, 1861, that the Maid of the Mist, with Captain Joel Robinson at the wheel sailed through the rapids on her way to Queenston. The boat had been sold on condition that she be delivered to the Montreal buyer. The trip was successful. the only visible damage was to her smoke stack which was broken off.

In 1883, Captain Matthew Webb, fresh from his triumph of being the first man to swim the English Channel, came to Niagara Falls to seek further fame and fortune. On July 24, he dove into the Niagara River from a rowboat that had approached within 1.83 km (2000 yds.) of the beginning of the rapids. The current soon carried him into turbulent water. He was seen by hundreds of onlookers, valiantly moving his arms and legs as he was carried along. He went under a huge wave and was not seen again until his body was recovered at Lewiston, New York opposite Queenston, four days later.

The mid 1880's brought the barrel fanatics to the Whirlpool Rapids. Carlisle Graham, a Philadelphia

Niagara Falls New York Public Library

cooper, was the first. Arriving in Niagara Falls, N.Y. with his hand-made oak barrel, he was the subject of ridicule when he announced he would go through the Whirlpool Rapids in the barrel. He made the trip on July 11, 1886, arriving safely at the Whirlpool, then going on to Lewiston. The whole trip took only thirty-five minutes. Graham, emboldened by his success, went through a second time, with his head out of the top of the barrel, in full view of the people watching. A big wave gave him a deafening slap on the side of the head, leaving him hard of hearing. He then made a third and a fourth trip.

Others caught the fever, George Hazlett and William Potts made the trip together. Then William Kendall, a Boston policeman, took some of the bloom off the barrel trips when he successfully went through the rapids wearing only a life preserver. George Hazlett talked Sadie Allen into making the trip with him in the late Fall of 1886. There was to be a fourteen year hiatus before the barrel fanatics would return to the Whirlpool Rapids.

The life-saving boats were next. In 1887 Charles A. Percy made three trips in a special boat with air chambers, one of them with Wm. Dittrick as passenger. On the third trip he lost his boat. In 1888 Robert Flack, in a boat named "Phantom", filled with a secret bouyant filling, drowned when the boat overturned and stayed upside down while it went around and around in the Whirlpool. Flack's "secret filling" was excelsior and wood shavings. In 1889 Walter G. Campbell was lucky, he was thrown out of his boat at the first turbulence, and got safely ashore because he was wearing a lifejacket. Peter Nissen, in his boat "The Fool Killer", the smallest steamboat afloat, - made the trip without a head of steam. The smokestack was carried away. Nissen survived and his claim to fame is that his stunt was the first to be recorded on movie film. The Edison Movie Co. filmed the event.

The Pan American Exposition, held in Buffalo in 1901, brought the barrel fanatics back. Fifteen years after his first trip, Graham made his fifth successful trip through the rapids. He arranged a new version of the trip. Maude Willard and her dog would use Graham's barrel to go through the rapids to the Whirlpool. There Graham would join them and the three, Maude, Graham and the dog, would go on to Lewiston in the barrel.

Maude was unlucky, the barrel got caught in the Whirlpool and went round and round for hours, out of reach of would-be rescuers who were trying to lasso the barrel from the shore. Finally, the barrel came

The second Maid of the Mist completed her last sightseeing trip in the Fall of 1860. The Company was in financial difficulties, business prospects for the future were clouded by the impending Civil War between the North and the South in the United States. The boat was sold at auction in 1861. It was purchased by a Montreal firm on condition that it be delivered into Lake Ontario. Captain Joel Robinson, with engineer James H. Jones and mechanic James McIntyre as crew, undertook the hazardous voyage on June 6, 1861, sailing the Maid of the Mist down the Niagara Gorge, through the Whirlpool Rapids and on to Queenston. The boat was tossed about in the rapids and lost its smokestack before arriving at Queenston. From there it sailed to Montreal and for many years served as a ferry on the St. Lawrence River between Quebec City and the Isle of Orleans.

close enough and it was pulled to shore. When the barrel was opened the dog jumped out. Maude was dead, suffocated when her pet dog pressed its nose against the only air hole, cutting off her air supply.

Maude's fate did not deter Martha Wagenfuhrer from being the first woman to try the feat alone. On September 6, 1901 she went through, and was rescued after circling the Whirlpool for an hour. This brought a temporary halt to the Whirlpool Rapids antics. It would be over thirty years before someone would make the trip again. The scene shifted to the Horseshoe Falls. You now had to go over the Falls in a barrel to attract attention![11]

Many of the barrel antics took place after the Park Commissioners had taken control of the area. Most

of the barrel stunts originated in the United States. Only a few stunts - Nissen's boat trip was one - originated at the Maid of the Mist landing on the Canadian side. The barrels and boats were landed on the gravelly beach at the end of the Whirlpool and hauled back up to the top, on Commission property, by way of the ravine.

On May 5, 1934, the Whirpool Rapids Incline and attendant buildings were destroyed by fire. In 1935 the Parks Commissioners entered into an agreement with Alonzo B. Robertson of Robertson Construction and Engineering Company of Niagara Falls, allowing him to lease the lands formerly occupied by the incline railway and the boardwalk along the rapids, with the right to operate the Great

Carlisle Graham, the first daredevil to navigate the Whirlpool Rapids in a barrel.

In 1901 Maude Willard successfully navigated the Whirlpool Rapids, but she suffocated when her barrel was caught for hours in the Whirlpool.

Martha Wagenfuhrer who successfully navigated the Whirlpool Rapids on September 6, 1901.

The parking shed, souvenir store and ticket office of the Whirlpool Rapids Incline, 1932.

Niagara Parks Archives

Great Gorge Trip

The Great Gorge Trip ticket office and souvenir store on the upper level at the Whirlpool Rapids.

Gorge attraction. The property, by the terms of the agreement, would after thirty years become the property of the Commission.[12]

The new owner constructed a 70 m (230 ft.) elevator shaft and a 73m (240 ft.) tunnel through the rock and talus to accommodate a high speed elevator and provide access to the lower gorge. A building faced with cut stone was built at the top of the gorge, at the end of the elevator shaft, to serve as a station and souvenir store. In 1937, Robertson Construction and Engineering leased the operation to a subsidiary company, Niagara Concessions Ltd..[13]

High water and ice often caused problems for the new owners. The original paths and walkways were

The boardwalk beside the Whirlpool Rapids in 1946.

The boardwalk beside the Whirlpool Rapids in the early 1980's. Low water conditions brought on by the diversion of water for electric power generation have left a large area along the riverbank, dry and accessible.

often undermined and washed away. Ontario Hydro and the Power Authority of the State of New York power plants went into full operation in 1957 and 1961. The water level in the gorge dropped considerably by the time both plants had diverted their allotted water for power generation. New boardwalks were built above the water level. The old path can still be seen in some places, higher up along the bank, showing clearly that the present boardwalk would be underwater if the river level were as high as in the 1920's.

Since 1961, when the water flow was reduced, great ledges of Whirlpool Sandstone have been left dry and bare. It is on one of these ledges of rock, smoothed and polished by millennia of rushing water that the tourist visiting the Great Gorge Trip can stand, closer than ever before to the awesome spectacle of the Whirlpool Rapids.

The agreement with Niagara Concessions was extended three years in 1964 when the original agreement expired, to compensate for the loss of business during the years of World War II. On December 1, 1967 the Niagara Parks Commission officially took over ownership and control of the Great Gorge Trip and the attendant building from Niagara Concessions Ltd. A new agreement was signed with Niagara Concessions, giving them the right to operate the Great Gorge Trip and the Scenic Boardwalk. The souvenir sales store, to be called the Whirlpool store, was to be operated by the Parks Commission. All of the assets in connection with this attraction were now under the ownership of the Niagara Parks Commission.[14]

In 1969 Ralph Grant, a former manager of this attraction, took over the remaining seven years of the Niagara Concessions lease and by a further agreement with the Commissioners operates the souvenir store as well. Mr. Grant brought with him a collection of barrels and other contrivances used by stunters such as George Stathakis and William Red Hill,

An observation point beside the raging Whirlpool Rapids.

Niagara Parks Archives

which make up an added attraction called the Daredevil Gallery.

The Whirlpool Rapids have had their share of barrel, boat and raft riders in contemporary times. William Red Hill, Niagara's famous riverman, made several trips through the rapids in a steel barrel during the mid 1930's.

In more recent times, tragedy and near tragedy have resulted from trips through the rapids. A movie made for television was being filmed in 1972 at Niagara Falls and permission was given the movie company to film in the gorge and send a wooden raft through the rapids, with a dummy strapped to a post on the deck. A stunt man, overcome with bravado, rode the raft instead, was thrown into the water, knocked unconscious and floated face down in the Whirlpool. He was picked up motionless and blue in

In 1975 a new venture with a larger raft carrying twenty-nine people including the crew, operated trips through the rapids, once again with permission only from the Niagara Frontier State Parks Commission. On one of the trips on August 29, the raft rode the big wave opposite the Great Gorge Boardwalk, stood on end, turned over and capsized, throwing all of the people aboard into the turbulent rapids. Three were drowned and others were injured, some seriously. Helicopters from both countries picked the people out of the Whirlpool and landed them on the Whirlpool Beach on a helicopter pad that had been laid out there in 1974. No more raft trips were made - the fun was over. An enquiry was made and litigation began, some of it still in progress. The Niagara Parks Commission's policy of steadfastly refusing permission for stunts and dangerous rides proved to be a

Man overboard on one of the raft trips in August 1972.

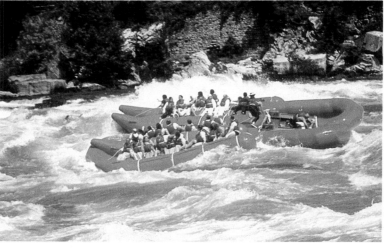

Herbert C. Force

the face when he was rescued. Fortunately he was revived. He had much more respect for the rapids and the river after that experience.[15]

On June 7, 1972, the first of a series of raft rides was made by the Niagara River White Water Tours, with the permission of the Niagara Frontier State Parks Commission on the American side. No permission was granted for this enterprise by the Niagara Parks Commission. The rafts could carry twenty passengers and a two man crew. A number of trips were made without incident, then there were several spills. On July 26, the raft capsized and six people were thrown into the river and had to be rescued from the Whirlpool. On August 7, after seven more people were dumped into the river, the raft ride was discontinued.[16]

wise one.[17]

In 1981 the Commissioners gave permission to A.B.C. T.V. who were filming a segment for the American Sportsman television programme, to allow four people - three men and a women - to go through the Whirlpool Rapids in kayaks. The trip was made without incident. The leader of the group said: "The kayak is the safest method of making the trip through the rapids".[18] The Commissioners gave permission for this venture on the basis that kayaking is a sport, not a stunt and this was to be a sports film.

Occasionally tourists visiting the Great Gorge Trip have ventured to explore past the end of the boardwalk, only to find that the elevator had stopped running for the day by the time they returned to it. In 1983 for the first time the failure of an elevator motor stranded a group of tourists below the bank for a number of hours before they could be guided to the top. This is an arduous climb. To prepare for any such future emergency a helicopter pad was built at the water's edge. From it people can be transported back to the top of the bank should the need arise.

The Commission is always mindful of the safety of those who venture down into the gorge and in 1977 and 1978 a geological reconnaissance survey was made of the gorge wall to ascertain the stability of the rock wall. As a result of this survey a maintenance program of rock removal was undertaken to ensure visitors' safety from intermittent and random rock slides. The work included controlled blasting, clean-up and general scaling of the gorge wall. Eight large masses of rock were removed in 1978 and further work was done in 1983.

The Whirlpool Rapids are accessible to tourists who wish to view them - not inaccessible as they were in Richard Bonnycastle's time. They are still treacherous and unpredictable and command the greatest respect of all who would challenge them.

A kayak in the Whirlpool Rapids during the filming of an A.B.C. television segment for the American Sportsman television programme, 1981.

Great Gorge Trip

Niagara Spanish Aero Car

A condition of the Niagara Falls Park and River Railway franchise required the Park Commissioners to acquire the land needed for the right of way which ran along the Chain Reserve.[1] Of all the land acquisitions made by the Commissioners, the most difficult was the acquisition of the Colt property for the railway right of way along the south side of the Whirlpool, extending south from the present day site of the Aero Car. It was known as lot 74 BF (Broken Front) in Stamford Township.

On December 24, 1868, the Dominion Government through its agent, Dr. Douglas of Fort Erie, sold about 2.8 ha (7 acres) of the talus in front of this lot to Samuel Colt for $250.[2] However the newly created Province of Ontario did not recognize this, claiming that ownership of the Chain Reserve had been transferred to the Province at Confederation in 1867.

The Colts developed the property soon after 1868, constructing an incline railway down the talus at Colt's Creek, to the bank of the Whirlpool. Here they laid out paths along the slope, adding wooden shelters with benches at intervals, to serve as resting places. Leander Colt designed and built the water powered "machinery" which operated the incline railway.

T. Holder, in his *Guide Book to Niagara Falls* of 1881 describes Colt's "machinery" as follows: "The method of operation is unique and novel . . . the power being derived from the weight of a stream of water entering a system of iron buckets revolving around an endless chain in such a way that the filled buckets carry the power to the cars, the nominal power of the water wheel being about 5 hp". "Carrying power to the cars" meant that the large wheel around which the buckets revolved was geared to a chain or rope windlass which pulled the car up the incline when the wheel was in operation, assisted by the weight of the descending loaded car.

On June 27, 1882, the Colts leased the facilities to Dr. W.H. Ferguson and Wm. Diefenbach. As early as 1889 the Commission was engaged in litigation to force the Colts to vacate the Chain Reserve and the talus slope. The Colts had blocked off access to the Whirlpool at the southern boundary of their property and charged a fee for the privilege of viewing the Whirlpool. While litigation was going on, a landslide damaged the incline and carried away some of the paths. On May 11, 1889, Superintendent Wilson wrote to Chairman Gzowski: "a further landslide damaged his (Colt's) repairs to the Pool".[3] Colt attempted to repair the damage but a subsequent landslide damaged the incline beyond all hope of repair.

On September 12, 1889 AEmilius Irving, the Commissioners' attorney, advised Superintendent Wilson that the Commission now had the legal right to dispossess Colt. They were still trying to move him in November of the same year.[4] The incline was not operating but the Colts held on and on. The Niagara Falls Park and River Railway roadbed was being laid in 1892 but Colt still wouldn't settle. On April 25, Superintendent Wilson wrote to Chairman Gzowski

Leander Colt's water wheel at the Whirlpool.

Picturesque Canada

The incline railway at the whirlpool, from a stereograph by C. Bierstadt circa 1880's.

advising that "a representative of the Niagara Falls Park and River Railway would visit Colt and try to secure the land amicably".[5] The meeting was not successful because the matter dragged on until 1895, when a settlement was made. The Niagara Falls Park and River Railway laid their tracks across Colt's land and the electric railway began operations on schedule on May 24, 1893. Colt and the Railway Company were evidently involved in litigation over the trespass because in 1895, Niagara Falls Park and River Railway tried to recover from the Commission costs of $961.21 which they had incurred in defending their case against Colt.[6] The Commission refused to pay. The Commissioners were not finished with the Colt family. The next confrontation would come in 1922 when the Commissioners would need more of the Colt property for the Niagara Boulevard.

Colt's Point became a stop on the Great Gorge Route Belt Line, as well as on the regular Queenston to Chippawa run of the International Railway

Digging the pit to house the Aero Car operating machinery, 1915.

The Niagara Spanish Aerocar Company

Aero Cable Car over Whirlpool.
Niagara Falls.

Marion Zeiger

The Aero Car landing platform at Thompson Point, with the operating machinery set in the gorge wall, circa 1916.

Marion Zeiger

The first trip of the Aero Car, August 8, 1916, being filmed by Mr. Oscar Simon for Mutual Weekly Movie Newsreel. Mr. J. Enoch Thompson, the Spanish Consul at Toronto, is shown helping Mrs. Thompson off the Aero Car at the Thompson Point landing.

Company - the Niagara Falls Park and River Railway had been purchased by the International Railway Company of Buffalo on April 18, 1899. Here passengers disembarked for a view of the Whirlpool. In 1913 the Park Commissioners were approached by a group of Spanish businessmen interested in building a cableway across the Whirlpool. The Commissioners called on Frederick Law Olmstead, the noted American Park designer, asking for his opinion of the venture.

Olmstead was not in favour of the proposed cable way route. He preferred a cableway that would go from the top of the gorge at Colt's Point to the Whirlpool shore opposite, below Thompson Point. In this way he felt the public would go down the Gorge at the Whirlpool then walk along the path at the river's edge, connecting with the Niagara Glen, where an

incline railway or an elevator would convey them back up to the top of the gorge. Then at the Niagara Glen they could board the Great Gorge cars and proceed to the next stop.[7]

The Park Commissioners chose to accept the Niagara Spanish Aerocar Company's proposal. The brilliant Spanish engineer, Leonardo Torres-Quevedo, designed and carried out the work. The basic design followed the principles of the installation at Mount Ulia San Sebastian in Spain. The terminals of the track cables are about 539m (1,770 ft.) apart and are at the same elevation, some 76 m (250 ft.) above the waters of the Whirlpool. The car was built in Bilboa, Spain with a capacity of forty passengers. The original installation cost $120,000. and operated for fifty years without major additions or alterations.

The system is a "to and fro" operation on six

Dignitaries riding the Aero Car, opening day, August 8, 1916.

Antonio Balzola, the contractor and secretary- treasurer of the Spanish Company, on the left; Leonardo Torres-Quevedo, the engineer who designed the Aero Car, on the right. This view is from the landing platform at Thompson Point, 1916.

2.54 cm (1 in.) lock coil track cables. Each cable is attached to an anchorage at the terminals and tension is maintained by a 9 tonnes (10 ton) counterweight at the Thompson Point station. An endless 2.23 cm (⅞ in.) plough steel wire rope driven by a 75 hp motor pulls the car which is suspended by a system of wires radiating from a semi-circular frame of metal tubing.

The aerial cableway began operations on August 8, 1916, in the presence of several hundred people. The *Niagara Falls Evening Review* of August 9, 1916 reported the event: "shortly after 3 o'clock Mrs. J. Enoch Thompson, wife of the Spanish consul at Toronto opened the cableway by breaking a bottle of champagne over the gate at the Thompson Point landing. The car made its first public trip. It was a pleasant sight to watch the car which carried four flags, the Union Jack, the Stars and Stripes, the French and Spanish flags. Mr. Oscar Simon, representative of Mutual Weekly, was engaged in taking motion pictures of the cableway and the crowd". Mr. Leonardo Torres-Quevedo the engineer and vice-president of the Company, and Mr. Antonio Balzola, the contractor and secretary-treasurer, were present.

From the beginning the Spanish Company had financial problems, due to a drop in tourist travel during World War I and a reluctance on the part of many tourists to try this new and daring trip. The

The Aero Car ticket office, Colt's Point Station, 1920.

Niagara Parks Archives

The Aero Car station at Colt's Point, circa 1970.

F.H. Leslie

The Aero Car over the Whirlpool, 1982.

Niagara Parks Archives

Niagara Parks Archives

The Aero Car terminal at Colt's Point, 1982, with the snack bar, souvenir store at the right. The ticket office and entrance to the Aero Car are in the canopied area.

financial agreements with the Commission called for payment of a minimum $3,500. a year in rent, plus a payment of 25% of gross receipts from $35,000. to $45,000.; 35% from $45,000. to $50,000. and 50% above $55,000.[9] After paying the minimum rental for 1914, 1915 and the first half of 1916, they requested a reduction. In 1917 the Commissioners reduced the minimum rental to $2,000. to continue through 1920.[10] In late 1919 the Aero Car operation was closed for a time due to a smallpox epidemic.

In 1920 the Commissioners agreed to a sub-lease of the enterprise to Wm. Laughlin, who was also manager at the same time of the Whirlpool Rapids Incline.[11] In 1923 earnings improved due to the opening of the Niagara Boulevard which allowed motorists to drive from Niagara Falls to Queenston for the first time. The special concession, reducing the minimum rental was cancelled and the sum of $3,500. was required. James Schiller, a lawyer, acted on behalf of the Spanish Company, Estudios y Obras de Ingenieria, until his death in 1941. The Harold Brooker family ran the operation until 1961 when A. Blake Robertson purchased the Aero Car assets. He negotiated with the Spanish Consul in New York, who acted on behalf of the Spanish Company.

In 45 years of operation the track, or carrying cables, had been replaced only once, after 35 years of service. On acquiring the property Mr. Robertson undertook a major overhaul of the equipment. The ancient Buick engine which had served as auxilliary power for 45 years was replaced in 1961 when a modern 60 hp engine connected by chain drive and friction clutch was installed. The operator could then change to auxiliary power in minutes. Limit switches were installed which automatically cut off the power and applied the brakes when the car reached either station. With these limit switches and signal lights the operator who is 549 m (1800 ft.) from the loading platform could determine the precise homing position of the car. The landing platforms were redesigned for safer access and egress. Aluminum wheels were used to lighten the weight of the car so that more passengers could be carried.[12]

In November of 1968 the Commissioners decided to build a structure adjacent to the Aero Car station to provide for a retail store, refreshment counter and washrooms. The original frame ticket office and souvenir store was torn down. Mr. Robertson sold the Aero Car installation late in 1968 to the Niagara Parks Commission and they took over the operation of the venture with their own staff beginning with the 1969 season.

After the end of the 1984 season the Aero Car was completely renovated and upgraded to meet today's standards. The carriage was not changed but the wheels, electrical circuits, track cables suspension system were all changed. For many years to come the Aero Car will continue as one of Niagara's prime attractions - the best way to view the swirling turbulent waters of the Whirlpool.

Whirlpool

The Whirlpool is mentioned in early writing as the "Twelve Mile Pond on the St. Lawrence" - a pond twelve miles from Lake Ontario. The Niagara was not considered to be a river, but a continuation of the St. Lawrence River. In 1782 Archibald Thomson and Jacob Bowman settled side by side on the Twelve Mile Pond, having received their grants of land from the Crown upon disbanding from Butler's Rangers.[1] When Archibald's brothers, James and John, emigrated from Scotland in 1785, John was granted lots 41 and 58 by the Land Board and his brother Archibald gave him a portion of his land so that John's property abutted James Park's on the rim of the Whirlpool.[2]

When the Land Titles were being prepared some officials misspelled the Thomson name, writing in "Thompson" instead. To avoid confusion the family accepted Thompson as their name. The Whirlpool was not accessible until John Thompson and his wife Jeannet built a log house and barn on the high bank, just north of the Whirlpool and John cut a rough road through the forest connecting their farm with the Portage Road. They called their farm Whirlpool Farm.[3] The year was 1785. John erected a stone house in 1802 and a stone barn in 1806. He built a saw mill on the gorge bank where a small stream fell into the gorge.

It was not long before curious travellers were making a side trip from the Portage Road, through the Thompson farm, to see the Whirlpool. The earliest written record of a visit to the Whirlpool was made by Mrs. Simcoe, the wife of Lieutenant-Governor John Graves Simcoe, recorded in her diary in 1793. " I rode to the Whirlpool, a very grand scene halfway between Queenston and the falls, where the current is so strong that Eddies are formed in which hewn timber trees carried down the falls from the sawmill upriver spin round and round. Vast Rocks surround this bend of the River and they are covered with Pine and hemlock spruce, some cascades among the rocks add to the wild appearance."[4] On August 15, 1795 she wrote: "The Governor drove the children to see the Whirlpool and I rode part of the way, we carried our tent and provisions as yesterday and dined on the Point from whence the Whirlpool and the opposite Bank of the River on which is a mill, form altogether a very fine Scene . . . In the bay or Whirlpool . . . are now a number of logs collected by Canby at his Saw Mill above the Falls . . . Where they whirl about and probably will continue to until the end of the World".[5]

In 1848 the Crown granted Thompson permission to build a stairway down the steep bank at the point near the Whirlpool exit, to allow visitors to get to the lower river bank. He was not allowed to charge for the privilege but was to be content with whatever revenue he could make from the sale of light refreshments.[6] Mrs. A.H. Walker, a direct descendant of the Thompsons, has in her possession a visitors' book from the 1850's which lists the names of hundreds of visitors who viewed the Whirlpool from this vantage point. Thompson kept a record of people who visited the Whirlpool before he built the stairs. In the period from June to November 1845 no fewer

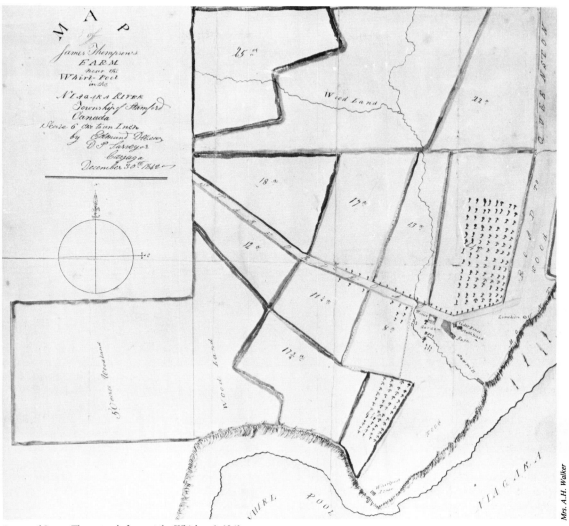

A map of James Thompson's farm at the Whirlpool, 1842.

Mrs. A.H. Walker

than 1500 people crossed his farm property to view the Whirlpool. They came from such places as New Orleans; Halifax; New Brunswick; Havana, Cuba; Dublin, Ireland; Boston; Delaware; Philadelphia; Wyoming; England and Scotland.[7]

At the curve of the Whirlpool is the St. David's Buried Gorge, the preglacial course of the river. It is composed of glacial debris, sand and gravel, and is cut by the ravine made by Bowman Creek - the name given to the stream which drained the countryside and flowed into the Whirlpool at this point. Over the years the stream eroded the soft gravelly soil, creating a long gradual sloping ravine with steep sides - it was the dividing line between John Thompson's and Jacob Bowman's property. This long

sloping ravine leading into the lower gorge was a convenient route for the Timber rattlesnake to use when entering or leaving the lower gorge. The Timber rattlesnake was common to this area in early days, and liked to hibernate in the caves and crannies formed by the fallen blocks of limestone. Each Fall thousands of these snakes would come into the lower gorge, hibernate through the winter, then return via the ravine to the countryside above to spend the summer months. They were a menace to both the Indians and the early settlers. Hazel Mathews in her book *Mark of Honour*, described the method commonly used by early settlers to get rid of the Timber rattlesnakes. She wrote: "In the Gorge below Thompson's is a large den of rattlers of uncommon

Ontario Archives

The Thompson farmyard at the Whirlpool in the early 1900's. The house is partly concealed by the large stone barn. Slits in the barn were for ventilation.

size. Whereas the Indians set fire to dry leaves in order to kill the snakes when they were emerging from hibernation, the settlers made war on them with the help of their hogs. Some five hundred were killed by an organized expedition in the gorge''.[8]

John Thompson cleared some areas of his land for grain and fodder, other areas he cleared and planted apple trees. He sold apple trees to other farmers, and bartered them as well for goods. Mrs. A.H. Walker has in her possession the "Debtors Account" of a tailor who exchanged apple trees with Thompson for a suit of clothes. The account showed a debit of £7 15 s 6 p for a suit and a credit to Thompson of £7 10 s for 100 apple trees, leaving Thompson owing 5 s 6p.[9] Along with other farmers in the area, Thompson used his oxen and wagon to haul goods on the Portage Road. In return for his services he received a "Portage Credit" which he exchanged for goods at the portage merchants' stores.

Thompson had a further source of income. Beginning in the early 1800's he made use of the limestone which was easily accessible - there was an exposed ridge of limestone along the front of his property close to the edge of the gorge. He quarried the limestone and processed it in a lime kiln,

producing agricultural lime. At one time he had two kilns in operation. He sold the lime in bulk to nearby farmers who then used it on their land. Packed in barrels it was also sent by boat to Toronto. The size of the quarry grew as more and more limestone was quarried. During the War of 1812, the quarry was considered important to the war effort and a guard was posted. One of the sentries, standing on the gorge bank at the Point, was shot at and killed by a sharpshooter from the American side.[10] It was a breach of truce and the American General Van Rensselaer wrote to General Isaac Brock expressing regret for the incident.[11]

The Queen Victoria Park Commissioners purchased land from the Thompson's at the Niagara Glen and also for the right-of-way for the Niagara Falls Park and River Railway. The Railway Company laid its tracks in a curve around Thompson Point so that passengers could get a view of the Whirlpool while riding by in the cars. The ravine was an obstacle that had to be bridged and a steel trestle was built, to carry the tracks across the gap.

When the Park Commissioners took over, the area around Thompson Point was a wasteland of bare rock. In 1897 the Point was renamed Whirlpool

Niagara Falls Park and River Railway trestle across Bowman Ravine at the Whirlpool. In 1903 the trestle was buried when the ravine underneath it was filled with rock debris excavated from the wheelpit of the Canadian Niagara Powerhouse.

Niagara Falls Heritage Foundation

The Whirlpool and the Electric Railway, circa 1900. From a water colour by William Armstrong. The trestle which carried the tracks across the Bowman Ravine is visible in the top left background.

Amon Carter Museum, Ft. Worth, Texas

The Whirlpool Bazaar at Thompson Point circa 1911.

F.H. Leslie

Point and the Superintendent wrote: "A beginning has been made to remove the nakedness of the Whirlpool Point. As the rock formation at this point is practically at the surface of the ground, the first thing to be done was to give the whole area a coating of soil, in which trees and shrubs could find a foothold, and on which grass would grow". In 1900 a rustic summer house was built and passengers on the Niagara Falls Park and River Railway could make a stopover to view the Whirlpool from this point.

In 1903 the Bowman Ravine was filled in with rock debris excavated from the wheelpit of the Canadian Niagara Powerhouse. The Power Company transported the debris in railway cars over the electric railway tracks and paid the Railway Company, now the International Railway Company, to get rid of the debris.[12] The trestle was buried to the track level. The old roadbed of the electric railway is still visible at the trestle site and there are two cut stone markers that remain exposed at either end of the buried trestle.

In 1914 J.W. Midforth, who had restaurant and souvenir privileges at Queenston Heights Park,

received a lease from the Park Commissioners permitting him to sell souvenirs and refreshments at Whirlpool Point. In 1915 the lease was extended and included photographic privileges. After 1918 the Commissioners began operating this concession using Park staff.

In 1916 the Hydro Electric Power Commission of Ontario purchased the Thompson property, along with other properties along the whole front of the gorge from the Whirlpool to a point near Queenston Heights, for the Chippawa-Queenston Power Canal and Powerhouse. They used the land they required for the canal which runs parallel with the gorge from the Whirlpool to the Powerhouse. The limits of the canal can be seen from the Niagara Parkway as you travel from the Whirlpool to the Niagara Glen and beyond. In 1918 the Commissioners were advised by the Hydro Electric Power Commission that there were 130.3 ha (322 acres) of land available in this area, suitable for park development. In 1919 to facilitate the construction of the Niagara Boulevard from Niagara Falls to Queenston Heights the Commissioners bought this land. The next year this

Milton J. Washburn

The Whirlpool from an air view taken in the 1920's before the massive diversion of water for electric power generation lowered the river level. On the American side of the river, the roadbed of the Great Gorge Route is clearly visible.

An air view of the entrance to the Whirlpool, 1980.

Niagara Parks Archives

Whirlpool Reversal Phenomenon

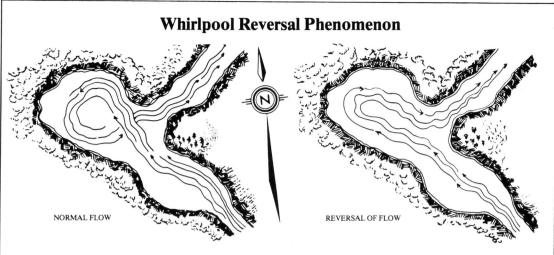

NORMAL FLOW   REVERSAL OF FLOW

NORMAL FLOW

The rush of water enters the pool and is carried down past the river outlet on the right. It then circulates counter-clockwise around the pool, and approaching the entrance finds itself cut off from the incoming stream. Pressure (hydrostatic pressure) builds up from behind, forcing it down under the incoming stream and it emerges near the outlet in dark boiling slugs of water.

REVERSAL OF FLOW

At times of extreme low water, caused by a combination of natural conditions and increased diversion of water for electric power generation, the Whirlpool shows no circular motion at all and becomes a "whirlpool" in name only.

When the flow of the river goes below 17,500 cbm (62,000 cu. ft.) per second the direction of the flow becomes clockwise, influenced by the sandstone ledge which exists under its entrance on the Whirlpool's right side.

Low water conditions can be seen very early in the morning during the summer months and from November 1 to March 31 when maximum water diversion is allowed.

---

new park area was named Niagara Glen Heights. It was surveyed and its physical contours were plotted as a basis for a preliminary study to be undertaken to determine its eventual development. The Niagara Boulevard (to-day called the Niagara Parkway) was completed from Niagara Falls to Queenston Heights in 1922 and motorists were able to visit Whirlpool Point as well as the other points of interest along the way to Queenston. Stairways and connecting paths were built on the sloping bank which covered the Bowman Creek Ravine gap, leading down the ravine to the beach at the Whirlpool shore. From there a connecting path was laid out along the lower rim of the Whirlpool, below Whirlpool Point and on to the Niagara Glen, creating a nature trail between the two points of interest. The Whirlpool Beach is still a favourite haunt for fishermen and from the Aero Car station to Colt's Point, they can be seen standing along the shore. Their numbers increase when salmon are running, at other times they fish for bass,

pike and even sturgeon.

In 1936, K.M. Broman, Superintendent of Aboriculture, submitted two plans for an arboretum at Niagara Glen Heights. The one adopted was on the principle of a golf course layout. Trees and shrubs were planted by the apprentice gardeners to beautify the area, keeping in mind the "golf course" plan. It was 1947 before work on the golf course began on 70.8 ha (175 acres) of the Niagara Glen Heights.

Over the years hundreds of thousands of people have visited the Whirlpool, beginning with those hardy travellers who detoured from the Portage Road and went through the Thompson Whirlpool Farm property to reach the Point. In future thousands will come to view the Whirlpool, certainly less turbulent and awe inspiring since the massive diversion of water for electric power generation began in the 1900's. It is not at all the Whirlpool Mrs. Simcoe saw and described in 1793, but it is still spectacular.

Niagara Glen

The Niagara Glen is a geological wonderland, acres of tumbled rocks which fell from the cliffs above. Here about 8000 years ago the unbroken crest of the Falls was eroding southward from Queenston-Lewiston and was about to be separated by a higher central limestone mass.

Possibly about 100 years later the crest was separated and fed by two channels - a higher thinner current on the west side, now the Canadian side, and the rest of the original stream on the east side, the present American side. In the centre was a long thin island, now reduced to a mass of debris by erosion. A dry gorge was caused on the western side when the faster erosion of the larger eastern stream cut off the small western stream's flow from the rear.

The area of the river bed that was cut off and left dry is now known as Wintergreen Flats, and it is on this table of land that the Niagara Glen picnic area is located. Approximately 7,000 years ago, erosion in varying depths, by two separate cataracts in sequence, produced a major falls with a 76 m (250 ft.) drop and a minor falls with a 15 m (50 ft.) drop over the low Whirlpool Sandstone. Then there was a sudden widening of the gorge, which may indicate that all of the Great Lakes except Ontario, began to use the Niagara channel as an outlet to the sea by way of the present St. Lawrence River. This widening can be seen from the south, upriver side of the Niagara Glen Snack Bar and Gift Shop.

When the Queen Victoria Park Commissioners granted the Niagara Falls Park and River Railway Company a franchise in 1891 to construct and operate an electric railway to run along the gorge, the proposed route was to be along the river's edge from Queenston to Queen Victoria Park.[1] The Commissioners were required by the terms of the agreement to obtain title to the remaining portions of the talus slope not already in their possession so that the roadbed could be built.[2]

On April 26, 1888 the Provincial Government had granted the Queen Victoria Park Commissioners control of "all those pieces or strips of land which lie along the bank of the Niagara River . . . beginning at the northern boundary of the Park opposite the Clifton House . . . and as far as the Town of Queenston".[3] There were several areas where the ownership of the talus slope was in doubt, one of these being at Foster's Flats, about 1.2 km (¾ mile) north and down river from Whirlpool Point - the present day site of the Niagara Glen. Negotiations had been going on between the Commissioners and James Murray who claimed to have purchased the property from the Dominion Government.[4]

AEmilius Irving, the Commission's solicitor, prepared a report on Foster's Flats in which he wrote: "Twenty or thirty years ago a man named Foster built a saw mill on these flats at the edge of the river, and having it is said a license from the Crown, cut and removed heavy timber growing there, floating it down the Niagara River to Queenston. That licence expired and there are no traces of the mill at the present day. The entire Flat is still covered with timber of some value, but of small growth. There is but one point from the top of the cliff whereby descent can be made to the Flats, the cliff here being quite precipitous. Murray's account of his possession is that about 8 or 10 years ago he purchased about 110 or 115 acres of land described to him as part of lots 42 and 21 and one half of which was above the cliff and table land, and the other below forming the Flats - that he paid $5000 for the whole. He has recently heard that he has no title to the Flats, but he seems to have been cautioned at the time of purchase, or to have doubts. He knows that the Flats are the most valuable part of his property and he would consider it very hard if he should be deprived of his land."[5]

Walking in the Niagara Glen, early 1900's.

John Burtniak Collection

Looking through a pothole in the Niagara Glen.

John Burtniak Collection

Negotiations with Murray went on for several years before the matter was settled by arbitration. The Commissioners were authorized in 1894 to purchase the 22.5 ha (55½ acres) known as Foster's Flats at the arbitration price of $4146.44.[6] In 1891 the Park Commissioners had refused the Niagara Falls Park and River Railway Company's proposal for a route along the river's edge and the company then chose a route along the top of the gorge instead. The Commissioners had previously purchased from the Thompson's a piece of land directly in front of Wintergreen Flats on the upper level. Their control of the Flats and the land above was now complete.[7]

The Niagara Falls Park and River Railway began operating a single track line along the gorge beginning on May 24, 1893. In its first year of operation it carried 354,000 passengers. In 1894 the line was double-tracked and by 1896 it carried 499,015 passengers. With such a large number of excursionists passing Foster's Flats on the electric railway it became apparent to the Commissioners that this unusual area which they now called the Niagara Glen, should be opened up for the excursionists' pleasure and enjoyment.

Superintendent Wilson wrote in 1896: "A beginning was made this year in opening the beauty of the Niagara Glen to the public. Pathways were cut from the tracks of the electric railway to the edge of the cliff, a substantial stairway of some 70 steps, in short easy stages was constructed to the talus below. From that point to the water's edge a winding pathway of easy descent was made by which visitors can enjoy some of the delightful scenery in this romantic spot. It is proposed that this walk will be extended during the ensuing summer, and in time all the interesting portions of this remarkable work of nature will be made accessible."[8]

During 1897 paths were extended along the whole breadth of the Glen from Fisherman's Eddy- now called Cripps Eddy - to Gravelly Bay - now called Pebbly Beach. During the ensuing years, from 1900 to 1906, paths were constructed into what were previously inaccessible parts of the Glen, opening up areas with interesting rock arches, potholes and other geological and botanical features.

While thousands of excursionists were stopping off at the Niagara Glen for a picnic, many were reluctant to make the trip down to the lower level.

A resting place on the lower path along the river in the Niagara Glen circa 1906.

John Burtniak Collection

The prospect of climbing the paths and stairways for the return to the top dissuaded all but the most energetic. At one time the Commissioners considered the possibility of providing an incline railway into the Glen, along with an elevator at Whirlpool Point, with a pathway leading to and connecting with the Glen.[9] Nature lovers will agree that it is fortunate that no action was taken and the Glen remained accessible only to those willing and able to make the effort to climb down and back on foot.

Numerous cedar bark shelters with benches were built along the paths at different levels, affording protection from sudden showers and welcome shaded resting spots for tired climbers. Picnic shelters, called dining pavilions, with fireplaces, were erected on the lower level in 1906. They were built of wood in a rustic design and provided a pleasant place for a picnic. Vandalism was a problem, even in those days. In 1909 the Park Superintendent wrote: "In addition to the caretaker, police protection is now provided during the summer months and parties are guided where intricate paths might lead to confusion and much of the wanton destructin of ferns and flowers by careless parties is avoided."[10]

Even before the Glen was opened, it attracted

attention when the rumour spread that there was $100,000 in gold buried there. On June 8, 1892, three Americans from Saginaw, Michigan, arrived at the Prospect House in Queenston. Their actions were mysterious and it was not long before they began to excite comment. They were seen to scrutinize a map often and soon made their way to Foster's Flats. There was a suspicion at first that they were involved in an opium smuggling ring. Their nightly visits to the Flats could not be explained. Someone broke into their luggage while they were away on one of their clandestine trips, and found fifty small stout canvas bags which could have been used to carry away gold rather than opium.

They took innkeeper Jerry O'Leary into their confidence under solemn oath that he would keep their secret - they were looking for $100,000 in gold. They spent three weeks in the search without success. Fully .4 ha (one acre) of the lower plateau was reported to have been dug over to a depth of 1.5 m (5 ft.). This is impossible as the overburden in the Lower Glen is not that thick. There is only a relatively shallow layer of soil over the rock. The treasure seekers left town and the innkeeper who had been told their secret, began his own dig, hoping to

The upper path underneath the rock overhang at Wintergreen Flats, circa 1900.

John Burtniak Collection

find the $100,000 in gold. His work was for nothing.

A map of the Niagara Glen in the Niagara Parks Commission Engineering Department files, made in the 1890's places the area where the gold was supposed to be buried, as near Pebbly Beach. There isn't any overburden at all at Pebbly Beach, it is all rock. The innkeeper broke his promise - but he told only one person - a newpaperman![11]

The Glen, along with the bank of the Whirlpool, was a favourite haunt for the Timber rattlesnake. For those getting chills down their spines as they read this, there hasn't been a sighting of a Timber rattlesnake in the Glen since 1959. It is believed that they are now extinct in this area. The Glen rattlesnakes received international renown when they were the cause of the cancellation of a proposed international bridge contruction project in the early 1900's. There was a time in the late 1890's and the early 1900's when there were a great many applications for franchises to build bridges across the Niagara gorge. One American company proposed to build an arch bridge across the gorge at the Glen, the narrowest point in the whole gorge of the river. The Bridge Bill passed the New York State Assembly,

but died in the Senate when a senator argued that if a land connection were made by bridge with the Niagara Glen, the rattlesnakes in the Niagara Gorge would cross the bridge structure and infest the United States. The Bill was defeated.[12]

Ever since it opened the only means of access to the Glen had been by the electric railway. Many tourists were thus deprived of the opportunity to visit this most interesting and picturesque natural park. During 1923 the Niagara Boulevard (to-day called the Niagara Parkway) was built from Niagara Falls to Queenston. The portion between Niagara Falls and the Glen was completed in 1922 and touring motorists could then visit the Glen. A picnic shelter of the same pipe-frame design as those built at Queenston Heights Park and Queen Victoria Park was built on the Wintergreen Flats and hot water facilities were installed. A 15 cm (6 in.) water line was laid from the City of Niagara Falls and when the new Niagara Glen Inn, which housed a restaurant and the caretaker's apartment, was built in 1923, modern lavatory facilities were installed.

The Glen entered a new era of popularity, as more and more people arrived by automobile. By 1928 the

The Niagara Glen Inn erected in 1923.

John Burtniak Collection

Niagara Parks Archives

The picnic shelter at the Foster's Flats level, Niagara Glen, 1932.

The Glen Rapids from the river path, 1930's.

The Glen Rapids from the river path, 1983.

The Niagara Glen as it appears from the United States. The rock overhang on Wintergreen Flats is shown, prior to the scaling in 1959. The promontory, the Stern of the Great Eastern is at the right. Note paths. The picnic shelter is at lower right.

The scaled cliffs of Wintergreen Flats, 1960.

The Glen Restaurant and Souvenir Store, 1980.

The Park naturalist conducting a nature walk in the Glen 1979.

Commissioners were planning a new entrance to the Glen as they felt that many of the motorists missed it as they rushed by at speeds of 32.1 km (20 mi.) an hour or more.[13] The Depression of the 1930's saw fewer people travelling and attendance dropped there as it did elsewhere. The electric railway stopped operating at the end of the season in 1932 and from then on visitors to the Glen came by automobile or bus.

Ontario Hydro's Sir Adam Beck Generating Station Number 2 project affected the Glen, when in 1951 an access road was built down along the gorge wall, beginning at the northern end of the Wintergreen Flats picnic area and extending down the side of the talus past Pebbly Beach and on to the new generating station site. This road occupied about 4 ha (10 acres) of the talus of the Glen in the dry gorge area. Planting and reseeding along with the appearance of some natural growth has gradually covered the banks of this road with greenery.

The interesting but dangerously overhanging rock ledges of Wintergreen Flats cliff were a unique feature of the Glen, giving to the cliff wall the appearance of an amphitheatre. There was a possibility that a piece of this overhang could suddenly break away and crash into the Glen, as so many others had done over the 7000 years of the Glen's existence. The Commissioners had Ontario Hydro blast off and scale the cliff wall in 1959, removing the hazard. The spectacular promontory at the northeast end of the cliff, known as the "Stern of the Great Eastern" - named after a famous steamship of the 1890's - was straightened. The cliff is now safe, but much of the charm of the Glen at this point is gone.

Vandalism in the 1970's brought about many changes in the Glen. The last of the picnic pavilions on the lower Foster's Flats level was burned by vandals in 1971. The picnic tables on Wintergreen Flats were continually being thrown over the bank to the rocks below. Now they are on cement pads and double chained and locked to ring bolts set in the cement. Access to the lower level, used by fishermen through most of the year, has been controlled by the installation of chain link fences at the top of the stairways, with gates that are locked at night.

The river at the Glen has always been a favourite spot for fishermen, who fish from the rocks strewn along the river bank. On several occasions fishermen have been marooned when they jumped a small stream of the river to another large rock, at the same time a change in the amount of water diverted by Ontario Hydro, or the Power Authority of the State of New York, has caused the river level to rise, creating a larger and sometimes impassable stream of rushing water behind them, where only a small stream had existed before. In April 1975, a man and his daughter were marooned on a rock when the water level rose. Wilfred Derbyshire, Niagara Parks Chief of Police, swam out with a rope in an attempt to rescue them, but a helicopter was finally brought in to lift all three of them off the rock and take them to safety. Others have drowned when they have fallen off the rocks, made slippery by the algae which clings to the rocks. The river must be treated with great respect in this area of the Glen.

The Glen has been designated as a Natural Reserve where no flowers can be picked, no trees damaged. Serious contemplation of its natural wonders is encouraged however. In the late 1970's a programme of free guided nature walks was begun. A seasonal Park Naturalist conducts these walks. The Wintergreen Flats area is still a popular spot for picnics. In 1983 the old pipe frame picnic pavilion was demolished and replaced by a modern pavilion similar in style and facilities to those in other areas of the park.

Those who venture into the Glen to explore its depths will understand what Frederick Law Olmstead meant when he wrote in 1914: "The wild sylvan scenery of the Niagara Glen is extraordinarily beautiful and the rapids as seen at close hand by one strolling along the paths there or sitting quietly close to the water's edge are overwhelmingly impressive. One of the important elements of this impressiveness is the relief which the tourist feels here from a sense of being herded in droves and surrounded by familiar suburban conditions of trolley cars and other features unavoidable at the top of the cliff."[14] Considering the pace of today's living compared with that of 1914, those who make the trip down into the Glen will certainly agree that the solitude and beauty of the Glen today are as welcome and as restful as they must have been in 1914.

Queenston Heights Park

The first glimpse of Brock's Monument, towering 50 m (190 ft.) above the ground level of Queenston Heights was a welcome sight to the hundreds of thousands of excursionists who crossed Lake Ontario on the "Toronto boats" and sailed up the Niagara River to Queenston Heights for their annual Church Sunday School or Company employees' picnic.

Brock's Monument stands on the escarpment where 12,000 years ago the waters of the Niagara River first poured over into Lake Iroquois, the forerunner of today's Lake Ontario. The United Empire Loyalist settlers called this abrupt ridge which rises to a height of 107 m (350 ft.), "The Mountain" and the plateau above, through which the gorge of the Niagara River is cut, was called "The Land Above the Mountain". The land on the plateau occupied by Queenston Heights Park was part of the Crown Land Grant awarded to John Chisholm[1] and was part of Township Number 1, later Niagara Township and now the Town of Niagara-on-the-Lake, part of the Regional Municipality of Niagara.

The Heights are historic grounds, not only because of the battle which was fought there on October 13, 1812, but also because of their association with the Portage Road, the first King's Highway in Upper Canada. This road ran from Queenston, on the bank of the river below, up the escarpment and on to Chippawa on the Upper Niagara River above the Falls, where the waters of the Niagara become navigable again.

The Niagara Gorge and the Falls are impassable obstacles to shipping. As the transport of goods in the early days was done by water, it was necessary for shipments destined for the British outposts in the West, to be unloaded from ships and loaded on the wagons at Queenston, for transport over the Portage Road to Chippawa. There the shipments (flour, salt, hard tack, military supplies and manufactured goods for trading with the Indians) were loaded on ships to be taken to the British military and trading posts on the Upper Lakes. On the return trip, bales of furs obtained in trade with the Indians, were brought back to Queenston along the same route, on their way to Montreal and thence to England.

The village of Queenston was first called "The Landing", then "The West Landing" to distinguish it from Lewiston on the United States east side of the Niagara River. In 1791 Lieutenant-Governor John Graves Simcoe chose Newark (present day Niagara-on-the-Lake) at the mouth of the Niagara River, as his capital. He commanded the Queen's Own Regiment and he built barracks for a detachment of his regiment on the bank of the river at West Landing. The West Landing soon became known as "The Queen's Town" and from this came "Queen's Town", "Queenstown" and finally "Queenston".

J.C. Ogden wrote about Queenston in 1799: "There I have seen four vessels of 60 and 100 tons burden unloading and sometimes no less than sixty wagons loaded in a day, with loads they carry 10 miles to the Upper Landing at Chippawa."[2] Currency was scarce and in payment for their services the

Queenston Village and the Portage Road leading from the wharves up the Heights. A sketch copied from an old print circa 1800.

drivers, who were farmers from the area using their teams of horses and oxen to augment their farm income, received a "Portage Credit" of 1 shilling 8 pence per hundred weight of cargo. Each wagon held between 2,000 and 3,000 pounds. Later they used their credits to purchase food and supplies at the stores run by the merchants who controlled the portage franchise.

The War of 1812 brought Queenston into prominence when, on the cold windy morning of October 13, 1812, American troops crossed the Niagara River before dawn and made a surprise landing at Queenston. Although they outnumbered the British defenders, they were not able to break through the front defences of the village. Many Americans, officers and soldiers, were killed or wounded and the rest remained pinned down among the wharves or below the river bank.

Shortly after daybreak, a company of resourceful Americans led by Captain Wool, found their way along the river bank and up the escarpment by way of a little used fishermen's path, to the top of the Heights. At the Redan battery, halfway down the slope, was an 18 pounder cannon which could fire on Lewiston, the river, or on Queenston itself. Wool and his men overran the battery by charging the British from behind and above. Taking control of the Redan, the Americans now had a tactical advantage and

could fire on Queenston.

The British commander, Major-General Isaac Brock, immediately organized a counter attack, which failed after two attempts to retake the battery. Brock, resplendent in his red uniform, was killed as he led the first charge, shot in the heart by a sniper's bullet. His aide-de-camp, Lieutenant-Colonel John Macdonell, was killed leading the second charge. Later in the day British troops led by Brock's second in command, Major-General Sheaffe, gained the Heights and suddenly appeared at the rear of the American troops, trapping them against the gorge edge. Outnumbered and outmanoeuvred, the American force surrendered after a short skirmish. The British regained control of the Heights, the American invasion was repulsed, but Upper Canadians lost their leader, Isaac Brock.

Brock came to Canada in 1802, with his regiment, the 49th, after service in the Napoleonic War and in Denmark. He was placed in command of the army forces of Upper Canada and in 1811 was assigned a further responsibility as Administrator of the Government of Canada. His early victories over American forces at Michilimackinac and Detroit made him a hero of the war. He rallied Upper Canadians to the defence of their homeland and was a souce of inspiration and pride. His death was greatly mourned.

General Brock's Monument above Queenston. Drawn by W.H. Bartlett in 1838. Engraved by R. Wallis in 1840. Published by N.P. Willis in Canadian Scenery, 1842.

Brock was not forgotten when peace came. It was in 1824, on October 13, the twelfth anniversary of the battle, that more than 5,000 people gathered on the Heights for the dedication of a monument to his memory. The monument was a 39 m (130 ft.) high Tuscan column of Queenston limestone. The remains of Brock and his aide-de-camp, Lieutenant-Colonel Macdonell, were brought from Fort George where they had lain since the battle and were reinterred in the vault below the monument.

After the dedication of the monument, Queenston Heights became a point of interest for travellers, many of them Americans making a pilgrimage to the 1812 battle site. Some came on horseback, others came by stage-coach or horse drawn carriage, along the Portage Road from Niagara Falls and Buffalo. Those coming from Toronto and other Lake Ontario ports came by lake boat, landing either at Queenston or Lewiston. From Lewiston they were ferried across the river to Queenston by "horse-boat". (In a "horse-boat", a horse was harnessed to a treadmill located in the centre of the boat. The motion of the horse walking on the treadmill activated side paddle-wheels which propelled the boat through the water.)

For almost 100 years the lake boats were the principal means of transportation for those who visited the Heights. In 1842 the steamboat "Chief Justice Robinson" made daily trips between Toronto, Niagara and Queenston. Passengers were eager to use the steamers to avoid the long stage-coach ride around the end of Lake Ontario. At Queenston connections were made with the Erie and Ontario Railway, the first railway in Upper Canada. It began operating in 1838-39 and was completed in 1841, running from Queenston to Chippawa. It was a horse railway, its cars pulled by horses over wooden rails topped with iron straps.

The fine view from the top of the monument, of the winding river and the shining lake beyond, was popular and one summer the keeper took in £35 in admission fees. Thomas Fowler, who visited the monument in 1831, wrote: "On reaching it we demanded admission which was readily granted on paying the usual charge of 1 shilling York each. The base is a square form and contains a lobby which is occupied by the keeper as a barroom. Above the base

Queenston. Drawn by W.H. Bartlett in 1838. Engraved by C. Armitage. Published by N.P. Willis in Canadian Scenery, 1842.

it forms a round pillar with a staircase inside leading to a fine gallery which encircles the column a little from the top."[3]

On Good Friday, April 17, 1840, the monument was blown up by a charge of gunpowder, placed it is said by a "vagabond" named Lett, thought to be one of the Mackenzie rebels of 1837 who fled to the United States and returned for this act of destruction.[4] Planning began immediately for a new monument but it was ten years before construction began. In the meantime the old column stood forlornly with its broken iron railing waving in the wind. The bodies of Brock and Macdonell were moved from the vault after the explosion and reinterred in the Hamilton cemetery in Queenston.

A competition was held for the best design for a new monument and one of two designs submitted by Architect William Thomas of Toronto was chosen. On October 13, 1853, the anniversary of Brock's death, the foundation stone was laid for the new monument. The bodies of Brock and Macdonell were buried once again, this time in the vault which would be under the new column, where they still remain.

John Worthington of Toronto was the builder. Queenston limestone from the nearby quarry was hauled in large blocks to the site, where skilled masons cut and chiselled it into shape. The monument was not completed until the autumn of 1856. The monument enclosure, the laying out of the grounds, the massive entrance gates and the caretaker's lodge were not completed until 1857, with funds provided by the Province of Ontario.[5] The monument itself was paid for by public subscription. The completed monument was dedicated on October 13, 1857, when a crowd of two thousand people gathered on the Heights for the ceremony.

Until the beginning of the steam railroad era in the mid 1850's, Queenston was an important docking point for the lake steamers which sailed regularly from Hamilton, Toronto, Kingston and the American ports on Lake Ontario. In 1854 the Erie and Ontario Railway was converted to steam and the tracks extended to Niagara, now Niagara-on-the-Lake, bypassing Queenston. At the same time a railway was built connecting Lewiston on the United States side with Manchester, now Niagara Falls, New

Dedication ceremonies, second Brock's Monument, October 13, 1857.

Canadian Illustrated News

York. Without a railway connection Queenston was no longer used as a docking point on the lake route.

In 1888 when Queen Victoria Park opened, the Niagara Navigation Company was operating two side paddle-wheel steamers on the Toronto to Lewiston run. They were the "Chicora", a converted Confederate blockade runner formerly called the "Let Her B", and the "Cibola". The dock at Queenston was improved and a ferry service, using the small steamer "Ongiara" ferried passengers from Lewiston to Queenston.[6]

The opening in May 1893 of the Niagara Falls Park and River Railway connecting Queenston and the docks with Niagara Falls, sparked a revival of the lake boat traffic between Toronto and Queenston. During the next sixty years, hundreds of thousands of excursionists would cross Lake Ontario on the "Toronto boats" on their way to Queenston Heights and Queen Victoria Park. The "Cibola" burned while docked at Lewiston in 1895 and had to be scrapped. In 1896 the "Chippewa" joined the

Toronto run, replacing the "Cibola". Business boomed and three return trips were made each day.

In 1895 the Queen Victoria Park Commissioners turned their attention toward Brock's Monument and the Military Reservation surrounding it on Queenston Heights. The Niagara Falls Park and River Railway was carrying hundreds of thousands of passengers each year up the escarpment, passing the monument on their way to Niagara Falls. Many of these excursionists stopped off to visit the monument and there was a need for proper facilities to accommodate them.

Since 1867 the monument and 4.9 ha (12 acres) of land surrounding it had been cared for by the Province of Ontario, even though it was owned by the Dominion Government. At the Province's request in 1875 the Dominion Government transferred control of the monument and 12.5 ha (31 acres) of the Military Reserve to the Province.[7] During this time, all repairs to the shaft and foundation of the monument were made by the Province. The grounds,

The Chicora at Queenston Dock, 1903.

Ontario Hydro Archives

The Cibola launched in 1887, burned at the dock in Lewiston, 1895.

Metropolitan Toronto Library Board

In 1877 the Niagara Navigation Company was formed by three prominent Ontario men, Barbaro Cumberland, the Honourable J.J. Foy, and Sir Franklin Smith. A passenger service was instituted between Toronto, Niagara-on-the-Lake and Lewiston, using one boat, the Chicora. In 1888 a second boat was added, the Cibola and a ferry service was added between Lewiston and Queenston using a small steam ferry, the Ongiara.

Niagara Falls New York Public Library

The Ongiara, the ferry between Lewiston & Queenston. From a stereograph by American Views.

The Corona, launched in May 1896.

The Chippewa, assigned to the Toronto to Niagara-on-the-Lake run to replace the Cibola.

The view from the Heights, 1906.

however, had not been maintained and were over-grown and neglected.

The Park Commissioners asked the Province for control of the area. They proposed to clean up the grounds, lay out paths, provide drinking water and sanitary facilities and trim the trees at the edge of the escarpment to open up a view of the river and the countryside below. In 1895 the monument and the adjacent 12.5 ha (31 acres) were placed in the care of the Queen Victoria Park Commissioners.[8] This land transfer, coupled with the acquisition of the adjoining Ordnance lands from the Admiralty Branch of the Department of the Interior in Ottawa, plus the purchase of 5 ha (12½ acres) of land from Sir Casimir Gzowski, formed the nucleus of the beautiful Queenston Heights Park which we enjoy today.

On April 18, 1899, control of the Niagara Falls Park and River Railway was acquired by the Buffalo Railway Company which then became involved in a merger which produced the International Railway Company. With the completion of the Upper Steel Arch Bridge and the Lewiston-Queenston Suspension Bridge, tracks were laid across the bridges and the electric railway lines on both sides of the river were joined, creating a "Belt Line". This new line, part of the Great Gorge Route, allowed passengers to get off at various points, enjoy the sights, then board the next car to proceed further on the route. Queenston

Heights became a popular stopover along the route.

In 1907 the propeller-driven "Cayuga" was added to the lake steamer fleet, joining the "Chicora", "Corona'. and "Chippewa" on the Toronto to Queenston route. From time to time other companies tried without success to make an inroad into the lucrative passenger trade controlled by the Niagara Navigation Company. The "Turbina" and the "Northhumberland" were two of the steamers used in these ventures which failed.

In 1903 Park Superintendent Wilson wrote: "The Queenston Heights Park is becoming more and more an attraction for the better class of visitors, and the accommodations there provided for their convenience and comfort are being widely appreciated by Church and Sabbath School organizations. No difficulty has been experienced in maintaining order throughout the year."[9]

Recreational facilities were provided for the picnickers. Between 1895 and 1905 baseball and picnic gounds were laid out, and in 1900 a one-storey restaurant and refreshment stand was built. Climbing the 250 steps winding up the inside of the column of the monument was a popular recreational activity. To encourage more people to climb to the top of the monument, the admission price was reduced in 1906 from 25¢ to 15¢, resulting in a large increase in the number of climbers.

A view of the Niagara River from Queenston Heights. In the foreground are two of the 24 pounder cannons of 1807, obtained from the Department of National Defence in 1900.

Hugh C. Leighton Co., Portland Maine

The Park lacked a shelter for picnickers in case of inclement weather. In 1907, a large open-sided building constructed of fieldstone, with a shingle roof and smooth cement floor was built. As well as serving as a picnic shelter, it was used for dancing, the smooth finished floor being ideally suited for this pastime. The building became known as the Dance Pavilion and was later used for band concerts.

The Portage Road adjoining the Park Boundary was under the jurisdiction of the County of Lincoln. The County, against the wishes of the Commissioners, licensed private concessionaires allowing them to set up flimsy structures along the road at the Park entrance, from which they offered souvenirs and post cards for sale. Their aggressive tactics were an annoyance to the public. In 1910, after much negotiation, the Dominion Government granted this section of the Military Reserve, including the Portage Road, a total of 1 ha (2.4 acres), to the Commissioners and the vendors were soon dispossessed.[10]

In 1912 the Park encompassed 35.6 ha (88 acres). Of this 8.9 ha (22 acres) were purchased, the remainder is vested in the Commission, partly by the Province of Ontario and partly by the Dominion Government, for preservation and management.

The popularity of Queenston Heights as a site for group picnics suffered a setback in 1915. On Wednesday, July 15, of that year, a sudden storm followed by steady rain, abruptly ended a picnic being held by two Toronto churches. There was a rush of people to get on the first electric car going back to the shelter of the Queenston docks. One hundred and fifty-seven people crowded aboard a car with a capacity of 80 passengers. Grossly overloaded, the car sped down the hill, running out of control. On the steep curve in the village of Queenston, the car ran off the track, smashing broadside into a tree. Fifteen people were killed and many others were injured. This sad occurrence, while not the fault of the Park Commissioners, kept many picnic parties from coming to Queenston Heights during the remainder of that summer season. It was several years before this park fully regained its popularity as a group picnic site.

The 1920's saw many improvements in the Park. The restaurant was enlarged and the Commission took over the operation of this facility from the private concessionaire. The price of refreshments was lowered and service to the visitors was improved. To inform the public that the restaurant was under Commission management, the Chairman, P.W. Ellis, wrote a letter to the *Toronto World* on August 9, 1920. He wrote: "It is certainly worth a mention that in these days of high living costs the Commission provides picnickers with coffee and tea at 30¢ a quart. This price includes jugs, cups, cream and sugar."[11]

The Park Commissioners realized that many mothers who came to Queenston Heights for a day's

The International Railway Station and souvenir store at Queenston Heights Park, 1920.

Picnickers who have just got off one of the electric railway cars which brought them up the Heights from the boat dock at Queenston, are seen entering the gateway to Queenston Heights Park, circa 1920.

Edwin H. Hodge

The Nursery or Crèche, at Queenston Heights Park, 1927.

outing, were not able to participate in the picnic events, or visit Niagara Falls, because they had to care for their small children. In 1921, a crèche, or nursery, was established, with a trained nurse in charge. The first crèche was a double tent. Five cents an hour was charged for the service and children up to 2 years of age were required to stay in cribs. In 1922 operating expenses were $284.92, while receipts were $22.00 for the season.[12] This was truly a public service. As time went on more mothers took advantage of the service and in 1926 an attractive fieldstone building was erected to provide permanent quarters for the crèche.

The picnic grounds were moved to their present location west of the monument in 1917. In 1921, a picnic shelter was constructed of the same pipe frame design as those in Queen Victoria Park, and another was added in 1926. These open air shelters provided adequate protection for rainy days and allowed picnics to continue in spite of the weather.

The completion of the Niagara Boulevard, connecting Niagara Falls with the Heights in 1923, and the widening and grading of the roadway down the escarpment to Queenston, connecting with Highway #8A which led to Hamilton and Toronto,

made the Park more accessible to those visitors who were now coming by automobile. As their numbers increased, a new entrance for motor traffic was made to accommodate them, connecting with the old roadway into the grounds. Parking was provided in a new circular drive for patrons of the restaurant. While more and more visitors came by automobile, large numbers still came by the lake boats and the electric railway.

The provision of drinking water had been a source of frustration ever since the Park opened. Spring water existed at the bottom of the hill. Appropriately called "Brock's Spring", it was collected in a reservoir then force pumped to the refreshment pavilion. During extreme summer weather in 1920, water had to be hauled to the restaurant. Wells were dug but even at 91.4 m (300 ft.) they provided insufficient water. In 1923 the problem was solved when a 15 cm (6 in.) water line was laid from the City of Niagara Falls and a 45,460 litre (10,000 gal.) wood-stave, water storage tank was erected. Dependency on springs and wells ceased. As soon as a reliable supply of water was available, modern comfort stations were built. Then in 1926, the Commissioners created a delightful playing area for

The picnic pavilions erected in 1905.

The picnic area at Queenston Heights Park, circa 1920.

In 1926 a children's wading pool was constructed in the centre of the earthworks redoubt known as Fort Drummond.

Niagara Parks Archives

The spray pool 1983. This pool replaced the wading pool.

Harry Mottershead

The damaged arm from Brock's Monument, May 1930.

Edwin H. Hodge

The scaffolding around Brock's Monument, 1930.

Edwin H. Hodge

The weathered torso of Brock's Monument with scaffolding built around it, 1930.

Edwin H. Hodge

The replacement for Brock's damaged arm and torso, 1930.

Edwin H. Hodge

small children when they had built a 29 m (75 ft.) diameter concrete wading pool. It was built in the centre of the old 1812 earthwork redoubt, Fort Drummond. This wading pool became a popular spot for families with small children. In 1967 a new spray pool was installed on the site, replacing the wading pool. Three clay tennis courts were added to the playground area in 1928, providing recreational facilities for young adults. Two more clay courts were added in 1959.

During a heavy gale on the night of April 5, 1929, the outstretched arm of the figure of Sir Isaac Brock, which had stood atop the monument for 73 years, fell crashing to the ground. Fortunately no visitors were present and no one was injured. The arm lay in three pieces on the ground and was estimated to weigh 450 kg (1000 lbs.).

Plans were made to replace the arm, and to make whatever other repairs were necessary to the monument. A scaffolding of heavy timber was built around the column reaching up to the figure of Brock on the top. Subsequent inspection showed that the head and shoulders and the upper part of the torso of the statue were in a dangerous state due to weathering. The top section of the statue was completely removed and replaced. The whole shaft of the

monument was pointed with mortar to make it weatherproof, lightning arresters and a new railing were placed at the top of the column. The work was completed in 1930.[13]

The increasing popularity of the automobile, the construction of new highways, and the economic depression of the 1930's combined to cause a decline in lake passenger traffic. Where groups of excursionists used to come by boat, they now came by highway bus or automobile. The "Chicora" was retired in 1920. The International Railway Company abandoned its franchise and the electric cars stopped running after midnight on September 11, 1932. The excursionists who crossed the lake on their way to Queenston Heights and Niagara Falls on the "Corona", "Chippewa" and the "Cayuga" were then driven up to the Heights and to the Falls by Gray Line buses. Business decreased in the depression and the "Corona" and "Chippewa" were taken off the lake run in 1936. Only the "Cayuga" was left to sail the lake.

The demise of the electric railway led to the relocation of the ornamental stone entrance gates to Queenston Heights Park. When they were built in 1856 they had been located close to the caretaker's lodge. In 1909 they were moved and set up as a

The steamship Cayuga approaching the Queenston Dock on the day of the last run of the electric cars of the International Railway Company, September 10, 1932.

A view of the Niagara River from Queenston Heights, with the Cayuga approaching Queenston, circa 1957.

The Dance Pavilion used for many years by the Fred Willett Orchestra during the Band concerts held weekly during the summer months.

pedestrian entrance opposite the electric railway station. In 1941-42 they were moved back to their original location, where they are now located. Often unnoticed by passing motorists, they are on the east-west axis of the monument. An impressive view of the monument is seen by the motorist looking up from the roadway, through the gates.

Over the years many other improvements were made to the Park. Paths which were first topped with gravel, were later blacktopped. Some of the paths adjacent to the monument and the restaurant were made of flagstone. Additional parking space for cars was provided as traffic increased. In 1960 a new parking area to hold 300 cars was built on the north side of the new Portage Road. Picnic tables were placed adjacent to this new parking area.

Band concerts, held weekly on Sunday afternoons during the summer months, have been a feature of Queenston Heights Park for over 35 years. The bands were first housed in the Dance Pavilion. The increasing popularity of this summer musical event led to the construction in 1976 of a new band shell. Built at a cost of $135,105, it can accommodate 100 musicians. The band shell is cone-shaped, constructed of natural wood, cedar siding and shingles. The natural slope of the ground in front of the band shell gives the installation an amphitheatre effect.[14] The old Dance Pavilion was torn down.

The restaurant at Queenston Heights, constructed in 1900, had been poorly placed. Additions and alterations made in 1909, 1910 and 1921, had resulted in a building which was unsightly and out of keeping with its surroundings. In addition the equipment was obsolete and not adequate to cater to the increasing number of tourists coming to the Park. The Commissioners decided in 1939 to build a new restaurant on the brink of the escarpment. Here diners would enjoy a view of the countryside below, extending to Lake Ontario.

Work began in 1939 and was completed in June 1940. Built of Queenston limestone, with a red tile roof, the building was designed to be in architectural

The band shell erected in 1976 is large enough to accommodate 100 musicians.

Niagara Parks Archives

Alfred Reed
Queenston Overture
for Concert Band/Wind Ensemble

CONCERT BAND with Full and Condensed Scores	60.00
FULL SCORE	7.50
CONDENSED SCORE	5.00
EXTRA PARTS	ea. 2.00

PIEDMONT MUSIC COMPANY, INC.
Sole Selling Agent:

EDWARD B. MARKS MUSIC CORPORATION / Exclusive distributors of all printed products / Belwin Mills Publishing Corp. MELVILLE, N.Y. 11747

Niagara Parks Archives

Niagara Parks Archives

Dr. Alfred Reed, left, Fred Willett, right, on the occasion of the premiere performance of the "Queenston Overture" at the Queenston Heights Bandshell, June 27, 1982.

"The Queenston Overture" by Dr. Alfred Reed, was commissioned by the Niagara Parks Commission to commemorate the thirtieth anniversary of summer Sunday afternoon concerts by the Fred Willett Concert Band at Queenston Heights Park. The concerts are co-sponsored by The Niagara Parks Commission and the Musicians Performance Trust Fund with the co-operation of Local 299 of the American Federation of Musicians.

Dining on the outdoor patio at Queenston Heights Restaurant, 1950's.

The Queenston Heights Restaurant today.

The dining room at Queenston Heights Restaurant, 1980's.

View of the lower Niagara River from the Queenston Heights Restaurant.

Illumination of Brock's Monument at night.

Niagara Parks Archives

Niagara Parks Archives

Queenston Heights from the air, circa 1924. The Lewiston-Queenston Suspension bridge spans the river at top right. The playing field with ball diamond is in the centre foreground, and the restaurant is visible in the trees to the right. The roof of the Dance Pavilion is visible to the left of the monument.

Queenston Heights Park from the air, 1980. The restaurant is visible at centre right. The picnic pavilions are in the foreground and the spray pool is at the left.

harmony with the other buildings in the Niagara Parks System. For over 30 years it featured an outside patio dining room, with a view of the lower river. Improvements over the years have included the enclosing of this outside patio area with plate glass, so that the view is unobstructed. In 1974 air conditioning was installed and the interior was redesigned. Other interior changes were made in 1977. In 1980 the open verandah at the restaurant entrance was enclosed with glass, to provide an attractive waiting area. All of these improvements have combined to make this restaurant a beautiful setting for relaxed and enjoyable dining.

A milestone in park development was achieved in 1959 when an area of about 5 ha (12 acres) in Queenston Heights Park was equipped with landscape lighting. The landscape illuminator employed by the Commissioners described the project as follows: "For the first time on this continent or in Europe, a portion of a park with all its fabulous display of nature, has been fully treated with planned aesthetic lighting for nighttime enjoyment." This type of illumination is not to be confused with flood lighting. It is instead a subtle form of illuminating an area by the direct use of lighting units placed in trees. One hundred lighting units were installed and they are operated during both the summer and winter months.[15]

In 1960 the public washrooms were renovated and the old wood stave water storage tank was replaced by a 75,708 litre (20,000 U.S. gal.) steel tank. The old pipe frame picnic shelters of the 1920's were torn down in 1971 and replaced by two new picnic pavilions each seating 500 people. A new snack bar was built replacing the old refreshment stand. In 1972 an ornamental mall bordered by flower beds and benches was established, connecting the new picnic pavilions and the refreshment stand

F.H. Leslie

The Laura Secord monument erected in 1910 by the Government of Canada in memory of Laura Secord's heroic walk from Queenston to Beaverdams, to warn the British troops of an impending American attack on their position. The monument stands on the site of the first Brock's monument.

Harry Mottershead

The marker at the site of the Redan Battery.

Niagara Parks Archives

This marker is situated a few miles west of Queenston Heights on Highway 55. It marks the path to the Heights taken by Major-General Roger Hale Sheaffe and the British forces when they outflanked the American forces to gain a victory at the Battle of Queenston Heights, October 13, 1812.

This marker commemorating the part played by Indians fighting on the British side during the Battle of Queenston Heights, October 13, 1812 is located west of Brock's Cenotaph.

Brock's Cenotaph, marking the spot where General Sir Isaac Brock fell after being struck by a sniper's bullet during the Battle of Queenston Heights, October 13, 1812.

A bronze statue of "Alfred", General Sir Isaac Brock's horse, mounted on a 1.4 m (4½ ft.) high sandstone base and contained in a safety glass case, is located to the left of Brock's Cenotaph. The statue was sculpted by Ralph Sketch of British Columbia and was commissioned by Mr. and Mrs. Stewart G. Bennett of Georgetown, Ontario. It was accepted by the Parks Commission and officially dedicated on October 3, 1976.

Niagara Parks Archives

Metropolitan Toronto Public Library

The ruins of the Mackenzie House, circa 1920's.

The restored Mackenzie House looking at the north side.

The original home of William Lyon Mackenzie in Queenston lay in ruins for many years. During 1936 the home was reconstructed from data relating to construction in that particular period. On June 18, 1938, the Right Honourable William Lyon Mackenzie King, Prime Minister of Canada, formally opened the restored home in which his grandfather, William Lyon Mackenzie, resided during his stay in Queenston and where he established his newspaper **The Colonial Advocate**. A gold key was presented to the Prime Minister, with which he opened the door of the restored home. He then read a letter by William Lyon Mackenzie in which he noted that he had planted acacias (locust trees) in front of his home, the Prime Minister noting that those trees were today mature and sheltered the reconstructed home.

For many years, until 1958, the Township of Niagara Municipal Offices occupied Mackenzie House. When the municipality vacated the offices, the Parks Commission decided to establish a museum there to house and display the Kirby Collection which had been in Fort George since 1944 when the Commission bought it for $5,000. This collection comprised military memorabilia of Butler's Rangers, the War of 1812-14, the Fenian Raids, and the history of the Masonic Order in the Niagara Peninsula. When the Mackenzie House was closed after the 1974 season, the collection was moved to Oak Hall and displayed there until February 1981, when it was donated to the Niagara Historical Society Museum in Niagara-on-the-Lake. For many years the Queenston Historical Committee provided attendants during weekend hours at Mackenzie House. The house is no longer open to view.

On October 6, 1974 the Archeological and Historic Sites Board and the Province of Ontario, Ministry of Colleges and Universities, placed a historic plaque at Mackenzie House, commemorating the publication of **The Colonial Advocate** at the location in 1824.

area with the bandshell. The fieldstone building erected in 1926 for a crèche was remodelled to provide additional washrooms.

On October 1, 1969, the Federal Government took over responsibility for the operation and maintenance of Brock's Monument. It became part of Parks Canada. The Niagara Parks Commission still operates and has responsibility for the park area of Queenston Heights. In 1973 Parks Canada instituted a Battle of Queenston Heights Walking Tour. Markers were installed at historic sites

associated with the Battle of Queenston Heights, throughout the Park area and on the river bank below. This new Walking Tour added an interpretive dimension to the historic battleground.[16]

Queenston Heights has maintained its popularity as a picnic and recreation site. While the number of group picnics has declined in recent years the number of individual and family picnic parties has increased. Queenston Heights Park is the next most popular destination for visitors in the Niagara Parks, after Queen Victoria Park and the Falls.

Navy Island

New France had scarcely been ceded to Britain at the close of the Seven Years War in 1763 when a powerful confederation of western Indians led by Pontiac, the Chief of the Ottawas, carried out savage attacks on all the frontier outposts. The British posts were quickly over run by the Indians and destroyed, except for Fort Pitt, Fort Detroit and Fort Niagara. Lord Amherst, the British Commander-in-Chief, placed Colonel John Bradstreet in command of an expedition which would assemble at Fort Niagara and then move by water up Lake Erie to relieve Detroit. Bradstreet was instructed to build three small schooners on the river above the Falls of Niagara, to carry the troops and supplies up the river and up the Lake to Detroit. After a naval shipyard was established in 1763 on the small island above the Falls, it became known as "Navy Island". The sloops "Huron" and "Charlotte" and the schooners "Boston", "Gladwin" and "Victory" were built at Navy Island. They were the first vessels to navigate the Upper Great Lakes under the British flag.[1]

In the mid 1850's 40.5 ha (100 acres) of the island were cleared for farming and the rest was left in woodlands. Orchards were set out and in 1865, four families were living on the island. In 1876 a portion of the island was leased to private entrepreneurs who established a pleasure ground. A two-storey frame summer hotel was built on the eastern side of the island close to the United States. A dock was erected to accommodate the boat traffic which would bring the tourists to the island. The farm families were still living on the island in 1887, but there is no record of when they vacated the site.[2] The Queen's Hotel as it was called, was a popular resort until the early 1900's when the whole venture was abandoned. The hotel burned sometime around 1910 and was not rebuilt.

In 1938 the Parks Commission became concerned that the island might pass into private hands and they applied to the Federal Department of Mines and Resources for the right to occupy the island. A lease was granted and the Parks Commission took over jurisdiction of the 127.9 ha (316 acre) area. There were no immediate plans for development. The 1944 Annual Report of the Parks Commission proposed post war construction projects. It was suggested that a bridge would have to be built connecting the island with the mainland if the area was to be developed into a public park.

Navy Island was promoted as a possible site for the World Security Organization - The United Nations - in 1945. Prominent people on both sides of the border joined in a concerted effort to convince the United Nations founding committee that Navy Island was the best place for a headquarters for their new organization. On July 31, 1945 the Niagara Parks Commission entertained the United Nations committee and the local organizers at a dinner held in the Victoria Park Restaurant.[3] New York City was the site chosen for the new headquarters and Navy Island remained undeveloped.

The Parks Commission received a request from an individual in 1949, asking that the island be leased out as a private game preserve. The request was

An aerial view of Navy Island, 1968. The Cascades and the spray rising from the Falls can be seen at the top left.

denied, but the Commission took action to head off any further requests by declaring Navy Island a Wild Life and Crown Preserve. The action provided official protection to the natural habitat of the birds and animals on the island. On April 30, 1946, the District Game Warden had observed a bald eagle's nest during one of his trips to the island. This sighting provided evidence that there was wild life there in need of protection.

There was great concern in 1950 when eighteen deer carcasses were discovered on the island with no cause of death apparent. Investigation proved that the animals had died of starvation. The herd had become too large, the island was estimated to be able to support only from 25 to 30 deer. During some severe winters deer are fed by Government and Sportsmen's organizations, and a controlled hunt of the herd was undertaken in 1956 by the Department of Lands and Forests. In 1981 another controlled hunt was held under the supervision of the Ministry of Natural Resources. One hundred and twenty-one deer were killed, twenty-five swam to the mainland and twenty-five remained on the island. No deer dead from starvation were found after the 1981-82 winter.

Some camping is allowed on the island by permit and Boy Scout groups use it regularly. Supervised nature tours arranged by appointment are conducted during the summer months by the Park Naturalist.

The Mackenzie Rebellion
and Navy Island

When William Lyon Mackenzie attempted, with 800 half-armed men, to overthrow the government of Upper Canada in early December of 1837, at York, his rebel force was quickly routed by the loyal militia under Colonel Fitzgibbon, the victor of Beaverdams. With his followers defeated and dispersed, and a price on his head, Mackenzie fled towards the United States. He was closely pursued and narrowly escaped capture, but finally arrived at the bank of the Niagara River, a short distance below Fort Erie. Here, he was almost captured by his pursuers, but sympathizers rowed him across the river to safety in the United States.

At Buffalo the rebel leader was greeted by popular demonstrations and given promises of support, arms, food and clothing. He soon formed a connection with Rensellaer Van Rensellaer and Jefferson Sutherland, two Americans notorious for their strong anti-British prejudices. Subsequently they established themselves with a force that did not exceed two dozen men, on Canadian soil - Navy Island. It was on Navy Island that Mackenzie, on December 13, set up his short-lived and abortive "Provisional Government". Lands were promised to volunteers who would assist in an invasion of Canada; a reward was offered for the capture of the Lieutenant-Governor; and a flag, emblazoned with twin stars and a new moon breaking through the clouds, was adopted for the so-called "Canadian Republic". Several weeks went by, during which the rebels remained in undisputed possession of the island and attracted a considerable number of recruits. At the height of the rebel movement it was

estimated that there were between 200 and 300 people, mostly Americans, with Mackenzie on Navy Island. Meanwhile, Colonel McNab had taken up a position on the Canadian mainland with a force of 2,500 Canadian militia and there was sporadic firing across the river which was only 609.6 m (2000 ft.) wide at this point.[1]

Assistance given to the insurgents by American citizens provoked deep resentment in Canada and matters came to a head at the close of 1837. Information reached Colonel McNab that the rebels had purchased a steam-boat called the "Caroline", to facilitate their intended invasion of Canada. Actually, the boat had been chartered and was plying between the American shore and Navy Island taking supplies and reinforcements to the rebel camp. McNab determined to cut off this supply route. At midnight on December 29 he sent a small force under Captain Andrew Drew, a half-pay Royal Navy officer serving with the Canadian militia, to put the "Caroline" out of commission. The men crossed in small boats to Navy Island and, not finding the "Caroline" there, continued to the American side of the River, where they found the ship moored close to Fort Schlosser. During a brief scuffle in which one of the Americans was killed, the ship was boarded by the Canadians and her crew driven ashore. The captured steamer was then towed to midstream, set on fire and left to drift in the swift current which carried her, in a mass of flames, over the brink of the Horseshoe Falls. South of the border, immense indignation was aroused by this violation of United States territory

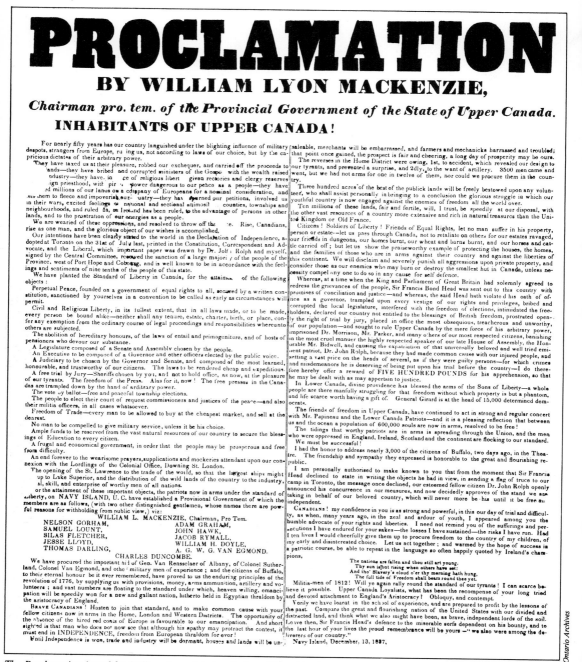

The Proclamation issued by William Lyon Mackenzie from Navy Island on December 13, 1837. It proclaimed the Provisional Government of the State of Upper Canada. The printer erred in calling it the Provincial Government.

and the situation was not improved when the British Government conferred a knighthood on Colonel McNab for his part in the action. Following the affair of the "Caroline", Navy Island was subjected to an intense bombardment and the rebels, finding their position too difficult to maintain, retreated to the American mainland on January 13, 1838, where they dispersed.

In the United States popular indignation over the "Caroline" was so great that war seemed imminent.

A $10.00 promissory certificate issued by the Provisional Government of Upper Canada in exchange for goods or services received.

The Burning of the Caroline. An oil on canvas by Nicolino Calyo. One wildly exaggerated report in an American paper, of this incident stated: "probably more than one-third of the thirty-three persons on board were wantonly massacred", when in fact only one man was killed in the skirmish.

The 43rd Monmouthshire Regiment encampment at Niagara opposite the American Fall, August 9, 1838. A water colour by Sir James B. Bucknall Estcourt.

Public Archives of Canada

The United States demanded redress from Great Britain for the violation of American territory. President Van Buren was determined to preserve the peace and he sent General Winfield Scott to the Niagara frontier to assume command of the state militia and prevent any further incidents. This did not prevent a series of raids over the Canadian border in 1838 and 1839 by Mackenzie rebels. In 1839 both Mackenzie and Van Rensellaer were convicted of having violated the neutrality laws and were imprisoned. The Patriot movement eventually died out after such futile provocations as the abortive attempt to blow up Brock's Monument at Queenston Heights in 1840.[2]

During the troubled times, the Canadian militia was reinforced by British regulars. The 43rd Monmouthshire Regiment was stationed at Niagara Falls and encamped on the high bank above the Horseshoe Falls from August 1838 to August 1839. The troops constituted a show of force and were meant to impress the Americans. A letter written by a member of the regiment at the time explains to what pains the Canadians went to impress their neighbours across the border: "Soon after the arrival of the regiment at the Falls, Governor-General Lord Durham arrived with his suite and he was joined by Lieutenant-Governor John Colborne. The Governor-General adopted the 'soothing' system with our neighbours over the water . . . willing perhaps, first to astonish, and afterwards to mollify the Yankees, he issued public notice of a grand review on July 17, and cards for 200 persons to dinner in the evening.

"An immense concourse, chiefly American, attended in the morning. Our force consisted of one Regiment of Light Infantry, about 600 strong, one squadron of the 1st Dragoon Guards, and two guns - the ground being kept by three companies of the 24th Regiment, and a troop of Her Majesty's Niagara Lancers - a most excellent and efficient corps, since disbanded. We gave the spectators a rapid field day, with liberal allowance of blank cartridges. Not many hours after we betook ourselves to dine at the Clifton Hotel".[3] This parade was held on the high bank above the Horseshoe Falls.

While the 43rd Regiment was stationed here, a number of its foot soldiers deserted to the United States. To prevent any soldier from leaving Canada by way of the row boat ferry, a guard was stationed at the landing place.[4] The crisis passed and the matter was finally settled during discussions between Daniel Webster and Lord Ashburton prior to the Treaty of Washington in 1842. Ashburton assured Webster that "no slight or disrespect of the sovereign authority of the United States" had been intended and that he regretted "that some explanation and apology for this occurrence was not immediately made".[5] The Americans for their part admitted that they had been too free in their support of Mackenzie.

On his release, after serving 18 months in prison in Rochester, Mackenzie engaged in journalism in which a strong anti-British bias was displayed. He returned to Canada under the amnesty of 1849 and resumed his political career.[6]

Niagara Parkway - Chippawa to Fort Erie

As you drive today from Chippawa to Fort Erie along the Niagara Parkway, only the presence of historic monuments by the roadside gives any indication of the activity which took place there in the early days of that road.

In the first survey of Willoughby Township made in 1787, a reserved strip of land one chain (20 m or 66 ft.) in width, that is, a "Chain Reserve", was left along the bank of the Niagara River as the Crown Reserve for Military purposes. The early settlers ignored the Reserve at times and built their fences right to the water's edge, using it as an extension of their own property. In 1791 the Land Board ordered the farmers who lived along the upper Niagara River to move their fences back from the shore, in order to leave the Chain Reserve for a public road. The Chain was used as the main travelled road between Chippawa and Fort Erie from the earliest days of settlement.[1]

As early as 1791 York boats loaded with flour, salt, hard tack, military supplies and manufactured goods for trading with the Indians, were rowed or poled upstream to Lake Erie. From there the cargo which had been loaded on board at Chippawa, the southern terminus of the Portage Road, was transported through the Upper Great Lakes in sailing ships, to British forts and trading posts in the West. Ships coming from the west, laden with furs obtained by barter with the Indians at trading posts, unloaded their cargo at Fort Erie, where it was transferred to York boats which sailed down the river with the current to Chippawa.

The road became strategically important during the War of 1812 when it formed part of the only supply route between Fort Erie and Fort George at the mouth of the Niagara River. The road had crude plank bridges over the six creeks - Frenchman's, Miller's, Baker's, Black, Boyer's, Ussher's - which flowed into the Niagara River between Fort Erie and Chippawa. On July 4, 1814, American forces numbering 8,000 men with their artillery and equipment, advanced along this road from Fort Erie, on their way to Chippawa. A British rearguard force hampered their progress by removing the wooden plank flooring from the bridges along the way. The advancing American forces had to replace the flooring with planks taken from nearby barns. Three weeks later the Americans were to take up the bridge floors they laid on July fourth, when they withdrew toward Fort Erie after the Battle of Lundy's Lane on July 26, 1814. At that time they burned every house and barn along the river road from Chippawa to Black Creek.[2]

After the opening of the first Welland Canal in 1829, the road became a tow path with oxen pulling large sailing ships up the river from Chippawa, the southern terminus of the canal, to Fort Erie. Traffic on this part of the River came to a halt when the canal channel was cut through from Port Robinson to Port Colborne in 1833. The Welland Canal then provided a through route between the Lakes and there was no longer any need for shipping to use the Niagara River route. However the tow path continued to be used as a road.

The United States Army at the Battle of Chippawa, July 5, 1814.

On July 3, 1814 United States General Jacob Brown sent Brigadier-General Winfield Scott and his Brigade numbering about 1400 men, across the Niagara River where they captured Fort Erie. By the next day the United States Army had been increased to 4000 men and early in the morning Brigadier-General Scott and his Brigade, with supporting artillery, advanced towards Chippawa. They camped overnight at Street's Creek (Ussher's Creek), about 3 km (2 mi.) south of Chippawa. British General Riall and a British force of about 1500 including militia and Indians, had advanced to meet the Americans and were camped at Fort Chippawa on the north side of Chippawa Creek.

Scott's Brigade was untested in battle, though it was the best trained and best disciplined unit turned out by the United States Army up to that time. The Brigade wore gray uniforms, normally worn by the militia, because there was a shortage of the blue cloth from which the uniforms of the regular United States Army were made. At 4 o'clock in the afternoon of July 5, Scott moved his Brigade across Street's Creek and advanced towards Chippawa. Riall had crossed the Chippawa Creek with his British force and prepared to do battle with the advancing American forces. When the Americans came into view, Riall incorrectly assumed that the force in front of him, dressed in gray, was militia and not regular soldiers. He did not treat them seriously and sent his men headlong towards the American line. Scott's men held fast and Riall who was expecting them to break and retreat at the first British volley, is reported to have exclaimed "Those are Regulars, by God". The British faltered under the American fire and broke when they were within only 73 m (80 yds.) of the American line. Riall and his forces retreated across the Chippawa Creek and sought protection behind the fortifications of Fort Chippawa. The British lost 415 killed, wounded and missing, the Americans, 328, in a battle that lasted not much more than one hour.

On July 8, the American Army, commanded by Major General Brown, advanced on a road cut through the woods from Street's Creek to the junction of Lyon's Creek and the Chippawa Creek about 2.4 km (1.5 mi.) from the mouth of the Chippawa. The Army bridged the Creek and crossed with its guns and supplies before being detected. The British forces, outflanked by this manoeuvre, hurriedly retired to Forts George and Mississauga, leaving the whole Niagara frontier, excepting these Forts, and Fort Niagara under American control. The American Army advanced and encamped within sight of Fort George, waiting for the arrival of heavy guns and ammunition needed for an attack on the Fort.

This stone, referred to as the "Ebenezer Stone" was one of the mill stones used in the mid 1800's by the Ebenezers to grind the flour in their grist mill. In 1842 the Ebenezers organized a community of about 800 people under the name Ebenezer Society and settled on the Niagara River just north of Black Creek. They built a wharf on the river for receiving and discharging cargoes. Besides their dwelling houses, which were built of logs, they had a store, blacksmith shop, sawmill, woolen mill, flour mill, tannery, cabinet shop and dining hall, buildings for weaving and dyeing and a community kitchen. Ebenezer blue, their own dye, was well known, as their chief industry was manufacturing cotton of high quality. They also built their own furniture. Hooked rugs and rag carpets were used on their floors. The Ebenezer women dressed alike with white caps and aprons, always wearing sombre colours of black, brown, grey and their famous indigo blue calico. They always wore hoods or sun-bonnets. Everything was held in common - all the property was owned by the Society, and the proceeds of their industries and business were shared by all members. Each village was governed by elders and trustees, who supervised the work done and kept books on the business activities. Eventually they left the area as quietly as they had come and moved to Amana, Iowa in 1859.

The Ebenezer Stone, marking the site of the Ebenezer colony on the upper Niagara River.

During the Mackenzie Rebellion of 1837-38, when the rebel, William Lyon Mackenzie, and his followers set up the Republic of Canada on Navy Island, every house from Chippawa to Black Creek billeted British soldiers. Ussher's Creek was the rendezvous at that time for a raid led by a Mackenzie rebel named Lett, who landed a small party and assassinated Captain Edgeworth Ussher, shooting him down in cold blood when he opened his front door in response to a knock.[3] It was from Ussher's Creek also that an expedition set out on the night of December 29, 1837 to intercept Mackenzie's supply ship, the "Caroline". The subsequent burning of the "Caroline" with the loss of one life, caused an international incident, and tension along the border was high for almost a year.

On June 2, 1866 the road was again the scene of military activity when the Fenians invaded Canada and set up a camp at Frenchman's Creek. After commandeering livestock and food supplies from nearby farms, they marched toward Ridgeway. Here they met a platoon of Canadian troops and in the resulting skirmish both sides retreated. The Fenians returned to the United States where they were promptly arrested. One body of Canadian reinforcements arrived by train at Niagara Falls and proceeded along the Portage Road, then up the river road past Chippawa, pulling a heavy cannon. The cannon was their undoing - when they attempted to cross the bridge over Ussher's Creek the cannon, which was too heavy for the bridge, crashed through the bridge platform. The delay in getting the cannon out of the creek and back on the road was so great that they reached the scene of action after the battle was over.[4]

Stage-coaches used the road, carrying passengers between Chippawa, Fort Erie and Buffalo, with a stage-coach line in operation as late as 1896. For a short time the "Red Jacket", a Tally-Ho coach drawn by four horses, made one trip each way daily between Buffalo and Chippawa. The coming of the Tally Ho was announced by the blowing of a traditional posthorn. Because the roadway was in such bad condition and the Park Commissioners were not yet ready to put in a good road, the coach on its Canadian route ran along the upper river for only a few miles above Chippawa. Then it turned west to the first concession road where a direct road led

F.H. Leslie

Slater's Point Dock on the upper river south of Chippawa, circa 1900. Here passengers transferred from the Buffalo steamer to streetcars of the Niagara Falls Park and River Railway for the journey to Niagara Falls or Queenston Dock.

south in a straight line to Fort Erie and Buffalo.[5]

On October 26, 1891, the Provincial Government gave the Queen Victoria Niagara Falls Park Commission title to the Chain Reserve along the upper Niagara River, from Fort Erie to Chippawa. The Annual Report for 1894 mentioned the erosion of the river bank but it was 1898 before the report was prepared on the condition of the shore line. A system of groynes was suggested along the shore, to attempt to reclaim the land that had washed away. The estimate for the work was so great that no work was done at that time. In 1899 some land was purchased where the road had become narrower by erosion to an impossible width for a roadway.[6] In 1900 the Park Commission made an agreement with the Fort Erie Ferry Railway Company. The Company was awarded a franchise for an electric railway between Chippawa and Fort Erie along the Chain Reserve, conditional on the bank being protected and a road being constructed. Plans were prepared and approved by the Provincial Public Works Department, but the railway company didn't begin construction and the franchise lapsed.

In 1902 and 1903 small amounts were spent by the Commission acquiring more land for the roadway.[7] In 1904 the Commissioners reported "a heavy spring flood of ice, along with high water, caused erosion of the clay banks of the upper river. The erosion was so great that the existing roadway along the shore was in danger of being entirely cut away".[8] Contracts were let to dump rip-rap in places were erosion was the worst, to try to check the damage.

The Commissioners then went on to propose the construction of a boulevard from Queen Victoria

Park to Fort Erie, not only to check erosion, but also to provide a connecting link with the Old Fort Erie which the Commission leased from the Dominion Government in 1901. During the years, 1905, 1906, and 1907 more rip-rap was placed along the shore. In 1908 the Provincial Government authorized the issue of debentures to the limit of $100,000. The proceeds of these debentures were "to be applied by the Commissioners primarily toward the preservation of the bank of the Niagara River between Fort Erie and the southerly boundary of the Park against erosion, wash or other action by nature affecting or which may affect the same, and the construction of an esplanade on and along the said bank for public purposes, and of such width as may be determined, and for the purchase of such lands as may be necessary or the acquisition thereof by expropriation".[9]

In the spring of 1908 after the issue of debentures, the Commissioners were able to undertake the active purchase of lands and the construction of the boulevard. Surveys were made and after much discussion it was decided to acquire a minimum width of 30.5m (100 ft.) as far as the northerly boundary of the Village of Bridgeburg (Fort Erie North) and to extend from the Village of Chippawa into Queen Victoria Park by a new entrance closer to the river. The general rule for the roadway was to be a 4.6m (15 ft.) minimum for lawns and shrubbery adjoining the river, then 9m (30 ft.) of roadway and the remainder in lawns and shrubbery.[10]

The first section of the roadway extending south from Chippawa for about two kilometres (one and a quarter miles) was completed in 1908. A 12.2m (40 ft.) span bridge at Frenchman's Creek was

A plank bridge along the upper Niagara River road before the construction of the Boulevard.

The upper river road near Frenchman's Creek, circa 1920.

Scenes along the upper Niagara Parkway to-day.

completed that same year, and the section extending some 4.4 km (2.75 mi.) downstream from Bridgeburg was begun. Difficulties were encountered in purchasing the land required for a wider boulevard, and by 1910 only two sections of the boulevard had been completed and were in use.

In 1910 expropriation proceedings were begun against those farmers who were holding out for a better price, and who had in fact placed an exhorbitant value on their land. The average price paid by the Commission was two hundred dollars an acre (.40 ha) while the prevailing price was seventy-five dollars an acre (.40 ha). The Park Commissioners also paid ten dollars for each tree that was cut down.[11]

After the property was expropriated work began immediately on the two middle sections, Chippawa to Black Creek and Miller's Creek to Black Creek. The six bridges along the route required spans varying from 9.1 m (30 ft.) to 21.3 m (70 ft.) in length. The Commissioners reported in 1913 that they were "pleased in being able to report the practical completion of the Boulevard from Queen Victoria Park to Bridgeburg". It was not until 1915 that the road was completed through the villages of Bridgeburg and Fort Erie, when agreement was reached on the apportionment of costs. The Boulevard then extended from Chippawa to the Ferry Dock at Fort Erie, running along the river except for a 1.6 km (1 mi.) detour at the old shipyard property, which was being used for structural steel manufacturing.

In the winter of 1926 the Commissioners received a complaint about snow drifts on the Boulevard. Superintendent Jackson replied that the Commissioners regarded the Boulevard as a pleasure road for summer use.[12] It was not until 1927 when the Peace Bridge between Fort Erie and Buffalo was opened, that the upper Niagara Boulevard began to attract its full measure of automobile traffic. Before that time motorists had to take the Buffalo-Fort Erie Ferry across the Niagara River. The Ferry was slow when the time spent in the line-up waiting to board was considered.

With the increase in traffic from Buffalo by way of the Peace Bridge, the 5.5m (18 ft.) roadway, which had been considered more than adequate, proved to be too narrow, and a wider roadway with a heavier base was built in 1927 and 1928. It was 7.3 m (24 ft.) in width and had an asphalt surface. Between 1928 and 1939 the bridges over the creeks were rebuilt and the approaches widened.

The Boulevard required only routine maintenance until high water conditions in 1943 and 1944 again eroded the bank and more rip-rapping with stone was done at the river's edge. A constant program of rip-

rapping with large stone is required even in the present day, to prevent erosion of the bank.

When the Niagara Boulevard was first planned it had been expected that adjoining property would remain as farm land. However the frontage along the Boulevard was soon being subdivided into smaller lots, raising the possibility that there would be driveway entrances on to the road every fifty feet or so. The Park Commission solved this problem by offering in 1929 to build and maintain service roads parallel to the Boulevard on condition that ' an additional width of 9.14m (30 ft.) be transferred to the Commission to accommodate the proposed service roads.

The Townships of Willoughby and Bertie set different limits regulating the distance that homes should be set back from the service roads. The general set back was about 22.86 m (75 ft.). Building restrictions were also imposed by the Townships controlling commerical establishments along the Boulevard. By that time a number of motels and cabins had been built, catering to the tourist traffic which passed along the Boulevard from Fort Erie.

In 1955 a uniform system of roadway signs was adopted for the Boulevard, incorporating the letters NPC, for Niagara Parks Commission, in each sign. No attempt was made to restrict parking along the river side of the Boulevard and motorists parked indiscriminately, resulting in damage to the turf. In 1957, recognizing the need for designated parking facilities and not wanting to discourage the use of the river bank for picnicking, the Commission began a program of constructing small parking areas along the upper river, some accommodating as few as six or eight cars, with picnic tables placed conveniently close by.

In 1939 Regulations were drawn up restricting the use of display signs adjacent to the Boulevard and in 1942 through traffic by commercial vehicles was prohibited. The proximity of the river and the popularity of boating and sailing led the Commission in 1941 to issue licences for the use of temporary, rather than permanent docks. This was not a hindrance to boat owners, but rather a help, because of the destructive force of the spring ice runs which regularly damaged permanent dock installations.

The building of the Boulevard increased the value of the adjoining properties. The fine view of the river, was the attraction which provided the incentive for the erection of large residences, which in turn increased the demand for building lots at proportionately higher prices and also tended to discourage the erection of inferior structures. In 1973 the name of the Boulevard was changed to the Niagara Parkway.

Niagara Parks Archives

In 1982 the Niagara Parks Commission purchased the building on the Niagara Parkway in Fort Erie known as Bertie Hall. During the siege of Fort Erie in 1866 by the Fenians, the house was commandeered by enemy soldiers. This historic house was built in the mid 1830's by William Forsyth as a family home. Forsyth had been owner of the Pavilion Hotel at Niagara Falls and had sold his holdings in the Niagara Falls area to the firm of Clark and Street before moving to Fort Erie around 1833. It was named for Sir Peregrine Bertie who supported the passing of the Canada Bill in the British House of Lords on May 30, 1791.

Bertie Hall is constructed of stone and brick, the bricks being hauled by horse and wagon from Hamilton. It has a deep cellar hewn out of solid rock. Double parlours with high ceilings open off the main hall. There are four black Italian marble fireplaces in Bertie Hall, one in each parlour, one in the master bedroom and one in another room, probably used as a guest room.

Bertie Hall is leased to the Town of Fort Erie which in turn has sub-let it to the Mildred M. Mahoney Silver Jubilee Dolls' House Foundation, to house the Mildred M. Mahoney Silver Jubilee Dolls' House Gallery. The Gallery is open to view by the public for a nominal charge.

Mather Park - Mather Arch

The southern entrance to the system of parks and parkways under the jurisdiction of the Niagara Parks Commission is in Fort Erie. It encompasses Mather Park including its gardens, the seawall, Mather Arch and Old Fort Erie.

The 30.4 ha (75 acres) of land area of Mather Park were once part of the 404.7 ha (1000 acre) Ordnance Reserve which surrounded Old Fort Erie. Park Superintendent Wilson in 1896 described the area as beach land, often under water, and noted: "The protection of the shore of the lake will be very important, but also an expensive work, as the whole reach of the frontage . . . will require to be substantially rip-rapped and the back of the wall filled with soil to a level to be determined on. Stone for the wall may however, be quarried on the spot.[1]. In 1901 when the Park Commissioners received title to the lands on which Old Fort Erie stood, they did not acquire the land occupied by the present Mather Park. This land along the river between Fort Erie and the Old Fort belonged to Alonzo C. Mather.

Alonzo C. Mather was a wealthy manufacturer and inventor from Chicago who planned to build a bridge across the Niagara River, connecting Buffalo with Fort Erie. In 1902 the New York State Legislature gave Mather permission to build his bridge. However Mather could not obtain the necessary land for the American terminus of his bridge because the United States War Department controlled Fort Porter where Mather wanted to locate the American terminus. No bridge was built at that time.

In 1919 a public commission called the Buffalo and Fort Erie Peace Bridge Authority was formed, with representatives from both sides of the border. The purpose of the Authority was to erect a bridge from Buffalo to Fort Erie, to commemorate the one hundred years of peace between Canada and the United States. The bridge, named the Peace Bridge, was opened to traffic in 1927.

Mr. Mather's plans for his bridge included a Gateway Park at each terminus. In 1926, Mr. Mather deeded 5.5 ha (13.6 acres) of the property he had set aside for the Canadian terminus of his bridge to the Queen Victoria Niagara Falls Park Commission.[2] The Commission planned a Gateway Park for this site. Work did not begin on this Gateway Park, to be call Mather Park, until November 1933. It was a "make-work" project carried out during the Great Depression, with joint funding supplied by the Federal and Provincial Governments. Construction began on the seawall at the river's edge extending from the boundary of the Town of Fort Erie to the Old Fort. When the seawall had been completed, and the dried-off portion behind it filled in and seeded, more than one mile of lake front land had been reclaimed, extending from the Peace Bridge to Old Fort Erie.

Mr. Mather made a donation of $35,000 towards the development of the Park and the erection of a memorial gateway on the site. The gateway, an impressive arch in a modern monumental style, was designed by architects Carl A. Borgstrom, H.S.M. Carver and E.L. Sheppard. It was built at the

Mather Park Gate, the southern entrance to Ontario's Niagara Parks. This view in the 1960's was taken while the Ontario Provincial Police had their Fort Erie Detachment office at this location.

Mather Arch, 1984.

Fort Erie swimming area north of Mather Park.

Niagara Parks Archives

High water during a spring storm floods Mather Park.

Niagara Parks Archives

junction of the Peace Bridge exit from Buffalo, the Niagara River Boulevard and the Queen Elizabeth Highway. On August 31, 1940, Mather Arch, the only one of its kind in Canada erected in honour of a living American, was officially dedicated. Mr. Mather died in 1941 and left a legacy of money and property to continue the work on Mather Park.

Work resumed after the end of the war and a parapet of stone and masonry capped with a cut stone coping, was built on top of the seawall. The same forces of nature - water, wind and ice - which destroyed the first two Forts in 1779 and 1803, breached the seawall at Mather Park in 1954, 1955 and 1979. In each case a southern gale raised the level of the lake and drove water and ice against the

wall and breached it.

In 1970 the Town of Fort Erie War Memorial was moved from its location in the town to the east side of Mather Arch, facing the Niagara River and Buffalo. Here each November eleventh, Remembrance Day services are held honouring Fort Erie's War Dead. A memorial plaque was erected on August 19, 1978, adjacent to the Arch, honouring the contributions made by Alonzo C. Mather to the Niagara Parks Commission. The plaque serves as a constant reminder of the generous gifts of land and money made to the Niagara Parks Commission by this philanthropist - gifts that made Mather Park and Mather Arch possible.

Niagara Parkway
Queenston to Niagara-on-the-Lake

The Niagara Parkway between Queenston and Niagara-on-the-Lake is one of the oldest roads in Upper Canada. In 1791 Prince Edward, Duke of Kent, the father of Queen Victoria, visited Canada and Niagara Falls. Colonel John Clark in his *Memoirs* recalled: "They arrived safe at Niagara and were welcomed by Governor Simcoe who paid the Prince every attention his limited accommodation would allow. From thence the party proceeded on horseback by the River Road, then partly opened by the troops".[1]

When Township Number 1 (Niagara Township) was surveyed in 1791 the Chain Reserve was laid out along the steep bank of the river. In this position it was not suitable for a road, but a road did exist along the top of the high bank, above the Chain Reserve, in 1791. The road was called a "given road" because it was built on land owned and occupied by nearby farmers, but "given" by them for use as a road.

In 1798 the first stage-coach route in Upper Canada was in operation between Newark (now Niagara-on-the-Lake) and Chippawa, using the given road from Queenston to Newark. An advertisement in the *Upper Canada Gazette* of May 1798 declared: "J. Fairbanks and Thomas Hind acquaint friends and the public in general that their Stage will continue to run between Newark and Chippawa on Mondays, Wednesdays and Fridays; to start from Newark at 7 A.M. of each day and return the same evening, provided four passengers take seats by 4 in the afternoon. Otherwise to start from Chippawa by 7 o'clock the following morning and return the same

evening. Each passenger is allowed fourteen pounds of baggage, and to pay one dollar. Way passengers to be taken up at sixpence a mile York currency. Good horses and careful drivers are provided, and that attention and despatch which are necessary to the ease, satisfaction and convenience of passengers may always be expected. Letters fourpence each".[2]

A York shilling was worth about 1½ cents and a pound $2.50.[3]

The road was a strategic military road during the War of 1812-14, connecting Fort George, the principal military post on the frontier, with other outposts along the Niagara River at Chippawa and Fort Erie. During the War of 1812 a military camp was located at Brown's Point about midway between Queenston and Fort George.

Sir George Head, in writing of his travels in this area in 1829, described the road as follows: "I was scarcely out of town (Newark), when I was surprised and pleased . . . that the road to the Falls of Niagara is one of considerable traffic, and better in consequence, than other roads in the country . . . As I rode parallel to the Niagara River, which rolled its course on the left hand below me, through a rich ravine, whose elevated banks were covered with ornamental shrubs, I called to mind the banks of the Garonne in the south of France, to which country it bore a striking resemblance. The rich diversity of foliage which prevailed on every side . . . the wild peach, cherry, sassafras, hickory, aspen, sycamore, etc."[4]

The need for an improved road from Queenston to Niagara was not pressing in the late 1800's because

Corona entering the Niagara River from Lake Ontario, on its way to Queenston.

A view of the Cayuga as seen from the Parkway, 1950.

The lower Niagara Boulevard before reconstruction, 1920.

Historic marker on the site of the Vrooman Point battery, used during the battle of Queenston Heights.

of the availability of railway and steamship facilities. The extension of the Erie and Ontario Railway from Queenston to Niagara in 1854, provided a transportation link between Niagara Falls and Niagara. Lake boats coming from Toronto in the 1890's docked first at Lewiston, then at Queenston, where they made connections with the Niagara Falls Park and River Railway which ran to Niagara Falls and Chippawa.

It was not until the 1920's and the increased use of the automobile that the Park Commission was approached by Niagara-on-the-Lake citizens, asking that the road along the river from Queenston be improved. The Park Commissioners had completed the Niagara Boulevard from Niagara Falls to Queenston and in 1923 decided to extend it to Niagara-on-the-Lake. The Commission experienced difficulty in acquiring the land required for the road. In 1926 an agreement was made with the Township of Niagara which had jurisdiction over the existing road, whereby it would acquire sufficient land for a 30.5 m (100 ft.) wide road. In return for this the Park Commission undertook to build and maintain the new road. By 1927 enough land was available and

construction began. The new road was completed during the same year with the exception of a short stretch which was to cross the Military Reserve near Fort George. It was 1931 before the Dominion Government gave a right-of-way across the Military Reserve and the last link of the Boulevard, a continuous road from Lake Erie to Lake Ontario, was completed.

The height of the river bank made it difficult for the Parks Commission to provide boat launching ramps for pleasure boats along the lower river. In 1961 a boat launching ramp was installed at the Deep Hollow in Queenston. Boat docking privileges were granted to the St. Catharines Boat Club on the river bank near Paradise Grove. The Boat Club installed docks for the use of their members.

Ample provision is made for picnickers in a number of parkettes located along the river bank. The well appointed picnic area at McFarland Point Park is also available for group picnics. On a fine summer Sunday the river bank along the Niagara Parkway, is crowded with picnickers enjoying the weather and the view of the lower Niagara River.

McFarland Point Park, picnic pavilion.

Niagara Parks Archives

Old Fort Erie

Early in North American history, convenient water travel, excellent fishing and fertile soils attracted Indian tribes to the Fort Erie area. However it was the abundance of flint in the rocky ledges of the local Lake Erie shoreline that kept the native people here on a continuing basis. From this stone they fashioned their tools and weapons. In two local discoveries in 1964 and 1965, archeologists unearthed Indian artifacts and skeletons showing that occupation of this area dates back to an Early Woodland culture around 1000 B.C.[1]

It was also for commerical reasons that the early French fur traders in Canada built a trading post here in 1750. Then, in 1764, shortly after the ceding of New France to Britain at the close of the Seven Years War, the British began construction of the first Fort Erie on the riverbank, somewhat north of the location of the present Fort.

In the summer of 1764 the British, under General Bradstreet, organized a retaliatory expedition against the western Indians in revenge for the attacks made on British outposts by the Indian forces under Pontiac. Bradstreet arrived at Fort Niagara in July, 1764, and on July 7 he ordered his chief engineer, Captain Montresor, to proceed to the outlet of Lake Erie and select a proper place for fortifications. Montresor reached Lake Erie the next evening and after a day spent in exploration finally chose the site of the first Fort Erie on the west bank of the Niagara at the head of Lake Erie. He described its location as "on the northwest side just at the discharge." On July 10 he reported to Bradstreet who approved the site,

and a week later Montresor set out with 500 men to build the new post. This first Fort Erie was a rectangular enclosure composed of four bastions with connecting walls or curtains, as they were called. Adjacent to the lake the two demi-bastions with their curtains were rubble masonry of moderate height. The remaining bastions and curtains consisted merely of upright timbers in the form of a loopholed stockade. There was no ditch of any kind. Log barracks, officers' quarters and a large storehouse were built within the enclosure, and ground was levelled for a parade.

In March 1779 a furious storm drove great masses of ice ashore, flooding most of the fort and making breaches in the curtain facing the river. What remained of the walls and palisades was so damaged that it was considered necessary to rebuild the fort in a different manner, with stone and mortar. The second Fort Erie, located somewhat farther south, was built by detachments of British regiments.[2]

The second Fort Erie withstood the assaults of wind and weather for almost a quarter of a century until February 5, 1803 when another notable storm breached its walls and filled the interior with masses of ice and water. In July of that year, Colonel Gother Mann, who commanded the Royal Engineers in Canada, inspected the post. He reported to Lieutenant-Colonel Hunter at Fort Niagara that the existing Fort was extremely defective in position and recommended that a new Fort of a more permanent nature should be constructed upon rising ground immediately to the rear of the old location.

Old Fort Erie and the Migrations of the Wild Pidgeon in the Spring . Watercolour by Edward Walsh, 1804.

Ruins of Old Fort Erie at the outlet of Lake Erie, 1838. From a watercolour over pencil by P.J. Bainbrigge.

The new fort proposed by Colonel Mann was to consist of four bastions connected with curtains in the form of a simple square with all works and buildings constructed of solid masonry. It was to be large enough to accommodate two or three hundred men. Colonel Mann's recommendations were forwarded to the Master-General of the Ordnance and on January 9, 1804, Colonel Hunter was authorized by Lord Hobart, British Secretary of State, to direct that "the proposed works be commenced and carried on gradually as circumstances might render expedient." Britain was preoccupied with the Napoleonic Wars in Europe and so military works in the Colonies were not given priority. Work was carried on for almost three years until the end of 1807, when it was stopped by order of Lieutenant-General James Craig on his arrival at Quebec.[3].

Fort Erie was still in an unfinished state when war broke out in 1812. It was garrisoned by regular troops and militia until May 27, 1813, when news was received of the capture by the Americans of Fort George and Newark. The fort was then dismantled, the magazines exploded, and the small garrison retreated to join General Vincent's forces at Burlington Heights. It was occupied by a regiment of the regular American Army until June 9, when after setting fire to the barracks and storehouses, they abandonded the fort. The British later re-occupied it and stationed a small garrison there.

On July 3, 1814 Fort Erie was attacked by an American force of 4500 men under Major-General Jacob Brown. The British garrison, under Major Buck consisted of only 175 men. Buck realized that his position was hopeless and he surrendered the Fort. The American force, leaving only a small detachment to guard the Fort, advanced along the river road toward Chippawa. On July 26, the American Army, considerably reduced in strength after the Battles of Chippawa and Lundy's Lane, returned to Fort Erie. On August 2, the British appeared before the Fort and prepared for an assault on the American position. The British attack began at two o'clock on the morning of August 15 and in the course of the action the British forces penetrated the Fort's defences and established themeselves inside Fort Erie around a captured artillery position. Extra supplies of gun powder were stored under the gun platform in a pit which also held a large amount of other ammunition. During the course of the fighting, this store of gunpowder and ammunition blew up, killing 300 officers and men of the British invaders. The remaining British withdrew from the Fort itself and took up positions outside the Fort, staying there until mid September, when they lifted the siege and withdrew to Lundy's Lane, leaving the Fort in American hands.

Fort Erie was held by the American Army for another month and a half until they decided that the retention of the Fort was of no further strategic advantage to them. In order that the Fort would be of no further value to the British, the bastions were blown up by mines and the buildings burned. Taking its stores and equipment, the American garrison withdrew to Buffalo. The British never rebuilt Fort Erie as a military post.[4].

In 1896 Superintendent Wilson reported: "numerous petitions have been presented to the Park Commissioners by municipal and other administrative bodies in the county asking that the grounds around the ruins of Fort Erie . . . should be taken over from the Dominion Government and improved and maintained under the jurisdiction of the Commissioners as part of the Niagara Parks System".[10] The original Ordnance Reserve surrounding the Fort was 404.7 ha (1000 acres). Some years before Confederation in 1867, the Reserve was laid out in small lots and nearly all sold off. In 1896 all that remained of the original tract were: 7.1 ha (17½ acres) surrounding the ruins of the Fort; a 10 ha (25 acre) plot formerly occupied by the Buffalo and Lake Huron Railway; and 3 ha (7½ acres) of beach land. The plot of ground containing the ruins of the old Fort fronted on the Lake but was separated from it by the beach and the highway which was called Lake Shore Road.

In 1901 the Commission was granted a license of occupation by the Dominion Government for the 7.1 ha (17½ acres) surrounding the old Fort. It was 1903 before an ornamental garden wire fence was erected along the front of the property and a woven wire fence erected along the northern border. A neat Credit Valley sandstone gateway was put in place opposite the centre of the face of the Fort. Over the years the stone walls had deteriorated, from weather and from vandalism. The best of the stones from the rear bastion had been removed to furnish building material for the Anglican Church which was being built in the north end of the village of Fort Erie. In 1903 part of the main wall had to be repaired with cement mortar, to repair the damage done by vandals who had removed stones from the wall and thrown them about the grounds.

The Parliament of Upper Canada voted the sum of $1,750 for a monument to be erected on the grounds. The monument, consisting of a 9 m (30 ft.) circular shaft of Canadian Granite with carved

The Gateway and monument, 1906.

The open picnic shelter built in 1907.

capital and finial and with two bronze tablets suitably inscribed to commemorate the events involving the Fort in 1812-14, was completed in 1905. An imposing 30.5 m (100 ft.) high galvanized steel flagpole was also erected that year.

A start was made in improving the grounds in 1905. Uneven areas were ploughed and seeded, maples and elms were planted. A large open shelter was built within the fortification in 1907. It was a twelve sided structure, 11.3 m (37 ft.) in diameter which provided shelter from inclement weather.[5] In the Annual Report for 1914 Superintendent Jackson put forward the first suggestion that the old Fort be restored: "The task of ascertaining the outline and form of this old structure might well be undertaken . . . to the end that the ruins may be rebuilt when occasion warrants it." 1914 was the first season that the upper Niagara Boulevard was opened for the whole distance between Niagara Falls and Bridgeburg. There was, however, no satisfactory connecting road

to join the neighbouring village of Fort Erie with the Fort.

As a patriotic gesture during the First World War a portion of the Park property was planted in potatoes and beans in 1918, yielding 152.88 hl (420 bu.) of potatoes and 1452 kg (3200 lbs.) of beans. There was little or no profit from the venture as the workers who looked after the crops had to travel from headquarters in Niagara Falls. The Park operated without an adequate water supply until 1922 when a connection was made with the Town of Fort Erie's water main, providing a plentiful supply of water for picnickers. A picnic pavilion, where hot water was available for picnickers, was erected in 1933. It had lavatory facilities and space for a lunch counter.

In 1937 under a joint agreement between the Provincial and Federal Governments, to create work during the Depression, the restoration of Old Fort Erie was begun. During the restoration the bodies of

An air view of Old Fort Erie.

Members of the Guard dressed in the uniforms of the British 8th Foot Regiment.

some one hundred and fifty British and three American soldiers were unearthed. Friend and foe alike were reinterred in a stone vault. The soldiers' monument, erected in 1905, was relocated and rebuilt on top of this vault.

On July 1, 1939 the Old Fort was officially re-opened. With garrisoned soldiers wearing picturesque uniforms of 1812, and carrying old guns of that date, reconditioned and ready to fire, the Old Fort was in gala attire. The Honourable T.B. McQuesten, Chairman, and the members of the Niagara Parks Commission were present for the occasion.

By 1951 major repairs had to be made to the restored Fort. A section of the bastion wall 21.3 m (70 ft.) long and 7.6 m (25 ft.) high which had collapsed due to a poor foundation, was replaced. A new steel flagpole was erected to replace the wooden pole which collapsed the year before, and the timber drawbridge was completely rebuilt.

Restoration of the Fort was founded upon careful research and painstaking workmanship. Some of the barrack rooms are furnished, while others are used as a museum to display collections of regimental badges, buttons and other military mementoes, including

military equipment of the period represented by the Fort. It also has a superb collection of sixty-two military prints from the collection of Sir Henry Pellatt. To explain to visitors the heroic seige of August 1814, a large scale model illustrates the British and American fortifications. Visitors are conducted through the museum's many display rooms by guards dressed in the 1812-14 period uniforms of the British 8th Foot Regiment, which built, defended and later beseiged the Fort. Several times during the day in the summer months, the members of the Guard carry out a program of manoeuvres, including the firing of cannon, changing of the guard and drill exercises.

Since 1979 more emphasis has been placed on the learning experience that the Fort has to offer, rather than its general interest value. A visit to Old Fort Erie is a visual exercise in the teaching of history. In crossing the drawbridge to go into the Fort, the visitor finds himself to all intent and purpose amongst the authentic surroundings of another age. While he is on the actual ground where the action took place, it is easier for him to associate with the events of the past.

Niagara Parks Archives

Since the 1960's a series of band concerts has been held at Old Fort Erie. At first the concerts were shared between the Fort Erie No. 1 Fire Company Band and the Royal Canadian Legion Band, with guest appearances from time to time by the Caledonia Pipe Band of Buffalo. Currently concerts provided by the Royal Canadian Legion Band of Fort Erie, under the direction of William Fenwick, are held each Sunday afternoon, from the last week of June until the end of August. The musicians play in the new bandshell which was officially dedicated on August 19, 1979. Concerts are free to the public and are paid for by the Niagara Parks Commission and the Musicians Performance Trust Fund.

Fort George, Navy Hall, Butler's Burying Ground

The Niagara Parks Commission and its predecessor, the Queen Victoria Niagara Falls Park Commission, were associated with Niagara-on-the-Lake and active in the restoration of its historic sites ever since the early days of the Commission. In 1896 Commission Chairman John Langmuir asked Superintendent Wilson to bring in a report on the Ordnance Lands at Niagara-on-the-Lake, including Forts George and Mississauga. The report was to comment on the advisability of the Queen Victoria Niagara Falls Park Commission acquiring control of these properties for Park purposes, and of preserving them from further deterioration. Two tracts of land were involved, the Garrison Reserve, an area of some 137.6 ha (340 acres) on which stood the ruins of Fort George, Navy Hall, and Butler's Barracks and the 24.3 ha (60 acre) tract at the mouth of the Niagara River, surrounding Fort Mississauga.

Superintendent Wilson's report in the Queen Victoria Park Commission's Annual Report of 1896 included estimated costs of acquisition and maintenance. No action was taken, the Commissioners chose instead to concentrate on preserving Old Fort Erie at the head of Lake Erie. In 1905 the matter was brought up again when Miss J. Carnochan, a school teacher and historian in Niagara-on-the-Lake, wrote to the Commission asking it to take charge of the Forts, George and Mississauga, as the Town of Niagara-on-the-Lake Council refused to do anything to preserve them. No action was taken on Miss Carnochan's request.

The Commission's first acquisition of land in the

Butler's Burying Ground, 1984.

Niagara Parks Archives

Niagara-on-the-Lake area was Butler's Burying Ground. This was the family burial plot of Colonel John Butler, the leader of Butler's Rangers. The Annual Report of 1907 stated: "The Legislature at its last Session passed an Act authorizing the

A view of Fort George from Fort Niagara, from an old engraving.

Fort George from the air.

Navy Hall, restored by the Niagara Parks Commission, now in the care of Parks Canada.

Commissioners to acquire, repair and preserve the small plot of ground near the Town of Niagara-on-the-Lake where Colonel John Butler, Colonel Claus and many others famous in the early history of the Province, lie buried. Upon examination it was found that this God's half acre had been greatly neglected, the head stones nearly all broken, the vault opened and desecrated and the burial ground an open pasture field".

After considerable negotiation the Commissioners purchased Butler's Burying Ground from the Dominion Government in 1909. The plot was fenced and restoration and improvements were carried out. The cemetery remained in the care of the Parks Commission until 1979, when as part of Parks Canada's Master Plan relating to historic sites in Niagara-on-the-Lake, the Commission entered into a lease agreement to enable Parks Canada to assume responsibility for the operation and maintenance of Butler's Burying Ground.

The economic depression of the 1930's resulted in "make-work" projects funded by the Federal and Provincial Governments. Under a cost sharing agreement with the Federal Government the reconstruction of Fort George was carried out by the Niagara Parks Commission, beginning in 1937. Fort

George, under the administration of the Department of National Defence, had been allowed to deteriorate. The palisade and wooden buildings had disappeared entirely; only part of the stone powder magazine remained. A decision had to be made as to which period in the history of the Fort would be represented by the restoration. Ronald L. Way, a professional historian who was involved in the restoration of Fort Henry in Kingston, was retained by the Parks Commission to undertake the research and he recommended that the Fort be restored to its original state when it was built by the order of Lieutenant-Governor Simcoe in 1797.

The awarding of all contracts was conditional upon the contractor hiring, wherever possible, persons who were on relief (today's term, welfare). According to Walter Haldorson, present Superintendent of Niagara National Historic Parks, wage scales for the restoration were quite different from today's wage scales: 35 cents an hour for unskilled labourers, 60 or 70 cents an hour for skilled tradesmen; a full $1.00 an hour for supervisors.

The restoration was completed in time for the Fort to be opened to the public on July 1, 1940. It was not until June 18, 1950 that the Fort was officially opened. The establishment of an extensive

The Niagara Parks Commission commissioned Elizabeth Wyn Wood in 1952 to design and sculpt a memorial to Lieutenant-Governor John Graves Simcoe and Mrs. Simcoe. This memorial depicts full figures of the Lieutenant-Governor and Mrs. Simcoe. It was erected in front of the restored Navy Hall and unveiled on July 29, 1953 by the Honourable Leslie M. Frost, Premier of Ontario.

Parks Canada

museum collection in the Fort was the occasion for this official ceremony. In 1953 the Niagara Parks Commission received from the Department of National Defence, the Crown Grant of the land on which Fort George stands. The Commission operated the Fort as a tourist attraction until October 1, 1969 when jurisdiction over the Fort was transferred back to the Federal Government, to the National and Historic Parks Branch of the Department of Indian and Northern Affairs to be operated as a National Historic Park.

In 1937 the Niagara Parks Commission undertook to restore one of the four clapboard buildings which had been erected in 1765 as a naval barracks for the Provincial Marine, called Navy Hall. About 1792 one of the buildings had been converted into a residence by Lieutenant-Governor John Graves Simcoe and was used by him during his stay in the area. Navy Hall, the only building remaining in 1937, was in an advanced state of deterioration. A

long low structure, with axe-hewn timbers covered with narrow board siding, it had been moved in 1864 from its original site on the river bank. The Commissioners decided to preserve the existing building rather than undertake a complete restoration. What was left of Navy Hall was moved back to its former location, and encased in a new stone building. The interior still reveals the axe-hewn and hand-sawn boarding of the original structure.

On November 1, 1969 Navy Hall was transferred from the jurisdiction of the Niagara Parks Commission to the National Historic Parks Branch, Department of Indian and Northern Affairs, of the Federal Government. The Administrative Offices of Niagara National Historic Parks were located in Navy Hall until September 1984, when they were moved to the Old Court House in Niagara-on-the-Lake. Navy Hall will be open to view starting with the 1985 season.

McFarland House
and
McFarland Park

In 1953 the Niagara Parks Commission acquired the McFarland or Taggart House and 12.14 ha (30 acres) of land, located on the lower Niagara Boulevard about 3.2 km (2 miles) upriver from Fort George. This red brick, Georgian style house was built in 1800 on land which was granted by the Crown to John McFarland on December 31, 1798. During the War of 1812 a British battery was emplaced behind the house to command the river. From the foot of the ravine north of the house a force under Colonel John Murray, consisting of Detachments of the 100th and 41st Regiments, Royal Scots, Royal Artillery and Canadian Militia, embarked in bateaux and crossed the Niagara River to a point above Youngstown, New York. They attacked Fort Niagara, killing or capturing all the members of its American garrison. The house was also used as a hospital during the war by both British and Americans in turn, as each had possession of the place.[1]

The Niagara Parks Commission, in recognition of the historic importance of the house and its surrounding property, began restoration in 1959. All of the rooms in the front part of the structure, which dates back to 1800, were refurbished. Floors were scraped, sanded and stained and walls were papered with appropriate wallpaper. The furnishings of the rooms were representative of the 1800's although the back part of the house was added much later. The house was opened to view on May 31, 1959 at a small admission charge. In 1973 a further and more complete restoration was undertaken.

The spacious grounds adjoining McFarland House, comprising 12.14 ha (30 acres), were made into a picnic grounds in 1957. A feature of this park when it opened was the hexagonal-shaped picnic shelter, built of stone and timber. It has a conical roof and a plexiglass dome. The floor is concrete and the shelter will accommodate 400 picnickers at the tables. The tables are unique as they were designed and built to fit the hexagonal shape of the shelter. Since 1957 similar shelters have been erected at Old Fort Erie, Queenston Heights and the Niagara Glen. In 1983 the McFarland park shelter was enclosed to provide protection from inclement weather.

The Park is divided by a deep ravine, and in order to provide pedestrian access, a substantial timber bridge was built across the ravine. Public washrooms and a store for selling picnic supplies are located in the rear of the McFarland House. A children's playground was installed in 1962 on the south side of the house. McFarland Park is a popular weekend picnic spot and on a sunny summer Sunday the Park is crowded with picnickers.

McFarland House front view.

Harry Mottershead

Inside restoration.

Niagara Parks Archives

Capture of Fort Niagara Plaque.

The curved timber bridge at McFarland Park, 1984.

Stoney Creek Battlefield and Battlefield House

In 1962 the Women's Wentworth Historical Society which had maintained Battlefield House for sixty-three years, deeded the house, formerly occupied by the Gage family, to the Niagara Parks Commission who restored it to the period of the 1830's. Battlefield House stands on the site of the Battle of Stoney Creek which took place on June 6, 1813.

The outlook for Upper Canada in the early summer of 1813 was bleak. War had been declared by the United States against Britain in June 1812, and Upper Canada was to be the prize. The American campaign of 1813 began on April 26, with Commodore Chauncey's successful naval attack on York, the capital of Upper Canada. Following this action during which most of the buildings in York were burned, the American Army under Major-General Henry Dearborn attacked Fort George at the mouth of the Niagara River. The British defenders, led by Major-General Vincent, realizing that they could not defend Fort George, retreated westward, along Lake Ontario to the safety of Burlington Heights, leaving the Americans in control of the whole of the Niagara Peninsula including Fort Erie.

An American force of 2000 men led by Brigadier-Generals Chandler and Winder, pursued the British, intending to destroy General Vincent's force. On June 5, 1813 they arrived at Stoney Creek where they established camp at James Gage's farm, making the Gage house their headquarters. The cleared and cultivated land of the farm was ideal for defence. On the left stood the escarpment and on the right a swamp and beyond that, dense forest. Running through the property was a tributary of Stoney Creek. Except for the bridge over this stream, the camp was protected from attack.

On the Afternoon of June 5, Isaac Corman was captured and then released by the Americans. During his captivity he obtained their countersign for the day, which he passed on to Billy Green, his brother-in-law. Green immediately relayed it to Lieutenant-Colonel Harvey who had already reconnoitred the American position and believed it to be vulnerable to surprise attack. Now, having the password, Harvey convinced General Vincent that a night attack on the American position would be successful.

Harvey's force reached the American sentry posts, which gave way without a struggle on hearing the countersign. The British rushed on to the flat meadow where they expected to find the American troops sleeping around the campfires, only to find that the fires were abandoned cooking fires and the sleeping troops were in a stronger position higher up on the ridge above the meadow.

In the ensuing action British casualties were 23 killed, 136 wounded and 55 missing, while the American losses mounted to 168 men, including prisoners.[2] Both American Generals, Winder and Chandler, were taken captive during the action. The Americans withdrew in great haste, leaving what equipment they could not destroy, not even stopping to bury their dead, and before noon that day they had deserted the battlefield and were retreating towards Fort George. Within three days of that battle, later to be known as the Battle of Stoney Creek, the situation along the Niagara Frontier had changed completely. On June 9 the Americans burned Fort Erie. On June 21 they evacuated Queenston after an aborted attack on Beaverdams. They retreated to a position behind the palisades at Fort George where they stayed until the coming of winter forced them to return to the United States.

After the Battle of Stoney Creek, the Gage family took the wounded from both sides into their house. The dead were buried by local people and soon the signs of battle disappeared. Dead horses, guns and baggage were removed from the field and only the presence of musket ball holes in the farm house itself remained as evidence of the fierce battle which had taken place.

Who were these Gages whose land was to become part of history? James Gage and his brother, William, were born in County Derry Ireland, in 1744 and 1746. They emigrated to New Windsor, in New York State. Here they married sisters, Mary and Susannah Jones. When the American Revolution broke out, the brothers were enlisted in the New York Militia and in June 1777, James was killed defending Fort Clinton against the British.[3] Mary and James had two children, James, aged three at the time of his father's death, and Elizabeth, aged one.

In 1789 Mary's younger brother, Augustus Jones, was appointed surveyor of Upper Canada. He moved to Saltfleet Township and was followed by Mary and her two children, and his sister and brother-in-law, Susannah and William Gage. The Gages took the oath of allegiance to the British Crown, were given free land, and set about a new life in the new country. In the difficult first years they had to clear the land, sow crops and build a log house.

The Battle of Stoney Creek Monument, erected 1913.

Niagara Parks Archives

Battlefield House restored, circa 1980.

Niagara Parks Archives

In 1796 both James and Elizabeth married, Elizabeth to Major John Westbrook and James to Mary Davis, daughter of a well-to-do United Empire Loyalist from North Carolina, who built a house and mills at Albion Mills. James and Mary remained on the farm with Mary Gage, James' mother. When the Americans bivouacked on their land on June 5, 1813 at least five of their children had been born and they had a comfortable farm house with two fireplaces and a loft upstairs.

In 1899, eighty-six years after the Battle of Stoney Creek, the Gage farmhouse was offered for sale, for $1900. At that time there was no memorial to mark the graves of those who died, no monument to remind future generations of the valour displayed by those who took part in this action. When the Pioneer and Historical Society of the County of Wentworth, composed entirely of men, refused to

buy the property, women who belonged to the Ladies Auxiliary of the Society, formed the Women's Wentworth Historical Society with Mrs. John Calder, grandaughter of James Gage, as its first president. They raised $900 to buy the house and Mrs. Calder signed a mortgage for the balance. They now possessed the farmhouse and about 1.8 ha (4½ acres) of land. The house was renovated and furnished as a museum with donations from the Gages and local families, and opened to the public as Battlefield House.

In 1910 Mrs. Calder and the Women's Wentworth Historical Society were able to purchase an additional 5.26 ha (13 acres) of the Gage's original Crown Grant of land.

Their next project was to raise a monument to commemorate the battle and the men who fought in it. This they persuaded the Dominion Government to

The dining-room, Battlefield House.

Niagara Parks Archives

The parlour with its open fireplace.

Niagara Parks Archives

The master bedroom, Battlefield House.

Niagara Parks Archives

A bedroom with a spinning wheel and cradle.

do The architect was Mr. J. Rastrick of Hamilton and the 30.5 m (111 ft.) monument was a copy of Nelson's monument at Calton Hill, Edinburgh. Although stonemasons were brought from Scotland, local stone from Queenston and Georgetown was used in the monument. On June 6, 1913, one hundred years after the Battle of Stoney Creek, the monument was unveiled. Queen Mary in Buckingham Palace touched a button and by telegraph connection of the Canadian Pacific Railway, the large Union Jack which covered the monument was released.[4]

In 1960 the Women's Wentworth Historical Society learned that 6.87 ha (17 acres) of land, known as the Smith property, immediately to the west of Battlefield House, was to be sold to developers. Unable to finance a purchase of this size, the Society asked the Niagara Parks Commission for assistance. The Commission had shown an interest in Battlefield Park by contributing toward the maintenance costs of the Park since 1924 with an annual grant of $1000, changed to $800 annually in 1933.

Arrangements were negotiated by the Niagara Parks Commission whereby the Federal Government agreed to contribute $25,000 toward the cost of acquiring the Smith property and $20,000 toward the preservation of Battlefield House. The balance, $30,000 was contributed by the Provincial Government. In addition the Federal Government made the necessary repairs to the monument and to the steps leading up to it. The Ontario Government provided for the building of a combined refreshment stand - washroom and for a timbered bridge over the creek.

The Parks Commission's Horticultural Depart-

ment cleared the acres of dead and diseased fruit trees and established turf; removed all the overgrown brush leading up to and around the monument; cleaned out the creek that winds through the property. A formal garden was designed and planted in front of Battlefield House; an Herb Garden was planted just north and east of the house, and foundation planting was carried out, using plant materials suitable to the 1800's. The Roads and Engineering Department of the Niagara Parks Commission constructed parking lots and laid out nature trails in the woods to the south. An underground watering system was installed. In 1961 Battlefield House was open to view and 1 338 visitors were recorded.

On January 19, 1962 the Women's Wentworth Historical Society transferred the deed of the original Gage house to the Niagara Parks Commission. An arrangement was made at the same time with the Federal Department of Northern Affairs and Natural Resources for the transfer of jurisdiction over the monument to the Commission.

Beginning in 1973 the house was restored to the period of 1790 - 1835. Old paint and plaster were removed and paints matching the original colours were used. A museum section was installed with a 35 mm audio-visual presentation on the Battle of Stoney Creek. The cost to the Niagara Parks Commission was $75,083. The renovated house was re-opened on May 15, 1976. A fire on August 8. 1977, caused $25,000 damage to the roof and to the second floor audio-visual room. The House was closed for repairs during the remainder of the 1977 season and re-opened in May 1978.

In 1979 a curator was appointed at Battlefield House, one of whose priorities was to increase public awareness about the Battlefield and the House, within the Stoney Creek and Hamilton areas. Now the Battlefield House lives through participation tours. Children of all ages come into the House to try their hand at carding wool and using a drop spindle. They help prepare a dish for the bake pot, and they taste the result. They grind the herbs and dip candles. When they try on dresses and uniforms of an earlier period they engage in role-playing. Suddenly they are not only learning their history, they are a part of it.

Special events focus on the family. It is not unusual to see children from school tours coming back with their parents for special events so that the children can demonstrate how they, too, have learned to card the wool. The most important special event that takes place at the Battlefield House and Park is Military Heritage Day in June. Here in memory of the events of more than one hundred and seventy years ago visitors to Battlefield Park watch, as British and American armies once again re-enact the Battle of Stoney Creek.

A view from the Stoney Creek Battle Monument, looking toward Lake Ontario. Battlefield House is in the centre.

Niagara Parks Archives

Drummond Hill Cemetery and Lundy's Lane Battlefield

In 1909 the Ontario Legislature recognized the importance of the burying ground on Drummond Hill, the site of the Battle of Lundy's Lane, and proposed that it should be placed in the care of the Queen Victoria Niagara Falls Park Commission. A Statute was passed and in the same year the cemetery was transferred to the care of the Park Commission. In 1910 an additional .4 ha (1 acre) was added, making the total area of the cemetery 1.6 ha (4 acres).

In 1795 a log church for the use of all denominations, the second place of public worship in the Niagara area, was built facing Lundy's Lane on what is now known as Drummond Hill. There was a small burying ground adjacent to it. John Burch was buried there in 1797. His grave stone reads; "First interment in this yard". In 1799, Christopher Boughner donated a .20 ha (½ acre) plot of land which, with the church burying ground, became the nucleus of present day Drummond Hill Cemetery.

It was on these heights of Drummond Hill Cemetery that British General Phineas Riall chose to set up his artillery on July 25, 1814. The war between Britain and the United States had been going on for two years. After their defeat at the Battle of Chippawa on July 5, 1814, the British forces led by Riall, retreated to Burlington Heights at the western end of Lake Ontario, leaving the American Army in control of the whole of the Niagara Frontier, with the exception of Fort George. By July 24, the Americans, who had been threatening a siege of Fort George, decided to withdraw to their permanent camp at Street's Creek above Chippawa. Riall used this opportunity to advance with his troops and return to the Niagara area, anxious to engage the American Army and avenge his defeat.

This position on the heights gave him a commanding view over the Portage Road, the route the American Army would have to travel from Chippawa to engage him. From this vantage point he waited for the American reaction. It was 6 o'clock on the evening of July 25 before the American General Brown arrived with his force to attack the British position on the hill. Most of the ensuing battle took place in darkness with the American forces making repeated attempts to take the artillery position. It was midnight before the fighting subsided, with both sides exhausted. Although neither side could claim a victory - the British suffered 880 officers and men killed and wounded while the American casualties were 860 - this action checked the American advance into Upper Canada. The Americans withdrew to their camp at Chippawa and after a brief foray the next day to reconnoitre the area, they withdrew to Fort Erie and subsequently returned to the United States.

It was not long after the War of 1812-14 before the battlefield of Lundy's Lane became a pilgrimage site for Americans. By 1845 the first observation tower had been built on Lundy's Lane opposite the cemetery, overlooking the battlefield site. It was a 12 m (40 ft.) high tower, built of wood. At one time

The monument erected in 1895 by the Dominion Government.

between 1845 and 1893 there were five towers overlooking the battlefield, which remained a point of interest to Americans until the beginning of the American Civil War in 1861. After the Civil War, Lundy's Lane Battlefield and Drummond Hill Cemetery did not regain their former popularity because Gettysburg became the focus of attention for American battle pilgrims. Without the revenue from the admission fees from American tourists, the Trustees of the cemetery and the battlefield did not have adequate revenue for maintenance. The towers were dismantled and the upkeep of the cemetery was neglected.

In 1895 the Dominion Government erected a monument, a stone obelisk, flanked by cannon, in the cemetery close to Lundy's Lane and in 1901 the Ontario Historical Society erected a bronze bust memorial on the grave site of Laura Secord who was buried there in 1868. These monuments were located close together and the area around them was kept clean and neat, while the rest of the cemetery was left uncared for.

The results of years of neglect in the Drummond Hill Cemetery were obvious. Marble slabs that marked graves had crumbled and chipped. Inscriptions on some of the markers were almost indecipherable. In the clear areas without markers whole pioneer families were known to be buried, but every stone bearing their names was gone.[1] Work began in 1911

to clean up the Cemetery. The old graves were levelled. Unmarked graves were designated by neat stone slabs. Trees and shrubs were planted, paths were laid out and the whole area was contoured and landscaped for easy maintenance. In 1924 a brick building was erected adjacent to the church to serve as a caretaker's office and public washrooms.

In 1911 during the work of restoring and landscaping the cemetery, the bodies of nine American soldiers were discovered. They were re-interred with military ceremony under the auspices of the Lundy's Lane Historical Society, with representatives from American Historical Societies and the United States Army assisting. Memorial services conducted each year by the Lundy's Lane Historical Society on the anniversary of the battle, are attended by interested people and military representatives from both sides of the international border. Of particular interest are the graves of the unknown American soldiers, the grave of Laura Secord and the grave of United States Army Captain, Abraham Hull, the son of General Hull, the American commander at Detroit in 1812.

In 1937 the National Historic Sites and Monuments Board placed three tablets on the 1895 monument, bearing the names of the officers and soldiers of the regular regiments of the British Army and the Canadian Militia killed in action during the Battle of Lundy's Lane. In 1948 ornamenal iron gates were installed at the Buchner Place entrance off

The gravestone of Captain Abraham Hull, U.S. Army.

Niagara Parks Archives

Markers on the graves of the unknown American soldiers.

Niagara Parks Archives

Drummond Road. (Buchner is the modern spelling of Boughner, the name of the original donor of the land for the cemetery). During the 1960's there was a brief flurry of interest and some consternation when the Department of Northern Affairs of the Federal Government announced that it planned to establish a National Historic Park at the cemetery. The plan included the removal of historic Drummond Hill Presbyterian Church and public reaction to this resulted in the abandonment of the project.

All burial plots in Drummond Hill Cemetery were sold years ago, although grave spaces are still sold privately and burial rights are authorized by surviving families. There have been 345 interments in the Cemetery over the last 34 years (1950-1984).

Access to the cemetery was cut off from the east in 1956 when a 1.8 m (6 ft.) high chain link fence was erected, preventing casual pedestrian traffic through the cemetery. Because of vandalism, the fence was extended across the north end in the 1980's. The most recent addition to this fence was erected in 1983, running from Lundy's Lane south to the caretaker's office. The only entrance now is through the wrought iron gates at the end of Buchner Place. The Niagara Parks Commission encourages the public to visit this historic cemetery and battlefield site.

Horticulture

The Niagara area has long been noted for its varied and unusual flora. The largest area of the Niagara Parks System is nestled along the Niagara River, some of it protected by the Niagara Escarpment and all of it climatically tempered by the bordering lakes. This unique geographical location provides moderating weather conditions, not usually found at this latitude, which permit numerous species and varieties of exotic plants, including trees, shrubs, vines and flowers to grow, in fact, thrive, within this region.

As far back as 1888, a renowned botanist, David F. Day of Buffalo, New York, recorded 909 separate species of "flowering and fern-like plants", growing naturally in the vicinity of the Falls.[1] Further botanical studies were undertaken six years later, when 900 distinct plant species, composed of 105 plant families and 147 genera, were actually catalogued, mounted and preserved, by Roderick Cameron the Queen Victoria Park's Chief Gardener.[2] This work was the beginning of a modest Herbarium. During this same period, the Chief Gardener prepared a valuable flora collection of over 700 plant specimens. Some of these mounted specimens can still be viewed in the Herbarium at the School of Horticulture. In more recent years, the late George H. Hamilton, B.A. M.Sc., Botanist for the Commission, wrote **Plants of the Niagara Parks System.** It was published by the Commission in 1943, and has proven to be an excellent reference book for this area.

The Commission, from its inception, realized the importance of trees and other flora in future park development. As a result, a wide range of plant materials was imported and propagated and then utilized in park plantings. When the Park Commissioners took over the present Queen Victoria Park area, it was practically bare of trees. The Park staff planted 269 trees in Queen Victoria Park of different varieties including: Dover Elm, Sugar and Silver leafed Maples, Dogwood, Horse Chestnut, Basswood, Laurel leafed Willow, Norway Spruce, Quince, Mountain Ash, Walnut and White and Red Cedar.[3] Since the beginning of the Park a tree replacement programme has been carried out.

Several unusual tree plantings have taken place. In the 1830's when Captain Ogden Creighton had his estate at the north end of the present day Queen Victoria Park, he planted slips of willow trees brought from the Island of St. Helena, Napoleon's place of exile. It is not known if any descendants of those trees remain today. In 1937 "Acorns from Windsor Great Park in England were received as a Coronation memento and planted".[4]

Over the years, plant nurseries were established and staffed with trained gardeners. One of the earliest nurseries was situated on a parcel of land above the escarpment, just north-east of Jolly Cut and the present Skylon Tower. In 1934, this land was exchanged in part for the present site of Oakes Garden Theatre, then owned by Commissioner Harry Oakes.[5]

In 1956, tragedy struck the tree population of the

The Centennial Tulip developed for the 100th Anniversary of Ontario's Niagara Parks.

Niagara Parks Archives

Elm trees affected by Dutch Elm disease circa 1959. One of the entrance gates to the Ontario Hydro Tunnels is at left centre.

Niagara Parks Archives

The main log of the damaged Black Walnut tree removed from Queen Victoria Park. It was sold for $3500 and shipped to Italy to be made into walnut veneer. This log was 122 cm (48 in.) in diameter and 5.18 m (17 ft.) long.

The Black Walnut tree removed from the Park was estimated to be from 170 to 180 years old.

Niagara Parks, when the first American Elm (Ulmus Americana) fell to the dreaded Dutch Elm disease. Knowing full well that the disease would spread, immediate steps were taken by the Horticultural Department to seek out the best method of control from Government Plant Pathology Stations. An extensive and time consuming inventory of trees on Commission property revealed that the elm population on accessible lands was approximately 8,350 trees, representing over 15 per cent of the total Park hardwoods. Although the recommended control programme of spraying and removing and burning diseased elms was rigidly followed, 1,083 trees were lost in the next seven years. Since that time, the removal and decline of this majestic tree species has been continuous, today only a handful of specimens remains. Fortunately, the death of these trees was gradual, permitting the Commission to replant with other species and varieties from its nurseries.

Since 1888 when the Park Works Department had responsibility for the care of 62.2 ha (154 acres) of Queen Victoria Park, the Horticultural Department's responsibility has grown to include the 1130 ha (2792 acres) of the present day Niagara Parks. It is also responsible for property deeds, leases, easements and surveys; and issues licenses and permits for docks, shore wells, water lines, and sewers on Park property. In 1888 when the Works Department looked after the Park grounds in addition to its other duties, such as laying out roads and paths, repairing Park bridges and equipment, it employed one Chief Gardener and an average of seven workmen a day the year round. The staff of the Horticulture Department to-day has grown to 65 employees. Augmented by 148 seasonal employees. There are 36 students at the School of Horticulture.

In 1950 the Annual Report of the Niagara Parks Commission carried this statement; "There are wild natural areas in the Niagara Parks. There are formal garden areas unsurpassed in beauty on this continent. There are areas designed for quiet enjoyment, wooded and secluded yet readily accessible, within easy walking distance of a car parking area, where the things of nature, God's handiwork, practically untouched by man, may be studied and enjoyed".

An Easter display of lilies in the Greenhouse, 1966.

Willis E. Beese

The tulip bed in front of the illumination battery, 1968.

Willis E. Beese

Greenhouse - Conservatory

Niagara Parks have long been famous for picturesque gardens, floral displays and special indoor conservatory exhibitions.

Following old European traditions, Commission gardeners have for years produced unusual plantings. These intricate floral designs utilize colourful dwarf foliage plants, such as Alternanthera, Santolina and Echeveria. This type of gardening is referred to as "Carpet Bedding", and dates back to the Romans. One of the best examples of this ancient floral art, is on the face of the Floral Clock, where about 19,000 plants are used annually.

The main attraction to the Niagara area is, of course, the Falls themselves. However, once the majestic cataracts have been viewed and photograped, it is equally true that visitors linger to gaze at and admire the well manicured lawns, restful vistas and colourful floral gardens. Over the years, these ornamental displays have inspired hundreds of visitors to landscape and improve their properties. Evidence of this can be found in the many telephone calls and letters received, along with the personal contacts made with staff, requesting floral plans and the names of flowering trees and shrubs, complete with cultural information.

The first Commissioners realized that the success of any ornamental park undertaking, was to have available high quality and unusual plant materials. Unfortunately, these two prerequisites are not found at all commerical greenhouse and nursery outlets. The obvious answer to this problem is to grow your own. With this in mind, two small wooden framed greenhouses were erected in Queen Victoria Park in 1894, directly opposite the powerhouse of the Electrical Development Company. Although this was a beginning, the greenhouses soon proved to be inadequate in size, both as a source of annuals and for the propagation and production of tropical exhibition materials. Three years later, in 1897, a modest 18.3 m by 6 m (60 ft. by 20 ft.) public conservatory was constructed, along with a plant propagation house and fernery.

These facilities sufficed until 1909, when it was necessary to add to the existing buildings.

In the early 1940's, a section of one of the oldest greenhouses collapsed, seriously injuring a gardener. Due to World War II, construction materials were at a premium, consequently rebuilding was delayed.

Finally, in 1945 the Commission constructed a new, modern 1021.9 m^2 (11,000 sq. ft.) conservatory, complete with growing houses, spacious work rooms and long needed public washrooms. The entire complex was centrally heated with hot water and boasted one of the first steam soil-pasteurizers. The latter was instrumental in reducing soil borne plant diseases and insects as well as eliminating unwanted weed-seeds.

Construction of the new greenhouse complex was not without its problems, as excavations for the basement and boiler were hampered by shallow bed rock and large river boulders, some weighing up to five and six tons. Dynamite was used to blast away

The Greenhouse of 1894, with the nursery on the left and the home of the Chief Gardener hidden in the trees to the right.

The new Greenhouse, 1953.

The new Visitors' Centre at the Greenhouse, 1981. The Spirit of Park Hall Fountain is on the right.

Niagara Parks Archives

these obstructions, making way for the giant boilers and large hot water mains.

As the Niagara Parks increased in size, more and more flowering plants were required to beautify the ornamental areas. This necessitated the construction of several small growing houses that were attached to the existing complex.

Finally, in June 1980, a spacious Visitors' Reception Centre and Garden Shop, complete with modern washrooms, was aesthetically attached to the front of the existing show houses. The new structure of glass, wood and stone, covered 522.5 m² (5,625 sq. ft.), with the central glass dome rising to 12.2 m (40 ft.). This permits the growing of full size palms and other tropicals. The new building is an ideal setting for special flower shows at Christmas and Easter and has become one of the main features in the Park.

In 1937-38, the outside display gardens received approximately 40,000 plants from the greenhouses. In the spring of 1983, over 150,000 annual and perennial plants were flatted up by the greenhouse growers and planted throughout the park system. In addition to the bedding plants, over 5,800 exhibition pot plants were grown and displayed in the public show houses. This ensures a year-round floral show for the touring public.

Unlike commercial greenhouse growers who produce fairly common and easy to grow varieties in assembly line fashion, the Commission has always emphasized quality. It has also encouraged the propagation of unusual species and varieties of flowers. Its gardeners have been trained to produce the very best in the way of exhibition plant materials. Floral exhibits sponsored by the Commission are sought after and welcomed by managements of both the Canadian National Exibition and the Royal Winter Fair in Toronto. The Commission has exhibited fall Chrysanthemums at the Royal for over 40 years. Its graceful and trailing Cascade mums have become one of the features at this prestigious show.

Visiting horticulturists and commercial greenhouse growers from foreign lands, have for years lauded the quality and size of the Calceolarias, Cinerarias and Poinsettias produced in the green-

The Niagara Parks Commission floral display at the 1978 Canadian National Exhibition.

houses. Equally appreciated have been the standard Fuchsias, Hydrangeas and Lantanas. So great has the interest been in these colourful mop-heads, that special printed growing instructions were prepared for distribution.

In more recent years, Commission gardeners have developed a new strain of Schizanthus. This world renowned exhibition pot plant is commonly called "Butterfly Flower". For over twenty years, gardener Louie Bereszynski crossed and re-crossed varieties by hand pollination, to produce four attractive new varieties. Not only are the colours different, but the florets are double the size of those Schizanthus varieties available through commerical seed houses in Canada, the United States and Great Britain. The Niagara Parks Commission's Schizanthus seeds are sought after by both private and public greenhouse growers. However, only a limited number of seeds are produced each year, therefore only a few requests can be filled.

Public attendance at the greenhouse has grown from approximately 3,200 visitors in the year 1937 to more than 365,000 visitors in 1983.

Spring flowering bulbs in the Main Show House of the Greenhouse.

Niagara Parks Archives

The new strain of the "Butterfly Flower" - Schizanthus - developed by Niagara Parks gardener Louie Bereszynski, shown here examining the blooms.

Niagara Parks Archives

Schizanthus blooms at the Greenhouse.

Niagara Parks Archives

A floral display, all produced from seed, taking from five to fifteen months from seed to show: Cyclamen, Schizanthus, Cineraria and Calceolaria.

Niagara Parks Archives

Large tropical palm trees featured in the Greenhouse Reception Area.

Early Spring flowers which were forced for display: Forsythia in the background, with Tulips and Daffodils.

Spring Flower Show: Easter Lilies, Blue Cinerarias, Yellow Calceolarias.

Marble Fountain in the Centre Display House with a March and April Spring Flower Display.

A Fall Chrysanthemum show of Exhibition and Bush Mums in the main display house of the Greenhouse.

Niagara Parks Archives

A Christmas Display of Poinsettias

Niagara Parks Archives

Oakes Garden Theatre and the Rainbow Gardens

For almost one hundred years, from 1833 until 1932, the site of present day Oakes Garden Theatre was occupied by the first and second Clifton Hotels. The first Clifton Hotel was built in 1833 by Harmanus Crysler. It became renowned as a tourist hotel, commodious, well furnished and elegant. It was destroyed by fire on June 26, 1898. For seven years the ruins were left undisturbed until the second Clifton was built in 1905. The builders of this hotel took advantage of the contours of the land, making it a five-storey hotel where it faced the River road and the American Falls. In 1899 the Lafayette Hotel was built alongside the northern wing of the Clifton. Together they occupied the whole block between Clifton Hill and the Bridge Lot, located opposite the exit from the Upper Steel Arch Bridge. On December 31, 1932, fire broke out in the northern wing of the hotel and could not be controlled. By the next morning the fire had destroyed all but one room width of the west wing, at Falls Avenue.

Due to the uncertainty of depressed economic conditions, the owners of the Clifton Hotel decided to terminate the business and dispose of the property. It was bought by Harry Oakes, who then bought the Lafayette Hotel and had it demolished. In the words of the Annual Report of the Parks Commissioners of 1933: "This whole plot of ground, approximately 460 ft. by 330 ft. in size would add largely to the Falls View Bridge entrance to Ontario if obtained for public use".[1] The Falls View Bridge was another name given to the Upper Steel Arch Bridge.

Harry Oakes, who was a Parks Commissioner,

presented the Clifton and Lafayette sites to the Parks Commission, in exchange for "a small plot of land above the steep hill at the rear of Queen Victoria Park proper".[2] The Commissioners were pleased with the exchange and the annual report stated: "The Commission is deeply indebted to Mr. Oakes for the exchange, by which the Province of Ontario gained greatly".[3] The Parks Commission also received a narrow strip of land along the Niagara Boulevard between Chippawa and Ussher's Creek. The following year, the Annual Report for 1935-1936 had this item: "A suitable design to convert this into a park entity in the form of a garden theatre has been secured and accepted. The work has been started, to be carried on over a period of years, as funds permit".[4]

Oakes Garden Theatre, built in the form of an amphitheatre, was designed by the firm of Dunington-Grubb and Stensson. It is constructed on varying levels, taking advantage of the contours of the ground and incorporating a foundation wall of the former Clifton Hotel. It is fan-shaped, with the stage so placed that the panorama of the Falls forms a natural backdrop, while at the rear there is a curved pergola connecting two open pavilions, one oriented on the axis of the Horseshoe Falls, the other on that of the American Falls. In front of the pergola is a broad curved lawn. Sloping terraces, rock gardens, lily ponds, shrubbery and wide promenades adjoin the amphitheatre, the whole being surrounded by an ornamental stone wall.[5] Ornamental iron gates, made by craftsmen in the Niagara Parks workshop,

Oakes Garden Theatre from the air, 1984.

were installed. Parks staff laid out flagstone walks, installed an underground watering system and a fountain. They also constructed specially designed benches which have opposing seats sharing a single back.[6]

Oakes Garden Theatre was laid out using Parks staff and the apprentices from the School of Apprentice Gardeners. The formal gardens utilize carpet bedding; Golden Privet, Santolina, Althernanthera, Korean Box, and Red-Leaf Japanese Barberry, are used to create patterns in living colour after a rigid geometric design.[7] There is a Japanese garden with lily ponds at the rear of the pergola. Over the years ducks have been placed in the ponds at Oakes Garden Theatre during the summer months.

The goal of the Parks Commission had been to provide an attractive and suitable entrance to Ontario and Queen Victoria Park at the terminus of the Upper Steel Arch Bridge. Clifton Gate House was opened in 1937, the Clifton Gate Memorial Arch was dedicated in 1937 and Oakes Garden Theatre was officially opened on September 18, 1938. The Commission's goal had been attained but now the entrance was in the wrong place as the Upper Steel Arch Bridge was destroyed, pushed off its abutments by ice on January 27, 1938. The Rainbow Bridge built to replace it, would be built with access ramps at a higher level, out of sight of the new Park

entrance.

After the opening, Oakes Garden Theatre was the scene of a number of choral programmes, with the Mendelssohn Choir of Toronto, the Bach Choir of Hamilton and the Schubert Choir of Brantford performing. Inclement weather spoiled the first two concerts, keeping attendance below expectations. Two band concerts, featuring the Niagara Falls Kiltie Band, were also presented under the auspices of the Commission. In the intervening years, other concerts and band performances have taken place in this garden setting, but it never did fulfill its potential as a site for concerts, because of the uncertainty of the weather and the noise of the traffic which passes along Clifton Hill and the River Road adjoining the Oakes Garden Theatre.

Oakes Garden Theatre is a fine example of the blending of architectural and horticultural skills. A walk through the Gardens is a restful and rewarding experience. There is ample opportunity for photography and it is a popular spot for wedding pictures.

The Rainbow Gardens and the wide stairway which separates them from Oakes Garden Theatre, have been built on land which in the past supported a variety of buildings and services. So great have been the changes that visitors coming to Niagara Falls after an absence of fifty years would have great

Centre, the first Clifton Hotel, built in 1835, on the site of present day Oakes Garden Theatre. When the survey was made in 1891 for the Niagara Falls Park and River Railway, it was found that the hotel encroached more than thirty feet on the Chain Reserve, obstructing the road. Litigation was underway when the Hotel burned on June 28, 1898. The second Clifton was built in 1906, farther back, clear of the road allowance. In the right foreground is the livery stable of the Clifton Hotel. Brundage's Livery Stable is at top left centre, the Customs House is at the top of the road down the gorge to the ferry (Maid of the Mist) dock. Site of present day Queen Victoria Park is in the background.

Niagara Parks Archives

The second Clifton Hotel, opened in 1906, on the site of present day Oakes Garden Theatre. The Lafayette Hotel, to the right of the Clifton, is under construction. The Canadian end of the Upper Steel Arch Bridge and the ticket office are at the extreme right. Behind the ticket office is a roller coaster, part of the amusement park which occupied the present site of the Sheraton Brock Hotel, until 1907. Clifton Hill is at the left of the Clifton Hotel. On the left, on the edge of the gorge is the Clifton Incline, now the Maid of the Mist Incline. One of the Maid of the Mist boats, built in 1885 or 1888, is in the river below.

difficulty in orienting themselves.

The land on which the stairway leading to Falls Avenue stands, was the property of the Clifton Suspension Bridge Company and was known as the Bridge Lot. It was here that the great stone anchorages of the Upper Suspension Bridge were located. The anchors which held the cables, were firmly embedded 5.49 m (18 ft.) below the surface of the ground. The Bridge Lot was a convenient short cut between Front Street (River Road) and Falls Avenue. It was kept open, except for one day a year, when the gate was locked and a guard posted to prevent anyone from using the pathway. This is a requirement of law - a pathway over private property becomes a public highway by common use if it is used for one year as such. It must be closed at least one day a year to have it remain private property.

Over the years the site has been occupied by several hotels, an electric railway terminal, a dance hall, two automobile garages with new car dealerships, a service station and various restaurants and souvenir stores. Eventually it became a shoddy, rundown area which gave a poor first impression to visitors entering Niagara Falls from the Upper Steel

Arch Bridge. After the collapse of this bridge in 1938 there were major changes. The Ontario Department of Highways bought or expropriated, all of the property extending from the Bridge Lot to Bender Hill. The Niagara Falls Bridge Commission razed the old buildings and built the Rainbow Bridge access ramps, the Carillon Tower, the Bridge Commission's Administrative Offices, and the Rainbow Bridge Plaza on the land. The Parks Commission agreed to accept responsibiltiy for the original cost of the construction of the gardens, including the flagstone walks, steps and flower beds, balustrades and ornamental stonework. The figure agreed upon was $140,000.[8] On April 1, 1968, the Province of Ontario, as a matter of policy, transferred the administration of the Rainbow Bridge Plaza Complex to the jurisdiction of the Niagara Parks Commission.[9]

These bridge structures and the beautiful formal gardens occupying the area today are a more attractive use of the land than the conglomeration of commercial buildings which stood there for more than seventy years.

A view looking south toward Queen Victoria Park, 1983. The Rainbow Bridge Plaza, the Rainbow Gardens and Oakes Garden Theatre are on the right.

Looking north on River Road from Clifton Hill, 1920's. The second Clifton Hotel is on the left, beyond it the Lafayette Hotel. The ticket office, (building with spire), for the Upper Steel Arch Bridge, is on the site of the present Clifton Gate House. Note the open-sided street cars near the ticket office.

Niagara Parks Archives

A view along River Road looking north, from the corner of Clifton Hill, the same viewpoint as previous picture. An example of Parterre Gardening in Oakes Garden Theatre. The low green hedge is Korean Boxwood, surrounding beds of Fibrous Rooted Begonias, with standard orange flowered Lantanas in the centre. The Linden trees on the upper level are pleached.

A photo taken from the Upper Steel Arch Bridge of the buildings at the Canadian end of the bridge in 1925. The four-storey building at the extreme right is the only building in this photo still in existence today. It is now the Niagara Falls Museum, where the artifacts from Thomas Barnett's Museum are on display.

The scene at the Canadian end of the Upper Steel Arch Bridge, 1925. This area is now the Rainbow Gardens. The Bridge ticket office with the cone roof is at the left end of the bridge, Customs and Immigration buildings at the right end of the bridge. The Oneida Community building at left centre on high ground, is on the site of present day Maple Leaf Village. The Queen's Hotel, centre, was later moved to St. Paul Street in Niagara Falls and rebuilt.

Scroll Bedding on the lower level of Oakes Garden Theatre. The low hedge is Korean Boxwood, the hedge surrounding the Japanese Yew trees is Golden Privet. The Japanese Yew cone shaping is called Topiary.

Niagara Parks Archives

The Fish Fountain in the Formal Gardens of the Rainbow Gardens, 1978. A hedge of Korean Boxwood surrounds the bed of Fibrous rooted Begonias with Standard Fuchsias in the centre.

Niagara Parks Archives

Oakes Garden Theatre from the air, 1963. In the foreground are gates and a stairway on the former Bridge Lot. The exit from the former Upper Steel Arch Bridge was located at the bottom of the Bridge Lot and directly in front of the Memorial Arch.

The raised formal gardens at the entrance to Oakes Garden Theatre. Beds of Fibrous Begonias, with standard Lantanas in the centre, surrounded by a low clipped hedge of Korean Boxwood.

Niagara Parks Archives

The lower fountain flower bed in Oakes Garden Theatre
has red Cannas, yellow Coleus, blue and green Heliotrope
and standard pink Fuchsias, edged with Korean Boxwood.

The Amphitheatre and Pergola. Urns are filled with
colourful annuals.

Niagara Parks Archives

Niagara Parks Archives

The Japanese Garden, with a natural area, a lily pond and a wishing bridge, Oakes Garden, 1978.

School of Horticulture

In 1908 Parks Superintendent, John H. Jackson, recommended to the Commission that an educational programme should be established within the Parks to train young Canadians in the art of gardening. The need for such a program was evident as parks, cemeteries and commercial nurseries, had to rely solely on immigrants, and as emigration from Great Britain and Europe had been drastically curtailed, there was now an urgent need for qualified gardeners.

The proposition was discussed by the Commission on several occasions during the ensuing years. In 1919, the Commission purchased 130 ha (322 acres) of surplus land that the Hydro Electric Power Commission had acquired for their Queenston-Chippawa Power Development project. The land stretched in a narrow band along the gorge between the Whirlpool and the Niagara Glen. In 1936 a portion of this property, 40.47 ha (100 acres), located opposite the Niagara Glen, became the site of the first "Training School for Apprentice Gardeners".

The name was changed in 1951 to the "School of Gardening" and then, in 1959, as teaching facilities and curriculum expanded, the institution was officially renamed the "School of Horticulture". The training program followed the long practiced gardener apprenticeship offered at Kew Gardens in England, based heavily on practical experience.

Enrolment commenced in 1936, with a class of eight young men. Official "Indentures" were signed by the Commission, the apprentice and his guardian, binding the apprentice: "To Learn the Art, Trade or Mystery of a Gardener after the manner of an apprentice and to serve for the term of three years".

These were the years of rough development at the School under the capable leadership of the first School Superintendent, K.M. Broman. The new apprentices could truly be called pioneers, as the property was not choice agricultural land. The soil texture was a heavy clay, and the top soil shallow, with numerous outcroppings of rock. This made cultivation, trenching, tree planting and grading very difficult, particularly when most of it had to be accomplished by hand.

Eventually, the apprentices were housed in a residence called "The Bothy". It had two dormitories and four semi-private rooms. The apprentices grew, harvested, stored and canned much of the food consumed. Besides vegetables and fruits, they raised their own pigs, chickens, wild geese and ducks. There was also a work horse, "Old Queenie", to help transport building materials, move and contour the soil and cultivate the nursery. Trenches for water lines, drains and deep stone sumps, were all hand dug by these young students.

In addition to providing free room, board and laundry, the Commission paid each apprentice five dollars per week subsistence allowance.

Besides participating in an extensive landscape development program, the apprentices propagated literally thousands of trees, shrubs and perennials which were used later to help landscape other acreages throughout the park system.

Even with the hard work schedule, the students

"The Bothy" with the original Murray house at the far right, behind the trees. The stone addition, used as students' quarters was added in 1938-1939.

Niagara Parks Archives

The original Lecture Hall, later the students' recreational centre. Originally it was the Niagara Falls Park and River Railway Station at Queenston Heights. It was dismantled in 1936 and transported to the School where $2,750.99 was spent during 1936-1937 in rebuilding it for use as a lecture hall.

Niagara Parks Archives

The class of 1955 getting ready for the day's work.

Niagara Parks Archives

entered into a physical exercising program each morning at 7:00 o'clock, led by the School Superintendent, who introduced these Canadian lads to a form of Swedish isometrics. This exercise was approached as fun and finished with a run up the Niagara Parkway, to circle an elm tree in front of the Niagara Glen, and then back to "The Bothy" for breakfast.

In 1968, the Commission increased the total enrolment at the school from 24 to 36 students. It then became necessary to enlarge the living accommodations by building an addition to "The Bothy".

An important milestone in the history of the school was reached when the first woman graduated in 1976, having entered the training program in April

The rose garden with the original fountain, circa 1950. The old Lecture Hall is in the background. The rose garden contains both Hybrid Tea and Floribunda roses.

The Lecture Hall dedicated March 1, 1962.

1973.

The school has grown in stature over the years, and to the credit of the Commission, graduates now number 350, and occupy many key horticultural positions throughout Canada and the United States.

In 1966, the Commission was honoured by the Parks and Recreation Association of Canada for its outstanding contribution in training horitcultural and parks personnel.

At the present time, the students are totally responsible for the overall maintenance of the nearly 40.47 ha (100 acres) of ornamentals and turf.

The School Herbarium has grown in size and is properly housed in steel cabinets. The collection contains upwards of 4,000 plant specimens with approximately 2,000 individual species or cultivars represented.

There are more than 2,500 species and cultivars represented in the living collection of ornamentals growing on the grounds. The total number of plant specimens under cultivation has been conservatively estimated by the staff at 20,000, making it one of the finest and most extensive collections in Canada.

Over the winter of 1982-83 a Visitors' Reception Centre was constructed. It includes a retail shop where seeds and plants not usually available in other garden outlets, are for sale. A major re-alignment of the Niagara Parkway in front of the school made it possible to increase the size of the parking lot.

In 1983 more than 300,000 people visited the Niagara Parks School of Horticulture. This unique educational institution with its well appointed grounds, has become one of the most popular tourist attractions in the Niagara Parks.

An air view of the School of Horticulture and the grounds, 1984. The new parking area is in the foreground, with the Lecture Hall directly above it in the centre, and the new Visitors' Reception Centre is to the right and to the rear of the Lecture Hall.

Niagara Parks Archives

The English Knot Gardens. Red and Yellow Coleus and large Yellow Marigolds.

A third year student explaining the plants to visitors, Red and Yellow Coleus with a standard Orange Lantana in the centre.

An annual flower bed of Celosia, with the Centennial fountain in the centre.

Niagara Parks Archives

A visitor in a wheel chair admiring the flowers at the School of Horticulture. The Centennial fountain is in the centre.

Niagara Parks Archives

Floral Clock

In 1950 Ontario Hydro built a Floral Clock on the north side of the Sir Adam Beck Generating Station No. 1. It was inspired by the famous floral clock built in 1902 in Princes St. Gardens in Edinburgh, Scotland. Westminster chimes and speakers are housed in the ivy-clad tower which rises above the clock dial at the rear. They intone the quarter hour, and strike on the hour.

In 1977 The Niagara Parks Commission assumed responsibility for security patrols and the design and planting of the Floral Clock. Ontario Hydro continued to provide mechanical maintenance. The 19,000 plants required to make up the floral design on the face of the clock are grown in the Niagara Parks Greenhouse. A 3.03m (10 ft.) wide water garden pool stocked with gold fish curves along the 26m (85 ft.) front of the clock. It is a gesture of good luck to toss a coin into the pool — good luck for the local charities who are the recipients of all coins retrieved from the pool.

An air view of the Floral Clock, 1984.

Lilac Gardens

Lilacs have always been popular in the Niagara Parks. As early as 1888, Superintendent James Wilson reported planting Syringa (Lilacs) in the vicinity of the Falls. In 1972, it was necessary to remove several very old clumps of Lilacs growing in Queen Victoria Park. The annual rings confirmed their age at 51 years, dating their planting time as 1921.

In succeeding years, Lilacs were utilized in many locations throughout the park system, both as ornamentals and for erosion control. Two small Lilac gardens were eventually developed in the late thirties, one directly across from the Niagara Glen and the other at the School of Horticulture, adjacent to the old quarry pond. Unfortunately, these two sites lacked good soil depth and proper drainage. Consequently, the plantings suffered and only the School plantings remain.

In 1966, just prior to Canada's Centennial year, the Commission was the recipient of a gift of thirty-five hundred dollars from the American Rotary Clubs of District 709. These funds were to be used for the sole purpose of establishing a Centennial Lilac Garden, honouring Canada's 100th birthday.

A site of some ten acres was selected near Smeaton's Cove, between the Floral Clock and the Lewiston-Queenston Bridge. This location was ideal, having a good depth of soil and being slightly undulated, with sufficient contours to make it interesting. The acreage was part of the old Larkin farm apple orchard and some of the old trees were carefully retained. Today, the property has been

A scene in the Centennial Lilac Gardens.

Niagara Parks Archives

fully developed into one of the finest Lilac gardens in the country. The collection contains over 1,200 mature shrubs with over 225 different varieties represented.

Although work on the gardens commenced in

1966, they were not fully developed until the spring
of 1981. At that time the chairman of the Commission,
James Allan, and several American Rotary officials,
unveiled a beautiful bronze plaque commemorating
Rotary's contribution toward the establishment of
the Centennial Gardens.

These gardens have proved to be a new tourist
attraction, as hundreds of flower lovers visit the
gardens each May and June.

*French Hybrid Lilacs growing on their own roots
and not budded root stock.*

Recreation In The Parks

The recreational facilities provided by the Commissioners for the enjoyment of today's visitors to the Niagara Parks cover a wide range of activities. Active recreation includes such sports as swimming, boating, camping, golf, tennis, cross-country skiing, tobogganning, hiking nature trails and fishing; passive recreation includes listening to band concerts, and viewing the scenic beauty of the Falls, the gorge and the floral gardens. Today, as in the early days, the nearby residents of Niagara Falls and the Niagara area are the chief benefactors of the facilities for active recreation.

In earlier years in the Parks, other facilities were available at times. Skating rinks were established in 1894 on spring fed ponds located near the main gate "affording great pleasure and enjoyment for winter visitors to the area as well as local residents."[1] In later years skating was provided on the ice on the large pond in the gravel pit which was located in the Flats area, south of the present Greenhouse-Conservatory. The pond was kept cleaned off for skating and at certain times hockey was allowed. These activities were supervised by the Chief Constable, who "kept everything in order".[2] The gravel pit pond was used for swimming in the summer.

In 1899 "a request was made by some of the leading citizens for a portion of the Park to be set aside for lawn tennis. A two court ground was selected . . . which proved to be a desirable addition to the facilities already afforded by the Park".[3] These grass courts were still in use well into the 1930's.

Tennis courts were also provided at Queenston Heights Park.

A map of Queen Victoria Park dated 1905, shows a number of active recreational facilities within the Park area: a bicycle path, cricket crease, tennis courts, lawn bowling green, a baseball field and a large area identified as a "Recreational Area". The Park Superintendent reported in 1907: "The lawn tennis grounds have been much used . . . the cricket crease has also been a great service . . .".[4] The Recreational Area referred to was in the location of the present Greenhouse-Conservatory. When this area of the Park was restored to Park use in 1922 after completion of the third Ontario Power Company conduit, two clay tennis courts were installed. Other facilities included nature paths and a fountain. Only the fountain located south of the present Greenhouse-Conservatory remains, and it is still in use.

Band concerts have been a tradition in the Niagara Parks. "Several programmes kept as souvenirs tell of band concerts in Queen Victoria Park. The personnel of most of the bands were military men; for example, on July 15, 1895, the 15th Battalion Band played . . ."[5] Visiting bands played at the band stand in Queen Victoria Park on many occasions, and continue to do so. Presently two bands alternate playing in Queen Victoria Park each Tuesday evening during the summer months, the Niagara Falls Concert Band and the St. Ann's Symphonic Band. The Niagara Falls Concert Band

In 1899 two courts for lawn tennis were laid out in Queen Victoria Park, opposite the American Falls.

was formed in 1871 and was known as the Clifton Citizens Band. This band first performed in the Park in 1963, when it played at the unveiling and dedication of the monument erected to the memory of King George VI. St. Ann's Concert Band was formed in 1954, and gave its first Niagara Parks concert in July 1959, under the direction of Captain Arthur Williams. Since 1969 Kenneth Norton, B.A., M.E.D., has been its conductor.[6] These concerts are jointly sponsored by the Niagara Parks Commission and Local 298 of the American Federation of Musicians with grants from the Musicians Performance Trust Fund.

Queen Victoria Park no longer has active recreational facilities. The tennis courts were removed and in 1972 the picnic pavilions were dismantled and

picnickers were directed to other Niagara Parks picnic areas. From a modest beginning, when swimming, skating and tennis facilities were provided in Queen Victoria Park, recreational facilities within the Niagara Parks have expanded to include today: two golf courses, a marina, supervised swimming areas, a wading pool, numerous boat launching ramps, tennis courts, cross-country skiing, to-bogganning and sports fields. During the winter of 1984-1985 a skating rink is planned for the Whirlpool Golf Course, to complement the cross-country skiing and tobogganning that are allowed there.

The Annual report of 1956 had this to say: "Commission policy is directed toward providing cultural and recreational enjoyment for all our visitors. Parks are for people".[7]

Queen Victoria Park
Picnic Grounds

The picnic pavilion and band stand in Queen Victoria Park. The Mail & Empire of May 25, 1909 reported that the Salvation Army Temple Band from Toronto was refused premission to play in Queen Victoria Park Sunday and Monday last, by Superintendent Jackson, because of the possibility that they would take up the usual collection. Permission was given to play on July 27, but no collection was to be taken. This picnic pavilion was built in 1895.

Picnic Scene in Queen Victoria Park, circa 1890.

The pic-nic grounds, as they were called in 1888, were located south of the Murray Street Ravine and adjacent to the old Barnett Museum - then called the Dufferin Cafe. In 1894 the grounds were considerably enlarged to accommodate the large numbers of excursionists who came from Toronto on the lake boats and on to Queen Victoria Park by way of the new electric railway. Gravel paths were laid out and a lofty pavilion of cedar work and elm bark was erected to serve as a picnic shelter and a band stand.

The picnickers often came in large groups: "Many of the excursionists coming to the Park are composed of several Sunday Schools and their friends" wrote Superintendent Wilson in 1894, "Others are employees of large manufacturing or mercantile aggregations. They usually supply their own provisions and desire only facilities for making tea and coffee, without expense. Some of these groups number from 1,000 to 1,500. It is apparent that a stove and tea kettle are not sufficient to meet their requirements especially since they want to enjoy refreshments immediately on arrival".[1]

To supply the needed hot water, a series of upright boilers of 727 litres (160 gallons) capacity was installed in the lower portion of the picnic pavilion. These boilers were connected by piping to heating coils which were fixed in large stoves which burned wood supplied by the Park staff. The boilers were tapped and an abundant supply of hot water was available, and furnished free. Cool spring water was also available. A comfort station, called "closet conveniences", was provided in connection with the large waiting room at the rear of the Dufferin Cafe. A matron was placed in charge of the ladies' toilet to provide information and keep the room clean and tidy.

In 1898 a large picnic shelter was constructed from iron pipe, and a custom-made canvas roof was installed.[2] The new shelter was located close to the high bank and served as a shelter and dance hall for many years. In 1904 the Dufferin Cafe was demolished, along with the old cedar and elm bark pavilion and the canvas awning - topped shelter. A Refectory and Shelter was built to the rear of the old Cafe site, which had an open area in the lower level which served as a picnic shelter, with picnic tables,

ARRANGEMENTS HAVE BEEN MADE FOR

MEALS AT PARK SIDE INN,

OPPOSITE MOWAT GATE, WHICH CAN BE HAD FOR

35 Cents.
★

TICKETS CAN BE HAD FOR

Niagara Falls Park and River Ry.

ON THE TRAIN AT REDUCED RATES.

God Save the Queen.

Bigley Co. Print Printer.

THE FIRST ANNUAL PICNIC

OF THE

EMPLOYEES OF THE BURROW, STEWART & MILNE CO.
LIMITED.

TO BE HELD AT

Queen Victoria Park, Niagara Falls, Ont.,

SATURDAY, JULY 30th, '98.

Bicycles and Baby Carriages carried FREE in Special Baggage Car.

Programme.

Hot Tea and Coffee Free on presentation of
of R. R. Ticket. Please return the Pitchers.

SONS OF ENGLAND BAND, UNDER H. A. STARES

Trains leave Locke St., at 7.45 a.m.; James St. at
8 a.m., stopping at Wentworth St.

TICKETS—Adults 75c. Children 40c.

JOHN DILLON,	R. SCOTT,	R. H. STEVENSON
Chairman.	Secretary.	Treasurer.

List of Games, Etc.

BASEBALL MATCH—Prize, 2 boxes cigars, value $3.00.

QUOIT MATCHES (first game)—Prize, set of nickel-plated quoits and bottle Scotch whiskey.
Second Game—Prize, set of nickel-plated quoits and bottle Seagram's whiskey.

100-Yard Race, married ladies (open)—1st set silver spoons, value $3.00; 2nd 1 silver butter knife, value 1.50; 3rd ¼ barrel flour, value 1.38.

100-Yard Race, employees' wives—1st set carvers, value $4.50; 2nd carpet sweeper, value 3.00; 3rd set silver spoons, value 1.50.

Old Man's Race, over 50 (shop)—1st ½ ton coal, value $2.00; 2nd pipe and case, value 1.50; 3rd pair fancy slippers, value 1.00.

Married Men's Race (shop)—1st ½ ton coal, value $2.00; 2nd 1 bottle wine, value 1.50; 3rd pair shoes, value 1.00.

Girls' Race, under 12 years (open)—1st book, value $1.00; 2nd candies, value 30c.; 3rd candies, value 20c.

Employees' Race, under 21—1st hat, value $1.50; 2nd pair cuff buttons, value 1.00; 3rd pipe, value 50c.

One Mile Open Race—1st pipe and case, value $2.50; 2nd box cigars, value 2.00; 3rd bottle wine, value 1.50.

100-Yard Dash (moulding shop apprentices only)—1st pair pants, value $2.00; 2nd cuff buttons, value 1.00; 3rd necktie, value 50c.

Young Ladies' Race (open)—1st toilet set, value $2.50; 2nd 2 boxes stationery, value 1.25; 3rd book, value 1.00.

Children's Race, under 10 years (shop)—1st candies, value 40c.; 2nd candies, value 35c.; 3rd candies, value 25c.

List of Games, Etc.
CONTINUED.

Fat Man's Race (shop)—1st pair shoes, value $2.00; 2nd box cigars, value 1.50; 3rd bottle wine, value $1.00.

Girls' Race, under 15 years (shop)—1st perfume, value $1.00; 2nd pair slippers, value 1.00; 3rd ladies' belt, value 75c.

Girls' Race, under 18 years (open)—1st pair slippers, value $2.00; 2nd perfume, value 1.00.

100-Yard Dash (open)—1st revolver, value $3.00; 2nd brass picture frame, value 2.00; 3rd bottle wine, value 1.00.

Three-legged Race (open)—1st box cigars, value $1.50; 2nd bottle wine, value 1.50.

Committee Race, 100 yards—1st box cigars, value $2.50; 2nd bottle Seagram's whiskey, value 1.50.

One Mile Bicycle Race (shop)—1st cyclometer, value $2.00; 2nd cyclometer, value 1.50; 3rd foot pump, value 1.00.

Standing Jump (shop)—1st clock, value $1.25; 2nd pair shoes, value 1.00; 3rd bottle wine, value 1.00.

Running Hop, Step and Jump (open)—1st cash $2.00; 2nd box cigars, value 1.50; 3rd bottle wine, value 1.00.

Standing Jump (open)—1st box cigars, value $1.50; 2nd bottle wine, value 1.00.

Putting Shot, 16 lbs. (open)—1st box cigars, value $1.50; 2nd bottle wine, value 1.00.

Throwing Baseball (shop)—Prize pair shoes, value $2.00.

Prize Waltz (open)—Lady's gold ring, value $3.00.

Irish Jig (open)—1st box cigars, value $1.50; 2nd bottle wine, value 1.00.

Tug of War (shop)—¼ barrel lager.

Comic Song (open)—Prize bottle wine, value $1.50.

Programme for the First Annual Picnic of the Employees of The Burrow, Stewart & Milne Co., Saturday, July 30, 1898.

Niagara Parks Archives

The pipe frame picnic shelter of 1905, removed in 1972.

Niagara Parks Archives

hot and cold water and light refreshments available. In 1905 and 1906 picnic shelters, called dining pavilions, were constructed of pipe frames with corrugated iron roofs and cement floors. They were located on the north side of the Murray Street Ravine, close to the foot of the high bank. Each pavilion had its own hot water boiler, heated with either wood or coal. A baseball diamond was laid out just north of the pavilions and the area in front of the pavilions was available for races and games.

The picnic grounds in Queen Victoria Park were used by thousands of groups over the years. The first Church and Sabbath School groups came from communities within easy driving distance, travelling by horse-drawn carriages and wagons. Later, church groups came by the lake boats and the electric railway and finally, in later years, by automobile and chartered buses.

By 1972 it became advisable to relocate the picnic grounds from the congested area in Queen Victoria Park where parking for cars and buses was inadequate. The two out-dated pipe frame picnic pavilions were demolished. The picnic facilities at Queenston Heights, McFarland Point Park and King's Bridge Park were improved and picnickers were directed to those areas, where there was adequate parking.

Toronto Transportation Commission

Purchasing picnic supplies at the Refectory, Queen Victoria Park, circa 1920.

Whirlpool Golf Course

The 1917 Annual Report of the Queen Victoria Niagara Falls Park Commissioners stated: "As a result of the construction of the Chippawa-Queenston Power Canal, there will be an extensive area of land available, from the Whirlpool to the end of the Canal and adjacent to the Park system, suitable for Park development." This land, part of the former Thompson and Murray farm properties, was owned by the Hydro Electric Power Commission of Ontario. In 1919 the Park Commissioners purchased it - an area of 130 ha (322 acres) - to facilitate the construction of the Niagara Boulevard between Niagara Falls and Queenston.

The Commissioners called their new land acquisition "Niagara Glen Heights" and in 1920 they had it surveyed and plotted, with its physical contours noted, for the purpose of making a preliminary study for its eventual development. Two plans were submitted by K.M. Broman, Park Superintendent of Arboriculture, both for an arboretum. The one chosen was for an arboretum laid out on the principle of a golf course,[1] and so the 70.8 ha (175 acres) lying between the Whirlpool Road at the north and extending to the Niagara Glen on the south, were set aside for that purpose.

In 1925 the Chairman of the Commission, P.W. Ellis, writing to the *Toronto Mail and Empire* stated: "Construction of a 9 hole golf course will begin on November 26, 1925, and a great motor camp will be located on 20 acres of Park property near the golf course". Neither the golf course nor the motor camp was constructed.

The property was left in a natural state until 1937, when an arboretum was begun in the area near the Whirlpool, on the principle of a golf course layout. In the intervening years, the old Thompson farm house and barn had been torn down. In 1947 actual construction began on a golf course. The building of tees and greens which was done by Park staff under the direction of a golf course architect, required thousands of cubic metres of subsoil and topsoil. Without defacing the contours of the grounds, as much as possible of this material was obtained on the site. The North American Cyanamid Company trucked in thousands of cubic metres of material and provided a bulldozer from time to time, all at no expense to the Commission. A cut stone club house was begun in 1947, with locker rooms, bar, lounge and pro shop. The club house, located adjacent to the Niagara Boulevard, opposite Thompson Point at the northern terminus of the Niagara Spanish Aero Car, was completed in 1949.

The 6400 m (7000 yd.) course was officially opened on July 2, 1951 with an International Tournament featuring four prominent professional golfers, two from Canada - Stan Leonard and Bob Gray, and two from the United States - Dr. Cary Middlecoff and Jimmy Demaret. An 18-hole match was played and won by the American twosome. A crowd of over 10,000 watched the event. It was a most successful opening.

Over the years many improvements have been made to the club house and the golf course. In 1957 an underground watering system was installed for the

Whirlpool Golf Course with the 18th green in the background.

Niagara Parks Archives

Niagara Parks Archives

Players in the International Golf Match at the opening of the Golf Course, 1959. Left to right: Bob Gray, Canada; Dr. Cary Middlecoff and Jimmy Demaret, the United States; Stan Leonard, Canada.

The Whirlpool Golf Course from the air, 1984. The Chippawa-Queenston Power Canal is on the right, the Whirlpool is at the top left.

First tee at the Whirlpool Golf Course.

The Golf Shop at the Whirlpool Golf Course.

The Dining Room at the Whirlpool Golf Course.

Niagara Parks Archives

fairways, using water pumped from the Chippawa-Queenston Power Canal which runs along the western boundary of the course. In 1968 the club house was renovated, resulting in larger facilities for the golfers' lounge and the dining room. In 1970 the pro shop was relocated to a more convenient position near the first tee. Electric golf carts were offered on a rental basis for the first time in 1970 and proved to be very popular. Paved paths were required for the golf carts and by 1971, 1127.8 m (3700 ft.) of paths were provided for these power-driven carts.

Changes were made in the course layout in 1970 when a "three tee" marker system was initiated, with separate championship, ladies' and regular tees. In the Ontario Public Golf Course Championships, sponsored by the Ontario Golf Association, held at the Niagara Parks Golf Course that year, Ken Trowbridge of Brampton set a new course record of 67. The previous low of 69 was held jointly by two well known United States professionals, Dr. Cary Middlecoff and Julius Boros. A long range plan of shortening some of the more difficult par 4 holes was instituted in 1977.

During a major capital works project in 1967 the club house lobby was converted into a golfers' lounge and the original pro shop became a group banquet area. By 1980 seventy golf carts were available for rent and a new building was constructed on the west

side of the first tee to house them. A new golf retail shop was completed in 1981, offering a greater variety of golf merchandise for sale.

During the winter of 1978-79 the Commissioners increased the use of the golf course by setting up a program of winter activities. Cross country ski trails were laid out on the course and the club house was open daily for ski rentals, meals, refreshments, washrooms and shelter. The golf course became a popular spot for cross country skiing by school groups. Tobogganing and cross country skiing on the golf course were free. The mild winters and lack of snow reduced winter activities in 1980, 1981, 1982 and 1983.

In 1980 the name of the golf course was changed from the Niagara Parks Golf Course to the Whirlpool Golf Course. This was a memorable year when the one millionth golfer played the course during the middle of the season.

The Golf Course and the Dining Room are a regular stop on the Double Decker Bus Tours and more and more tourists are making use of the excellent dining facilties. The continued popularity of the Whirlpool Golf Course - an average of 33,300 golfers has played the course each year since it opened in July 1951 - confirms the Parks Commissioners' foresight in providing for this popular form of recreation.

Miller's Creek Campsite and the Marina

As early as 1925 the Park Commission had considered establishing a campground on Park lands at the Whirlpool. Chairman P.W. Ellis, in a letter to the *Toronto Mail and Empire*, wrote: "A great motor camp will be located on 20 acres of Park property. A central building will be erected to contain dining rooms, store and registration. Nearby will be a group of smaller buildings for showers and washrooms. Electric plates will be installed so that tourists can cook their own meals." This was an ambitious plan but it was never carried out. It was 1962 before campgrounds were actually established at Charles Daley Park and Miller's Creek on Commission property.

In 1957 the Commissioners purchased a 46.5 ha (115 acre) plot of land at Miller's Creek on the upper Niagara River near Fort Erie. In 1958 a parking area and a roadway were constructed, along with a ramp into the creek for launching small boats, and the area was opened as a picnic site. The Commissioners realized that the area's potential would not be reached until a water supply was made available and other facilities provided.

In 1962 a line was installed to draw water from the Niagara River and fifty-four campsites were laid out on 5.67 ha (14 acres) of land. Necessary service buildings and facilities were provided. An additional 24.3 ha (60 acres) of land adjoining the campsite were planted in Austrian Pine and other trees, including nut-bearing trees. The area was well used during its first season in 1963 and thereafter. In late September of 1968 the combination registration,

sales, washrooms and shower building was destroyed by fire and had to be rebuilt.

For some time, beginning in 1969, registrations for Miller's Creek campsites were taken at the Parks Information Centre located south of Table Rock House in the former International Railway Powerhouse and this ensured maximum use of the camp facilities. In 1971 the 24.3 ha (60 acre) wooded area adjoining the campsite was declared a "natural zone" and laid out in nature trails, providing a pleasant adjunct to the camp. The Commission, in 1973, followed a policy adopted by the Lands and Forests Department of the Provincial Government and allowed Senior Citizens free camping privileges. Each campsite at Miller's Creek has 232m² (2500 sq. ft.) of space with an electrical hook-up and a fireplace. Coin operated laundry facilities are available. Miller's Creek Campsite, about 4.8 km (3 miles) from Fort Erie and about 27 km (17 miles) from Niagara Falls is an ideal place for a camping holiday.

In 1957 the Niagara Parks Commission acquired from the Canadian Ship Building Company their shipyard property located on the upper Niagara Boulevard between Black Creek and Fort Erie. These 3.64 ha (9 acres) of land, owned by the Canadian Ship Building Company since 1903, were first used as a shipyard. In later years, the facilities were used for structural steel fabrication.

In 1965 the Commissioners decided to test public demand for a marina and installed a timber dock on the south side of what was the north slip of the old

Miller's Creek Campsite, the Marina is at the top of the picture.

Niagara Parks Archives

The Marina from the air.

Campsite at Miller's Creek.

The docking area at the Marina.

shipyard. Some small floating docks were installed. By 1968 the new boat-docking facilities had become so popular that the Commission undertook a major addition. A sea wall was installed as well as a dock with a gas pump at the river's edge, along with berths for fifty-four boats. In 1969, the first full year of operation, all fifty-four berths were rented. In 1970 a new concrete ramp was laid for the launching of larger sized boats, and a septic tank was installed. During the summer months seventy-seven boats were berthed at the Marina, and a winter storage programme was initiated.

It was found necessary in 1974 to construct a 30.3 m (100 ft.) retaining wall for shoreline protection and this was also used for small boat docking. Pilings were also installed to secure the docks. The Marina was fully rented for the 1974 season with a waiting list of forty-seven applicants in 1975. With such a large backlog of applications, the Commissioners felt justified in installing fifty additional spaces for boats in 1975. The north bay of the Marina was dredged in 1978. By 1981 some of the original timber docks were replaced with fibre glass docks constructed by Parks Commission employees.

Charles Daley Park

Charles Daley Park is located just west of St. Catharines on the shore of Lake Ontario between Fifteen and Sixteen Mile Creeks. In 1960 the Niagara Parks Commission purchased a non-productive 4.4 ha (11 acres) fruit and vegetable farm, which included 792.5 m (2600 ft.) of sand beach. Access at that time was directly from the Queen Elizabeth Way. Although now a picnic and camping park, the original purpose of this development was to provide "Day Use Recreational Facilities" for both local residents and tourists.

The site was very hilly, running out to a sheer drop or bluff at the lake, making farming difficult. The value of the property for park purposes was in the lake frontage, and the outstanding view which included the Toronto skyline. However, in its purchased state, these features were inaccessible.

Due to the uneven terrain, development was not easy. Large earth movers and bulldozers were used to reduce the height of the hills. In one instance, nearly 9.1 m (30 ft.) was cut from the crown of a hill to create the flat parking area. During 1961 the grading contractors met serious problems when they struck a deep layer of blue, gumbo clay and an underground spring, which mired the heavy machinery for days. The spring was actually an artesian well and eventually it was tapped and still produces potable water for the park's facilities.

In 1961 a 500 car parking lot was completed, along with service roads. A toll-gate booth, washrooms, refreshment stand, and a small maintenance service building were also built. To provide safe access to this new park from the heavily used Queen Elizabeth Way, the Ontario government constructed a service road connecting with Gregory Road to the east and the new bridge that spanned 15 Mile Creek. In 1961 and 1962 the steep slopes around the parking lot were sodded with 9,197 m² (11,000 sq. yds.) of sod cut at Queenston from the site of the new Lewiston-Queenston Bridge and truck marshalling yards, former parkland. Numerous shrubs and more than 200 ornamental shade trees were planted to landscape the property. To protect the lake frontage from erosion and storm damage it was necessary to purchase and place 49,200 tonnes (50,000 tons) of very large rubble along the shoreline, where there was no beach. The beach was cleared of tons of debris, which included dead trees, stumps, piles of rotting seaweed, dead fish and large boulders.

The Park, named in honour of Charles Daley, Chairman at that time of the Niagara Parks Commission, was officially opened on July 1, 1962. The Lincoln and Welland Regimental Band presented a concert for the occasion.

Unfortunately attendance at the park never came up to expectations as a day use facility. This was probably due to intermittent water pollution which from time to time caused closing of the beach for swimming. Demands were being made by the visiting public for more and more overnight camping facilities. As public campsite developments were practically non-existent in that area, a small section of the park was quickly converted to twelve tent-camping sites to help alleviate the problem.

Niagara Parks Archives

The first stages of the parking lot construction at Charles Daley Park. In the background is the Queen Elizabeth Way; in the centre is 15 Mile Creek; in the foreground is Lake Ontario.

Niagara Parks Archives

The levelled parking lot at Charles Daley Park. The bridge over Fifteen Mile Creek is shown under construction.

Charles Daley Park from the air. The Queen Elizabeth Way and the Service Road are on the right. The outlet of 15 Mile Creek is at top left.

Camping area at the Lakeshore.

Niagara Parks Archives

In 1972 the Commission negotiated with the Ministry of Transport and Communications for surplus soil fill, which was available as a result of the extension of the service road westward and the construction of a new bridge over 16 Mile Creek. The fill was used to reduce the size of 16 Mile Creek Pond and raise the general level of the lower floodplain by 0.9 m (3 ft.). This new elevated acreage was then developed into twenty-nine additional tent and trailer sites. Since that time thirty of the original trailer sites have been provided with electricial outlets. Since

1973 the Niagara Parks Commission has allowed free camping privileges for senior citizens.

With purchases made in the years 1962 and 1974 of adjoining property, including the two large ponds formed by the Creeks on either side, Charles Daley Park now encompasses 15.8 ha (39 acres) with 934.8 m (3070 ft.) of sand beach on Lake Ontario. It continues to provide both day use and overnight camping facilities for the general public in a very beautiful park-like setting.

Administration

The Legislature of Ontario appointed a Commission of three men to select the land for the new park to be created by the Niagara Falls Park Act of 1885. These three were Colonel Casimir S. Gzowski, an engineer, who was appointed chairman; John W. Langmuir, manager of the Toronto General Trust Corporation; and J. Grant Macdonald, chief executive officer of the London and Canadian Loan Association. They were called the Niagara Falls Park Commission. A fourth Commissioner, John A. Orchard of Niagara Falls, was appointed after the Queen Victoria Niagara Falls Park Act was passed in 1887. The name of the Commission was changed to the Queen Victoria Niagara Falls Park Commission.

On May 5, 1887, the Commissioners hired James Wilson C.E., as Superintendent of the Park. Shortly afterwards James Quillinan was appointed Accountant. While the immediate supervision of the Park was supposed to be in the hands of the Superintendent, in reality Chairman Gzowski involved himself in the smallest administrative details. The General Correspondence files of the Commission, now in the Ontario Archives, record that Gzowski handled even a fourteen dollar tender from a Toronto printer for the printing of tickets for the Hydraulic Elevator. On another occasion, June 1, 1887, the files record a terse telegram sent from Chairman Gzowski to the Superintendent which said only: "Cut the Grass". After the end of each month, the Accountant prepared the payroll and accounts payable statement and mailed the information with the unsigned cheques to Toronto. There the Chairman signed the cheques and returned them by mail to Niagara Falls for distribution through the Park Administration Office.

The size of the Commission varied over the years, from four members in 1888, five in 1899, six in 1907, seven in 1910, eight in 1914. It remained at eight until 1951, except for a brief period of one year when Harry Oakes was appointed as the ninth member in 1933.

Until 1934 membership on the Niagara Parks Commission was not directly affected by political change in the Provincial Government. The Commissioners served under either Conservative or Liberal Governments, either resigning of their own accord or dying while in office. Vacancies arose from time to time and were filled by men appointed by the Government in power. With the electin of the Liberal Government of Premier Mitchell Hepburn in 1934, the principle was accepted that all members of the Commission should be appointees of the party in power. The Hepburn Government appointed eight Liberals to the Commission. Justification for this was on the grounds that in this way the Commission was more directly responsible to the voters. In September 1944 after the return of the Conservatives to power in the 1943 election, a new Conservative Commission was appointed to replace the one appointed by the Liberal Government on 1934. The Honourable Charles Daley was appointed Chairman of this new Commission.

In January 1967 the Honourable James N. Allan was appointed Chairman of the Niagara Parks

The first Administration Building in use from 1887 until 1907 when the building was converted into police headquarters and public washrooms and the administrative offices were moved to the new Refectory.

Edwin H. Hodge

The new Administration Building, 1926.

Edwin H. Hodge

Commission. Following the February 10, 1967 Commission meeting, Mr. Daley and five Commissioners resigned. Mr. Allan and the four remaining Commissioners carried on the business of the Commission until July 13. At that time, a new Commission was appointed under the provision of the Niagara Parks Act as amended by Bill 74. Under the terms of Bill 74, there could be six to eight Provincial appointees. Two Commissioners were appointed for a three year period, two for two years, two for one year and the three municipal government representatives for one year, unless reappointed. The municipalities represented were the City of Niagara Falls, and the Counties of Lincoln and Welland.

In 1971 the establishment of the Regional Government of Niagara absorbed the former Lincoln and Welland Counties. An amendment to the Niagara Parks Act provided for the appointment of a representative from the Regional Government, plus a representative from the City of Niagara Falls, one from the Town of Niagara-on-the-Lake and one from the Town of Fort Erie.

Since the inception of Queen Victoria Park, there have been only eight Commission Chairmen: Sir Casimir Gzowski 1885-1893; John W. Langmuir 1893-1915; Philip William Ellis 1915-1929; R. Home Smith 1929-1933; Norman Somerville 1933-34; the Honourable T.B. McQuesten 1934-1944; the Honourable Charles Daley 1944-1967; James N. Allan 1967-86. Ms. Pamela V. Walker became Chairman on May 14, 1986.

The powers of the Commission are far from absolute. From its beginning, the approval of the Legislature was required for the purchase and sale of lands; the amending of by-laws; the levying of tolls; the appointment and dismissal of all permanent Park officials and employees. Today's Commission is still required to obtain approval by Order in Council for the purchase and sale of lands, the amending of regulations and to borrow money.

In the early years, the Commission met in Toronto an average of once a month. In 1916, the headquarters of the Commission were moved to Niagara Falls. The Commissioners met in the Commissioners' Quarters on the second floor of the Victoria Park Restaurant until 1970 when the Board Room was moved to the third floor.

The immediate supervision of the Park is in the hands of a General Manager, assisted by an Assistant General Manager, both appointed by the Commission. As in the case of the Chairmen, the Niagara Parks have been extremely fortunate in attracting able men to this top executive position. There have been five Superintendents or General Managers since the beginning of the Park: James Wilson C.E. 1887-1908; John H. Jackson C.E.,

The former Administration Building with the second floor addition, added in 1957. The Administrative Offices were moved to Oak Hall in 1982. This building is now occupied by the Niagara Parks Police and the Cash Office.

Offices of the Engineering Department in Oak Hall, 1983.

Niagara Parks Archives

Offices of the Accounting Department in Oak Hall.

Niagara Parks Archives

O.L.S. 1908-1934; C. Ellison Kaumeyer 1934-1941; Maxim T. Gray O.L.S. 1941-1968. Donald R. Wilson B. Sc.F., the present General Manager, has served since December 1, 1968.

Responsible to the General Manager are the Assistant General Manager and some Department Heads. The Department Heads who report directly to the General Manager are: Merchandise and Retail Operations Manager; Attractions Manager; Food Services Manager; Superintendent of Horticulture; Superintendent of Engineering; Controller; Director of Public Relations and Advertising. A Women's Affirmative Action Programme Advisor also reports directly to the General Manager.

Those reporting to the Assistant General Manager are: the Director of Personnel; Chief of Police; Superintendent of Golf Courses; Fort and Historic Sites Managers and Safety Training Officer.

At present there are 247 regular staff members employed by the Commission. The number of seasonal employees varies throughout the year, to a high of about 1200 in the summer. The total payroll amounted to almost eleven million dollars in 1983.

An Annual Report, outlining the Commission's activities for the year is submitted by the Chairman, through the Lieutenant-Governor, to the Legislature. In 1972 the Niagara Parks were placed under the Provincial Ministry of Natural Resources and from that time until 1982 the Annual Report was submitted through the Minister of Natural Resources to the Lieutenant-Governor and in turn to the Legislature. In 1982 jusrisdication over the Niagara Parks was transferred to the Ministry of Tourism and Recreation, and the Annual Report is now submitted through that Minister.

Finance

The Legislature of Ontario set out two founding principles for the Queen Victoria Niagara Falls Park, which were regarded as indispensable conditions: first, that the Park should not be a financial burden on the Province and therefore it should be self-funding; second, that as far as possible the Park should be free to the public.

The Commissioners were required to raise enough money each year to cover the costs of maintenance and to provide for the payment of interest on the debentures issued to pay for the land for the Park. They decided that entrance to the Park would be free, but that a toll would be charged for the use of "structural appliances", such as the Hydraulic Elevator which took people to the lower gorge to go Behind the Falls and for the use of guides.

At the end of the first year, when the Park's income was disappointingly low, it was evident that new sources of revenue would have to be found. The Commissioners decided in 1889 that the granting of a franchise for the operation of refreshment facilities would be not only a source of revenue, but would also satisfy public demand that light refreshments be made available in the Park. This franchise was granted to Samuel Barnett in the same year.

The tolls and food franchise fee still did not provide enough revenue to meet expenses. Chairman Gzowski felt that economic considerations were more important than the beauty of the Park and was adamant that expenses be kept to a minimum. Reducing expenses became a preoccupation with the Chairman and he kept up a steady stream of correspondence to the Superintendent on the subject. In 1889, Gzowski found that the Superintendent had spent $1301.80 on maintenance costs for June, and he wrote demanding that expenses for July be kept to $1,000.[1] When July's costs rose to $1250, Gzowski admonished Superintendent Wilson, saying that every month he promised to reduce expenditures, but never delivered on his promise. He singled out the payment of $15.35 for horse-feed, saying that this amount was too much for one horse's feed. Wilson replied, telling the Chairman that the $15.35 horse-feed was the cost for two months, not one![2]

The Chairman became so concerned when the bank overdraft kept increasing and the bank began pressing for payment, that he even considered asking the Province to change its policy and provide the Park with an annual grant until the financial situation improved. In the meantime other franchises were granted - in March 1890, a franchise for the development of power from the waters of the Niagara River above the Horseshoe Falls, and in 1891 a franchise for an electric railway.[3]

While these franchises brought in additional money, there still wasn't enough to clear the bank overdraft. The problem was solved, when the Province authorized the Commission in 1893 to make an issue of debentures in the amount of $75,000, increasing the total bonded debt to $600,000. Additional power franchises were granted in 1900 and 1903, increasing the Commission's guaranteed annual income from franchises.

In 1904, the total of all income received since the

founding of the Park, from tolls, restaurants, railway and three power franchises amounted to $620,777.78. The Commissioners were able to meet all necessary expenses for improvements and maintenance and to pay the interest on the debentures. The Province had not been called upon to pay a single dollar on behalf of the Park.

Today there are two main sources of revenue which allow the Niagara Parks Commission to be financially independent, first, water rental fees and second, income from Commission operated attractions, restaurants and gift shops.

Water rental fees, (payment for the privilege of using the water from the Niagara River to generate electricity), are authorized under the Niagara Parks Act. The Canadian Niagara Power Company paid $56,100 in water rental fees to the Park Commission in 1916 and the Ontario Power Company and the Electrical Development Company paid a total of $152,640. In that same year the Hydro Electric Power Commission of Ontario was formed. In 1917 this Power Commission purchased the Ontario Power Company and in 1920 it purchased the Electrical Development Power Company. It continued to pay water rentals to the Park Commission on behalf of these plants.[4]

The first power was generated at the Hydro Electric Power Commission's new Queenston Powerhouse in January 1922, but an agreement was not reached on water rental compensation to the Parks Commission until November 1, 1938, when a formal contract was signed. In the intervening period, interim payments were made by the Hydro Electric Power Commission for water used by the Queenston Powerhouse. While the amounts were included as income on the books of the Parks Commission, they were paid directly to the Provincial Treasurer. It was not until 1934 that the water rental fees from this powerhouse were paid directly to the Parks Commission. In that year, which was the heart of the economic depression of the 1930's, the water rentals from all the power plants totalled $421,031.36.[5]

Under the current agreement, Ontario Hydro (formerly the Hydro Electric Power Commission of Ontario), pays to the Niagara Parks Commission half the rate on the first million horsepower of electricity generated. All other water rental fees are paid directly to the Provincial Treasury. The Canadian Niagara Power Company, which is privately-owned, pays its water rentals, based on the amount of electricity generated, directly to the Parks Commission. Water rental rates are adjusted annually, according to the change in the annual consumer price index.[6] In 1986 The Niagara Parks Commission received $3,544,977 in water rentals.

The second main source of revenue for the Niagara Parks Commission is from Parks operated facilities such as restaurants, attractions and gift shops. Beginning in 1916 the Park Commission took over restaurant and refreshment facilities at the Refectory and operated them with Park staff. This was the beginning of Commission operated revenue-producing facilities in the Niagara Parks.

Today the Commission operates four restaurants, Table Rock, Victoria Park, Whirlpool and Queenston Heights; one cafeteria; nine snack bars; eight gift shops; two attractions, the Scenic Tunnel and the Niagara Spanish Aero Car; three historic sites; two golf courses; two campgrounds; one marina; two incline railways; five pay parking lots; and one People Mover transportation system.

The most popular attraction, the Scenic Tunnels, had a net income of $1,703,339 in 1986; the Niagara Spanish Aero Car $192,601; the restaurants $1,478,548; the gifts shops and snack bars $5,182,347; the parking lots $1,286,373. The net income from all Commission operated facilities was $10,002,382.

The Commission derives other income from the privileges granted private entrepreneurs to operate within the Parks system. These privileges are granted when the Commission feels it is not practical or economically feasible to operate the concession or to provide the service itself. In 1986 the total of $684,150 was received from these sources. The Maid of the Mist is the largest concession operated privately.

Of the total annual income of the Niagara Parks, water rentals make up approximately twenty three per cent. Income from self-operated facilities, concessions and other sundry sources makes up the other seventy seven per cent.

The foregoing is intended as an overview of the Niagara Parks Commission's financial history. Those wishing a more detailed explanation of the Parks' finances are referred to the publication *Ontario's Niagara Parks a History,* by Ronald L. Way, published by the Niagara Parks Commission in 1960.

GENERAL INDEX

Numbers in italics denote illustrations.

Acres, H.G. & Co. Ltd., 48
Act, Park, 26, 27, 28
Admiralty Branch, 220
Aero Car, Niagara Spanish, *40,* 151, *151,* 186, *189,* 190, *190,*
    191, *191, 193, 193,* 194, *194,* 195, 319
Agriculture, 237, 254, 262, 278, 311, 328
Albion Mills, 274
Alfred the Horse, 235, *235*
Amana, Iowa, 245
American Civil War, 279
American Falls, *21, 41, 47,* 123, *124, 133, 169,* 293
American Revolutionary War, 273
Arbitration awards, 25, 27, 28, 29, 44
Archeology, 258
Armstrong, William, painting, *The Whirlpool and the*
    Electric Railway, 199
Attractions: earliest: see Barnett Museum; Behind the Sheet
    of Falling Water; Burning Spring; Street's Pagoda; Queen
    Victoria Niagara Falls Park's: see Behind the Sheet (also
    called Behind the Sheet of Falling Water, Under the Falls);
    Hydraulic Elevator; Niagara Parks Commission's: see
    Aero Car, Niagara Spanish; Battlefield House; Forts:
    Erie, Old; McFarland House; Scenic Tunnel; private
    attractions: see Crown Jewels Exhibit; Great Gorge Trip
    and Daredevil Gallery; Maid of the Mist boats; Potvin
    Museum; Soundlight Productions

Bach Choir, 294
Bainbrigge, P.J., painting, *Ruins of Old Fort Erie at the*
    outlet of Lake Erie, 1838, 259
Baker's Creek, 243
Band concerts: see Concerts, band
Bands: Clifton Citizens Band, 314; 15th Battalion Band,
    313; Fred Willett Concert Band, 230; Lincoln and Welland
    Regiment Band, 328; Niagara Falls Concert Band, 313,
    314; Niagara Falls Kiltie Band, 294; St. Ann's Symphonic
    Band, 313, 314; Salvation Army Temple Band, 315;
    Shredded Wheat Co. Band, 121
Barnard, H.W., painting, *The Clifton Hotel on the Ferry*
    Road, 10
Barnett Museum, 12, *13, 17,* 18, *18,* 20, 21, 93, 174, 316
Barricades, wartime, 85, 94, 100
Bartlett, W.H., engraving after a water-colour, *General*
    Brock's Monument above Queenston, 215; Queenston, 216
Bath Island, 25
Battlefield House, 272, *274,* 275, *275,* 276, *276,* 277, *277*
    Museum, 276, 277
Battlefield Park, 276, 277
Battles: see Beaverdams, Battle of; Chippawa, Battle of; Fort
    Erie, Battle of; Gettysburg, Battle of; Lundy's Lane,
    Battle of; Queenston Heights, Battle of; Stoney Creek,
    Battle of
Beaverdams, Battle of, 273
Beck, Sir Adam, G.S. No. 1, 157, 160, *161,* 162; No. 2, 104,
    160, *161,* 170, 173, 212
Behind the Sheet, 9, 12, 13, 17, 18, 19, 21, 32, 166, 176; also
    known as Under the Falls, 83, 84, 349

Berlin, Ont., 158
Bertie Hall, 250, *250,* 344
Black Creek, 243, 245, 249, 324

Boulevard, Niagara: see Niagara Boulevard; Niagara Parkway

Boundary, International, 101, *169*
Boundary Waters Treaty, 168
Bowman Ravine, *199,* 200, 202
Bowman's Creek, 197
Boy Scouts of Canada, 238
Boyer's Creek, 243
Bridal Veil Falls, 84
Bridge, Ice: see Ice bridge
Bridge lot, 293, 296, 301
Bridgeburg, Ont., 246, 249, 262
Bridges: see Cedar Island; Clark Hill Islands; Cynthia
    Islands; International R.R. (Fort Erie); King's; Lewiston-
    Queenston; Mather (proposed); Niagara Falls Park and
    River Railway; Peace; Railway Arch (also called Canada
    Southern Railway, Michigan Central Railway, New York
    Central Railway, Penn Central Railway); Railway Can-
    tilever (also called Canada Southern Railway, Michigan
    Central Railway); Railway Suspension (also called Grand
    Trunk Railway); Upper Steel Arch (also called Falls View,
    Honeymoon, International Railway Co.); Upper Suspen-
    sion (also called New Suspension); Whirlpool Rapids
Bridgewater, 61
Bridgewater mills, 61, 63
Brock's Cenotaph, 235, *235*
Brock's Monument, 213, 215, 216, 217, 220, *226, 227, 232,*
    236, 242
Brown's Point, 254
Brush Electric Co., 117
Buchner Place, 280
Buffalo, N.Y., 239, 245, 249, 253, 260, 281
Buffalo and Fort Erie Peace Bridge Authority, 251
Buffalo Railway Co., 220
Burch's mills, 61, *80*
Burlington Heights, 260, 272, 278
Burning Spring, 61, *62,* 66
Burrow, Stewart & Milne, Ltd., 317, *317*
Butler's Barracks, 265
Butler's Burying Ground, 265, *265,* 267
Butler's Rangers, 196, 236

Calyo, Nicolino, painting, *The Burning of the Caroline, 241*
Camera lucida, *166*
Campbell Stark, Laurel, sketch, *Queenston Village and the*
    Portage Road, 214
Canada, Government of: 186, 203, 217, 221, 236, 246, 251,
    257, 260, 261, 267, 274, 276, 279; Administrator of the
    Government, 214; Department of Indian and Northern
    Affairs, National and Historic Parks Branch, 268;
    Department of Mines and Resources, 237; Department of
    National Defence, 267, 268; Department of Northern
    Affairs and Natural Resources, 276, 280; Department of
    the Interior, Admiralty Branch, 220; Provisional Govern-
    ment of Canada, 239
Canada, Upper, 213, 239, 254, 260, 272, 273, 278;

Canada Bill, 250
Canada Southern Railway, *25*
The Canada Southern Railway at Niagara Falls (painting;
    Robert Whale), *25*
Canada's Centennial, 48, 311
Canadian Carborundum Co., 153
Canadian Militia, 279
Canadian National Exhibition, *288*

Canadian Niagara Power Co., 45, 48, 79, 125, 147, 152, 154, *156*. 158. 159, 163, 169, 200

Canals: see Desjardins Canal; Welland Canal

Cantilever Railway Bridge, 131, 141
Carillon Tower, Rainbow Bridge, *45*
Carter Electric Co., 40
Catlin, George, painting, *Topography of Niagara, 79*
Cave of the Winds, 84, 176
Cedar island, 30, *31, 80,* 81, 82, 154, 176; Bridges, 81
Cemeteries: see Butler's Burying Ground; Drummond Hill
    Cemetery; Hamilton Cemetery

Centennial Lilac Gardens, 311, *311,* 312, *312*
Chain Reserve (also called Crown Reserve, Military Reserve),
    6, 7, 9, 12, 13, 19, 21, 26, 105, 140, 174, 186, 243, 246, 254,
    257
Chapman Murray Associates, Architects, 56, 74
Charles Daley Park, 324, 328, *329, 330,* 331, *331*
Chicago, 251
Chippawa, 102, *103,* 213, 243, 244, 246, 254, 257, 260, 278,

Chippawa, Battle of, 244, *244,* 260, 278
Chippawa, Fort, 101, 102, *102,* 104, 244
Chippawa Creek, 102, 244
Chippawa-Grass Island Pool, 170, 173
Chippawa-Queenston Power Canal, 102, 200, 319, *321,* 323
Chippaway, taken from the Mouth of the Creek (painting;
    Edward Walsh), *102*
Church, Frederic E., painting, *Niagara Falls, 23*
City of the Falls, 9, 10
Clark & Street (firm), 7, 9
Clark Hill, 63, 78
Clark Hill Islands, 63, *63*; Bridges, *63,* 64, *64,* 65; see also
    Cynthia Islands
Clifton, Town of, 11
Clifton Gate House, *42,* 43, *43,* 49, 294
Clifton Hill, 294
The Clifton Hotel on the Ferry Road (painting; H.W.
    Barnard), *10*
Clifton Incline Railway, 46, 111, 112, *112,* 113, *113,* 114,
    114, 296, *296*; see also Maid of the Mist Incline
Clifton Suspension Bridge Co., 296
Cockburn, James Pattison, paintings, *The Pavilion Hotel at
    Niagara Falls, 8; The stairway and path to the foot of the
    gorge near Table Rock, Niagara, 8*
Colt's Creek, 186
Colt's Incline Railway, 186, *187, 188*
Commission, Niagara Parks: see Niagara Parks Commission
Concerts, band, 229, *229,* 230, *230,* 294, 313, 315
Concerts, choral: see Bach Choir; Mendelssohn Choir;
    Schubert Choir
Confederation of Canada, 186, 260

Creeks: see Baker's; Black; Bowman's; Boyer's; Chippawa;
    Colt's; Fifteen Mile; Frenchman's; Lyon's; Miller's;
    Sixteen Mile; Street's; Ussher's
Crescent Island: see Cedar Island
Crown Grants, 268, 269, 274
Crown Jewels Exhibit, 90, 91, 92
Crown Lands Department, 21
Crown Reserve: see Chain Reserve
Currency, 254
Cynthia Islands, 63, 64; Bridges, 63, 64, 65, 66

Daredevil Gallery, 150, *150,* 184
Daredevils: see Stunters
Deep Hollow, 257
De Leuw Cather, (firm), 90
Depression, 251
Desjardins Canal, 11
Detroit, Fort, 237
Double Decker Bus Tours, 323
Drummond, Fort, 225, *225,* 227
Drummond Hill, 278
Drummond Hill Cemetery, 279
Drummond Hill Presbyterian Church, 280
Dufferin Cafe, *36,* 93, 94, *94,* 316
Dufferin Gate, 28, 66
Dufferin Islands, 30, 35, 47, 51, 52, 61, *65,* 66, *66, 67, 68, 69,*
    70, *70,* 71, *71, 72,* 152, 153, 154, *154,* 170
Dunington-Grubb & Stennsson, 293
Dunlap, William, painting *View of Niagara (from the Bank
    Above the Stone House), 13*

Dutch Elm Disease, 284

Early Woodland Culture, 258
Ebenezer Society, 245
Ebenezer Stone, 245, *245*
Edinburgh, Scotland, 276, 309
Edison Movie Co., 53, 177
Electrical Development Company, 79, 93, 285,   ; see also
    Toronto Power Co.

Engineerium, 157
Erie, Old Fort: see Forts: Erie, Old

Estcourt, James B.B., painting, *The 43rd Monmouthshire
    Regiment encampment at Niagara opposite the American
    Fall, August 9, 1838, 242*
Estudios y Obras de Ingenieria, 195
Explorers: Bréhant de Galinée, René de, 4,5; Brûlé, Étienne,
    3; Cartier, Jacques, 3; Champlain, Samuel de, 3; Dollier
    de Casson, François, 4; Hennepin, Fr. Louis, *4,* 5, 101;
    Lalemant, Fr. Gabriel, 3; La Motte de Lucière, Domini-
    que, 5, 101; La Roche Daillon, Fr. Joseph de, 3; La Salle,
    René Robert Cavelier, 5, 101
Exposition, Pan American, 177

The Fall of Niagara (engraving; van Vienan), *4*
Falls: see American Falls; Bridal Veil Falls; Horseshoe Falls
Falls Avenue, 296
Falls View Bridge: see Upper Steel Arch Bridge (also called
    Honeymoon Bridge; Upper Bridge)
Fenians, 245
Fensom Elevator Works, 83
Ferries: Buffalo-Fort Erie, 249; horse-boat, 215; Ongiara, 217,
    217, 218, *218;* row boat, *7, 105, 108, 242;* ferry landing,
    105, *111,* 242; ferry lease, 105; Ferry Road, 10, 11, 28, 105,

Festival of Lights, 121
Fifteen Mile Creek, 328, *329, 330*
Fisher, Alvan, painting, *The Great Horseshoe Fall, Niagara,
    7*
Fishing, 212
Flats, The, 30, 78, *78, 80,* 155
Fleming, Sir Sandford, Foundation, 157
Flora, 281, *282,* 285, *291, 292,* 294, *305,* 306, *307, 308,* 311,
    311, 312, *312*
Floral Clock, 309, *309,* 310, *310*

The 43rd Monmouthshire Regiment encampment at Niagara opposite the American Falls, August 9, 1838 (painting; J.B.B. Estcourt), *242*

Fort Erie, Battle of, 260

Fort Erie, Old: see Forts: Erie, Old

Fort Erie, Town of, 186, 239, 243, 244, 249, 250, 251, 253, 258, 269, 272, 273, 278, 324,

Forts: Chippawa, 101, 102, *102*, 104, 244; Clinton, 273; Detroit, 237; Drummond, 225, *225*, 227; du Portage, 101; Erie, Old, 246, 251, 253, 258, *261*, 262, *262*, 264, 265, Museum, 264; George, 243, 254, 257, 260, 265, *266*, 267, 269, 273, 278, Museum, 268; Henry, 267, Mississauga, 265; Niagara, 5, 77, 237, 258, 269; Pitt, 237; Porter, 251; Schlosser, 101; Welland: see Forts: Chippawa

Foster's Flats, 34, 203, 204, 206, *208*, 212

Franchises: Behind the Sheet, 34; electric railway, 33; Hydraulic lift, 34; photographic, 34, 84; power, 35, 152, 167,   refreshment, 34

Frenchman's Creek, 243, 245, 246

Front, The, 12, 13, *18, 19,* 21

Front Street, 296

Funambulism, 135, 136, *136,* 137, *137,* 138, *138, 139,* 140, *140, 141,* 142, 150, *151,* 176

Funambulists: Bellini, 140; Blondin, Jean François, Gravelet, 135, *136,* 137, 139, 176, 177, *177;* Calverley, Clifford, 141, *141;* Dixon, Samuel, 140, *140,* 141, 142; Farini, Enrico, 108, 135, 137, *137,* 138, *138,* 139; Hardy, James, 142; Leslie, Harry, ("The American Blondin"), 139; Peer, Stephen, 140, 141, *141,* 142; Petit, Phillipe, 150, 151; Rechatin, Henry, 150, 151, *151;* Spelterina, Maria, *139,140*

Gage family, 273

Gage House, 272, 274

Garrison Reserve, 265

Gateway Park, 251

General Brock's Monument above Queenston (engraving after a water-colour, W.H. Bartlett) *215*

General Electric Co., 120

Geology, 61, 166, 197, 203, *207, 210,* 212, 213

Georgetown, Ont., 276

Gettysburg, Battle of, 279

Goat Island, 23, 25, 47, 170, 172, *172*

Gorge, Niagara, 213

Grass Island, 144

Grass Island Pool: see Chippawa-Grass Island Pool; Grass Island Weir, 170

Great Gorge Route, *118, 153,* 178, 179, *181,* 183, *183,* 184, 188, 190, *201,* 220

Great Gorge Trip and Daredevil Gallery, 149, 150, *150*

The Great Horseshoe Falls, Niagara (painting; Alvan Fisher), 7

Great Lakes, 166, 170, 203, 237, 243

Great Lakes Dredge and Dock Company, 163

Greenhouse, 46, 78, 79, *159, 165,* 285, *286,* 287, *287, 288, 289, 290, 291, 292,* 313

Gregory Road, 328

Hackmen, 33, 174

Hamilton, Ont., 276;

Hamilton Cemetery, 216

Heriot, George, painting, *View of the Falls of Niagara,* 80

Highways, 213, 253, 328, *329,* 330

Historic markers: see Plaques

Historic monuments: see Monuments

Historic plaques: see Plaques

Historic restorations: see Battlefield House; Forts: Erie, Old; George; Mackenzie House; McFarland House; Navy Hall

Historical societies, 274, 276, 279

Hogg Island, 102

Hollow, The, 77, 155; see also The Flats

Horses, 303; see also Alfred the Horse; Surreys, *43, 45*

Horseshoe Falls, 7, *7,* 23, 31, 37, 53, 54, 79, 84, 117, *124, 125,* 144, *144,* 145, *145, 146,* 147, *147, 148,* 149, *149,* 150, 163, 166, 167, *167,* 168, *168,* 169, *169,* 173, 176, 178, 239, 242, 293

Horseshoe Falls Incline Railway, 48, *49*

Horticulture, *57, 58,* 59, 60, 202, 276, 284, 285, 287, 288

Hospital, Greater Niagara General, 149

Hotels, Bath House, 10; Brown's, 7; Cataract House, 23; Clifton House, 10, *10,* 23, 28, 43, 111, 174, 293, *295, 296, 297;* Eagle Tavern, 105; Lafayette, *41,* 43, 293, *296;* Pavilion, 7, *8,* 10, 79, 105, 250; Prospect House, 13, *14;* Prospect House (Queenston), 206; Queen's (Front St., later River Rd.), 299; Queen's (Navy Island), 237; Table Rock House, 12, 13, 86, 167, 174

House of Lords, 250

Hydraulic Elevator, *36,* 83, 84, 85, 86, *86, 161,* 173

Hydro Electric Power Commission of Ontario, 102, 120, 157, 158, 170, 200, 303, 319

Ice boom, 134, *134*

Ice bridge, 127, 128, *128, 129,* 130, *130,* 131, 132, *132,* 133, 134, *134*

Illumination, Falls, *52,* 117, 118, *118,* 119, *119,* 120, 121, *121,* 122, *122,* 123, *123, 124, 125, 126, 162*

Illumination Board, 120, 123

Illumination landscape, *232, 233*

Industries, early, 61, 77, 78, 152, 153, 198; U.S. mill district, *107*

Inspiration Point, *30, 33,* 38

International Board of Control, 169

International Boundary, 101

International Control Dam, 47, 115, 173, *173*

International Joint Commission, 170

International Niagara Board, Special, 169

International Niagara Board of Control, 168, 170

International Railway Co., 44, 45, 111, 118, 188, 190, 220, 221, 222, *222,* 227, *228,* 297, 324, Powerhouse, 33, *35,* 90, *153,* 324

International Waterways Commission, 168

Islands: see Bath; Cedar (also called Crescent, Long, Swayze's); Dufferin, (also called Clark Hill, Cynthia, Sutherland's); Goat; Grass; Hogg; Luna; Navy; Tower

Jolly Cut, 281

Kew Gardens, 303
King's Bridge, 102, *102;* Park, 101, 102, *103,* 104, 318
Kitchener, Ont., 158

Lake boats: Cayuga, 220, 227, 228, *228, 255;* Chicora, 217,
    218, *218,* 227; Chief Justice Robinson, 215; Chippewa,
    217, *219,* 227; Cibola, 217, 218, *218;* Corona; *219,* 227,
    255; Northumberland, 220; Ongiara, 218, *218; Turbina,*
    220; see also Ships, steam
Lake Erie, 168, 243, 257, 258
Lake Iroquois, 213
Lake Michigan, 169
Lake Ontario, 215, 257, 272, 328, *329*
Land Board, 196, 246
Larkin farm, 311
Lewiston, 1/6, 177, 214, 257
Lewiston-Queenston Bridge (also known as Queenston-
    Lewiston Bridge), 220, *232,* 328; Suspension Bridge, 31,
    232

Lilac Gardens; see Centennial Lilac Gardens
Lincoln County, 221, 334
Lions Club of Dunnville, 343
London, Ontario, 158

Loretto Centre, 7
Luna Island, 121
Lundy's Lane, Battle of, 49, 243, 278, 279; Monument, 279
Lundy's Lane Historical Society, 279
Lyon's Creek, 102

McFarland House, 269, *270*
McFarland Point Park, 257, *257, 271,* 318
Mackenzie House, 236, *236,*   Museum, 236
Mackenzie Rebellion, 216, 239, 245
Mahoney, Mildred, M., Dolls' House Foundation, 250;
    Gallery, 250
The Maid of the Mist (sketch; Ferdinand Richard), *106*
Maid of the Mist (boats), 46, 105, 106, *106, 107,* 108, *109,*
    110, *110,* 111, *113, 114, 116,* 137, 149, 176, 178, *178*

Maid of the Mist Incline Railway, 112, *114,*   see also
    Clifton Incline Railway
The Maid of the Mist landing (sketch; Ferdinand Richardt),
    106
Manchester, N.Y., 216
Maps, *11, 29, 35, 57, 79, 158, 169, 202*
Mather Arch, 251
Mather Bridge, proposed, 251
Mather Park, 251; Park Gate, *252,* 253, *253*
Memorial Arch, *42, 43,* 44, 49, 294, *301*
Mendelssohn Choir, 294
Military Reserve, Queenston Heights, 217, 221
Militia, Canadian, 239, 269
Miller's Creek, 243, 249, 324; Campsite, 324, *325, 326;*
    Marina, *325, 326,* 327, *327*
Mills, water power: see Industries, early
Minolta Tower, 48
Monuments, Alfred the Horse, 235, *235;* Battle of Lundy's
    Lane, 279, *279;* Battle of Stoney Creek, *273,* 274, 276,
    277; Brock's, 213, 215, 216, 217, 220, *226, 227, 232,* 236,
    242; Brock's Cenotaph, 235, *235;*
                                                    Laura Secord, *232,*
    234, *234,* 279, *279*
Motion pictures, 55, *55,* 177, 184, 190, 192; T.V. movies, 184
Mowat Gate, 28, *29*

Murray property, 304, *304,* 319
Murray Street ravine, 316, 318
Museums: see Battlefield House; Barnett Museum; Forts:
    Erie, Old; Museum; George, Museum; Niagara Falls
    Museum; Niagara Historical Society Museum; Potvin
    Museum
Musicians, American Federation of, 230, 314
Musicians Performance Trust Fund, 230, 264, 314
Mutual Weekly Newsreel, 190, 192

Natural Reserve, 212, 324
Natural zone: see Natural Reserve
Naturalist, Niagara Parks, 212
Navy Hall, 265, 268
Navy Island, 102, 170, 237, 245
New France, 258, 237
New York City, 237
New York Militia, 273
New York State Assembly, 207
New York State Reservation, 24, 25, 84, 130
Newark, 254, 260
Newspapers; *Colonial Advocate,* 236; *Daily Globe,* 135;
    Hamilton Evening Times, 13, 17; *Mail and Empire,* 120,
    315, 319, 324; *New York World,* 23; *Niagara Falls Gazette*
    (now called Niagara Gazette), 18, 19, 21, 118, 128, 130,137,
    138, 167; *Niagara Falls Review* (formerly called *Niagara*
    Falls Evening Review), 94, 192; *Toronto Empire,* l66;
    Toronto Saturday Night, 30; *Toronto World,* 221; *Upper*
    Canada Gazette, 254
Niagara, a view of the Flats and the Upper Cascades (painting;
    John Vanderlyn), *78*
Niagara (motion picture), 55, *55*
Niagara, Ontario: see Niagara-on-the-Lake, Ontario
Niagara, Regional Government of, 213
Niagara, Regional Municipality of, 213
Niagara Boulevard, 43, 44, 155, 188, 195, 200, 202, 207, 223,
    249, 256, 257, 267, 304, 306, 319, 324; Bridges, 245, 246,
    247, 249; see also Niagara Parkway
Niagara Concessions Ltd., 183, 351
Niagara District Art Association, 73
Niagara Diversion Treaty (1950), 170, 173
Niagara Falls: see American Falls; Bridal Veil Falls; Horse-
    shoe Falls
Niagara Falls, (painting; F.E. Church), *23*
Niagara Falls, (painting; Guerlok Rock), *16*
Niagara Falls, (painting; Robert H. Whale), *80*
Niagara Falls, New York, 120
Niagara Falls Bridge Commission, 296
Niagara Falls Ferry Association, 105
Niagara Falls Illumination Board, 120
Niagara Falls Kiltie Band, 294
Niagara Falls Museum, *299*
Niagara Falls Park and River Railway, 33 *33,* 34, *34,* 35, 66,
    152, 153, 167, 174, 186, 188, *190, 198, 199,* 200, 203, 205,
    212, 217, 220, 257, 295, *304;* Bridges, *65;* Powerhouse, 33,
    90, *153,* 324
Niagara Falls Power Co., 152, 154
Niagara Glen, 160, 190, 203, 204, *204,* 205, *205,* 206, *206,*
    207, *207, 208,* 209, *209, 210, 211,* 212, 269, 303, 304, 311,
    319,   proposed bridge, 207
Niagara Glen Heights, 202, 319
Niagara Historical Society Museum, 236
Niagara Mohawk Power Co., 154
Niagara National Historic Parks, 267, 268
Niagara Navigation Co., 218, 220
Niagara-on-the-Lake, Town of, 213, 216, 236, 254, 257, 265,
    267, 268

Niagara Parks Act, 150, 268, 332, 333, 334
Niagara Parks Commission, Administration, 332, *333,* 333,
    334, *335,* 335, 358, 359; administration headquarters, *40,*
    41, *74,* 74, 94, 100, 165, 333, 334; aims, 2; Engineering
    Department, 276, 284, *335;* (also called Roads and
    Engineering Department; Works Department); Finance
    Department, 336, 337; finances, 28, 29, 32, 33, 34, 35,
    44, 45; Horticultural Department: see Horticulture;
    leases, 43, 49, 71, 90, 178, 181, 183, 192, 195; parking
    and parking lots, 32, 47, 48, 51, 56, *56,* 90; Service
    Department: 79, 165; water rentals, 160, 162; see also
    Greenhouse; Queen Victoria Niagara Falls Parks
    Commission; School of Horticulture; individual
    attractions, parks, restaurants, stores and other buildings
Niagara Parks Golf Courses: see Whirlpool Golf Course;
    Oak Hall Golf Course
Niagara Parks Police, 41, *60,* 143, 147, 148, *148,* 149, *149,*
    151, 313
Niagara Parkway, 200, 243, 249, 250; see also Niagara Boule-
    vard
Niagara Spanish Aero Car: see Aero Car
Niagara Township, 213, 236, 254; see also Township #1
Niagara, a view of the Falls and the Upper Cascades (paint-
    ing; John Vanderlyn), *78*

Oak Hall, 73, 74, *74, 75, 76,* 359
Oak Hall Golf Course, 74, *76*
Oakes Garden Theatre, 10, *42, 43, 43,* 44, *45,* 124, 281, 293,
    294, *294, 297, 298, 300, 301, 302*
Observation Towers: see Towers
*Old Fort Erie and the Migrations of the Wild Pidgeon in the
    Spring* (painting; Edward Walsh), *259*
Oneida Community Ltd., *299*
Ontario, Province of, 186, 217, 236, 246, 251, 262, 267, 276,
    294; Department of Highways, 296, Department of
    Lands and Forests, 238; Plant Pathology Stations, 284;
    Public Works Department, 246
Ontario Bus Industry, 56
Ontario Golf Association, 323
Ontario Historical Society, 279
Ontario Hydro, 47, 48, 49, 79, 102, 104, 158, 160, *161,* 162,
    170, 183, 309
Ontario Legislature, 278, 342
Ontario Police, 141
Ontario Power Co., 35, *35,* 36, *36,* 45, *47,* 70, 85, 86, 93, 120,
    122, 131, 132, *154, 155, 156, 157,* 158, 159, *159,* 160, *161,
    162,* 313
Ontario Provincial Police, 252
Ontario Public Golf Course Championships, 323
Ontario Society of Artists, 23, 25
Ordnance Branch, 26; Lands, 220, 265; Reserve, 251, 260
Ornithology, 238

Pan American Exposition: see Exposition, Pan American
Paradise Grove, 257
Paragon Holdings Ltd., 90
Parks and Recreation Association of Canada, 306
Parks Canada: see Niagara National Historic Parks

Parkway, Niagara: see Niagara Parkway
Patriot movement, 239, 242
The Pavilion Hotel at Niagara Falls (painting; James
    Pattison Cockburn), *8*
Peace Bridge, 249, 251, 253
Pioneer Historical Society of the County of Wentworth,
    274; Ladies Auxiliary, 274
Plaques, Historic: Battle of Queenston Heights, *234,* 235,
    235, 236; Brock's Cenotaph, 235, *235;* Capture of Fort
    Niagara, 271; Fort Drummond, 225, *225;* Redan Battery,
    214; Vrooman Point Battery, *256*
Police: see Niagara Parks Police; Ontario Police; Ontario
    Provincial Police
Pontiac, 237
Port Robinson, Ont., 243
Portage Road, 61, 77, *79,* 101, 196, 213, 214, 221, 243, 245,
    278
Potvin Museum, 49
Power, hydraulic, 152, 153, 158, *187*
Power Authority, State of New York, 212
Powerhouses: Canadian Niagara Power Co., 154, 159;
    Electrical Development Co., 155, 157; International Rail-
    way Co., (also called Niagara Falls Park and River Rail-
    way Co. (also called Niagara Falls Park and River Rail-
    wayCo.), 153; Ontario Power Co., 155; Toronto Power
Princes St. Gardens, Edinburgh, 309
Princess Elizabeth Building, 46, *46*
Privy Council, Westminster, 44, 45, 158
Prospect Park, 25, 118
Provincial Marine, 268

Queen Elizabeth Way, 253, 328, *329,* 330, *330*
Queen Victoria Niagara Falls Park Commission:
    Administration headquarters, 11, 94, *95,* 100
    finances, 27, 28, 29, 32, 33, 34, 35; franchises, 33, 155,
    158, 160; leases, 34, 84, 85, 93, 94, 176, 195, 200; water
    rentals, 154, 160; see also Niagara Parks Commission
Queen Victoria Park, 11, 21, 27-60, *27-60,* 94, 100, 108,
    142, 152, 153, 160, 174, 176, 178, 186, 188, 190, 198, 200,
    203, 246, 265, 278, 281, 285, 293, 294, 311
Queen's Rangers, 61
Queenston, 33, *34,* 176, 178, 203, 207, 213, 254, 257, 273,
    276, 319, 328
Queenson (engraving after a water-colour; W.H. Bartlett),
    216
Queenston-Chippawa Power Development, 159, 160, 303
Queenston Heights, Battle of, 213, 214, *234*
Queenston Heights Park, 34, 200, 207, 213, 214, 217, 220,
    220, 221, *222,* 223, *223,* 225, *225, 226,* 227, *227,* 228,
    229, *229,* 230, *230,* 231, *231, 232,* 233, *233,* 236, 318
Queenston-Lewiston Bridges: see Lewiston-Queenston
    Bridge
Queenston Overture, 230
Queenston Village and the Portage Road (sketch; Laurel
    Campbell Stark), *214*

Railway Arch Bridge, 106
Railway Cantilever Bridge, 131, 141
Railway excursions, 128, 131

Railway Suspension Bridge, 106
Railways, electric: Fort Erie Railway Co., 246; International
    Railway Co., *35,* 44, 45, 111, 118, 188, 190, 220, 221, 222,
    222, 227, *228, 297* ; Niagara Falls Park and River
    Railway, 33, *33, 34,* 35, 66, 152. 153, *154, 156,* 167, 174
    186, 188, *190,* 198, *199,* 200, 203, 205, 212, 217, 220, 221,
    257, 295, *304;* Park and River Division, 111
Railways, horse-drawn, 215
Railways, steam: Buffalo and Lake Huron, 260; Canada
    Southern, *25,* 26; Canadian Pacific, 276; Erie and
    Ontario, 215, 216, 257; Great Western, 32; Michigan
    Central, 118, New York Central, 32
Rainbow Bridge, 49, 294, 296, *297*
Rainbow Bridge Plaza, 296, *297*
Rainbow Gardens, *43,* 294, 296, *297,* 299, *300*
Rapids View Parking Area, 56, *56*
Rattlesnakes, 207
Recession, Horseshoe Falls, 83, 86, *169*
Refectory, 20, 35, 41, 45, 49, 85, 93, 94, *95, 96, 97, 98, 99,*
    100, *161, 162,* 316, *318* ; see also Victoria
    Park Restaurant
Regiments, British: 8th Foot, *263,* 264; 1st Dragoon
    Guards, 242; 43rd Monmouthshire, 242, *242;* Light
    Infantry, 242; Niagara Lancers, 242; 100th, 269; Queen's
    Own, 213; Queen's Rangers, 61
Remedial Work: American Falls, 172, *172;* Horseshoe Falls,
    171, 173; see also International Control Dam
Reserve, Chain: see Chain Reserve; Military Reserve,
    Queenston Heights
Richard Strong Associates, 74,
Richardt, Ferdinand, pencil sketches, *The Maid of the Mist,*
    106; *The Maid of the Mist Landing,* 106
Ridgeway, Battle of, 245
Ridgeway, Ontario, 245
Robert Moses Generating Station, 173
Robertson Construction and Engineering Co., 178, 181
Rock, Guerlok, painting, *Niagara Falls, 16*
Rope walkers, see Funambulists,
Rotary Clubs of District 709, American, 311, 312
Royal Canadian Air Force, 73
Royal Canadian Humane Society, 131
Royal Winter Fair, 287
Ruins of Old Fort Erie at the outlet of Lake Erie, 1838 (paint-
    ing; P.J. Bainbrigge), *259*

Sailing ships: *Boston,* 237; *Charlotte,* 237; *Gladwin,* 237;
    Huron, 237; *Victory,* 237
St. Catharines, Ontario, 110, 328,
St. Catharines Boat Club, 257
St. Catharines, Thorold and Niagara Falls Toll Road Co.,
    12; Toll Road, 11, 12, 29
St. David's Buried Gorge, 197
St. Lawrence River, 203
Salvation Army, 128; Temple Band, 315
Scenic Tunnel, 47, 83, *85,* 86, 88, *89,* 169, 173
School of Apprentice Gardeners, 294, 303
School of Gardening, 303
School of Horticulture, 281, 303, 304, *304, 305,* 306,
    306, 307, 308, 311, *321*
Schubert Choir, 294
Scow, *159,* 163, *164,* 165, *165*
Secord, Laura, 234, *234*
Ships, steam: *Caroline,* 239, *241,* 245; see also Lake boats;
    Maid of the Mist (boats)
Sightseeing: air, Sky View Lines, 122, *122;* bus, 43;

Canada Coach Lines, *40,* 48; Double Decker Bus Lines,
    48, 323; Gray Coach Lines, 43; Gray Line Sightseeing
    Companies Association Ltd., 43; Highway King Coach
    Lines, 43; Niagara and Toronto Tour Co., 43; Van
    Dyke Sightseeing Co., 43; surrey, horse drawn, *43, 45;*
    Viewmobiles, 48, *49*
Sixteen Mile Creek, 328
Sky View Lines, 122, *122*
Slater's Dock, 66, *246*
Smeaton's Cove, 311
Snakes, Timber rattlesnake, 197
Soundlight Productions, 49
Spirit of Park Hall Fountain, *287*
Stage coaches, 215, 245, 254
*The stairway and path to the foot of the gorge near Table
    Rock, Niagara* (painting; James Pattison Cockburn), *8*
Stairways, Table Rock, 7 *8,* 9, 12, 13, *16,* 18, *18,* 19,
Stamford Township, 186
Steamships: see Ships. steam; Lake boats
Stoney Creek, Battle of, 272, 273, 276, 277
Streets: Clifton Hill, 43, 46, 52; Ferry Road, 10, 28;
    Fraser Hill, 48, 358; Front, 12; Jolly Cut, 41; Murray,
    10, 29; River Road, 294, 296, 341; Robinson, 10, 29,
    41; St. Paul, 299; Whirlpool Road, 314
Street's Creek: see Ussher's Creek
Street's Mills, 77
Street's Pagoda, *80,* 81, *82*
Stunters, over the Horseshoe Falls: Boya, Nathan (also
    known as William FitzGerald), 147, *148, 149;* Hill,
    William Red, Jr., 147; Leach, Bobby, 144, 145, *146;*
    Lussier, Jean, 147, *147;* Munday, Dave, 151; Soucek,
    Karel, 151; Stathakis, George, 147, 183; Stephens,
    Charles, 145; Taylor, Annie, 144, *144, 145;* Trotter,
    Steven, 151; through the Whirlpool Rapids: Allen,
    Sadie, 177; Campbell, Walter G., 177; Dittrick, Wm.,
    177; Flack, Robert, 177; Graham, Carlisle, 173, 177,
    178, *179;* Hill, William Red, Sr., *147,* 163, 165, 183, 184;
    Kendall, Wm., *142,* Nissen, Peter, 177, 178; Percy,
    Charles, *143,* 177; Potts, Wm., 177; Wagenfuhrer,
    Martha, 178, *180;* Webb, Captain Matthew, *142;*
    Willard, Maude, 177, 178, *180;* over the Whirlpool:
    Rechatin, Henry, 151, *151;* Rechatin, Janyck, 151, *151;*
Stunts: aborted, 147, 150; Commission's policy on stunts,
    140, 142, 150, 151, 184; Kayaking through the Whirl-
    pool Rapids, 184, *184; Michigan,* 7; Movie stunts, 184;
    parachute drops, 144, 145; proposed stunts, 150
Superman II (motion picture), 55, *55*
Surrey, horse drawn, *43, 45*

Table Rock, 6, *9,* 10, 12, 13, *16, 18,* 31, 33, 35, 37, *37,*
    38, *38,* 46, 47, *47,* 88, 117, 120, 159, 169, 173;
    Observation Platform, 88, *89,* 144; see also Table Rock
    House; Scenic Tunnel
Table Rock House, 12, *15, 35,* 41, 45, *47,* 48, 73, 81, 83,
    84, 85, 86, 87, 88, 90, 91, 92, 153, *153, 161,* 167
    South Building, *54.* 91, *92*
Taggart House (also called McFarland House), 269
Termination Rock, 83
Terrapin Point, 173
Thom(p)son Farm, 319
Thom(p)son Point, 186, 188, 189, *189,* 190, *190,* 192, *192,*
    196, 198, *198,* 200, *200,* 202, 203, 319
Tightrope walkers: see Funambulists
Toll Road, 11, 12, 29

*The Top of the Bank at the Road Leading to the Ferry
  Landing* (painting by an unknown artist), *111*
Topography of Niagara (painting; George Catlin), *79*
Toronto, Ontario, 217, 257, 328
Toronto boats: see Lake boats

Toronto Power Co., 46, 77, 79, 131, 152, *154*, 155, 157,
  158, 159, *159, 160*, 163, *165*

Tower Island, 170
Towers, Observation: *18*, 48, 81, *82*, 281; Battle of Lundy's
Lane site towers, 279
Township number 1: see Niagara Township
Township of Bertie, 249
Trading posts, 243, 258
Traffic studies: Del Can, 52, 56; De Leuw Cather, 48,
  51; Greater Niagara Traffic Survey, 47; Lanmer-Fenco,
  56; Master Plan for Traffic Improvements in Queen
  Victoria Park, 51, 56; Ministry of Transport and
  Communications, 51; Ontario Department of Highways,
  48; Richard Strong Associates, 48, 51, 56; Technical
  Advisory Committee, 51, 52: also called TAC4;
  Technical Co-ordinating Committee, 48
Training School for Apprentice Gardeners, 303
Transportation: buses, 227; see also Ferries; Lake boats;
  Railways, electric; Railways, horse-drawn; Railways,
  steam; Stage coaches; York boats
Treaties: Boundary Waters Treaty, 168; Jay Treaty, 101;
  Treaty of Washington, 242

Under the Falls: see Behind the Sheet; Behind the Sheet of
  Falling Water
Unions: Carpenters', 342; Musicians', 230, 314
United Empire Loyalists, 152, 213, 274
United Nations, 237
United States, 239, 242, 278; Army, 102, 243, 244, *244*,
  260, 272, 278, 279, *280;* Army Corps of Engineers, 172;
  Coast Guard, 163; Congress, 168; Senate, 170; State
  Survey, 24; War Department, 251
*The United States Army at the Battle of Chippawa, July
  5, 1814* (painting; The United States Army in Action
  series), *244*
Upper Steel Arch Bridge, *42*, 43, 44, 49, 121, 131, 140,
  144, 220, 293, 294, 296, *297*
Upper Suspension Bridge (also called New Suspension
  Bridge), 31, 296
Urban Transport and Development Corporation, 56
Ussher's Creek (also called Street's Creek), 243, 244, 245,
  293

Vanderlyn, John, painting, *Niagara - a view of the Flats
  and the Upper Cascades,* 78
Victoria Park Restaurant, 20, *97, 98, 99,* 100, *100, 162*
  ; see also Refectory

Victoria Place, 73
Vienan. van. engraving, *The Fall of Niagara, 4,* 5
View of Niagara (from the Bank Above the Stone House)
  (painting; William Dunlap), *13*
View of the Falls of Niagara (painting; George Heriot), *80*
Viewmobiles, 48, *49*

Walsh, Edward, paintings, *Chippaway, taken from the
  Mouth of the Creek, 100; Old Fort Erie and the
  Migrations of the Wild Pidgeon in the Spring, 259*
Wars: American Civil, 279; American Revolutionary, 101,
  273; Napoleonic, 260; Seven Years, 258; War of 1812-
  14, 198, 214, 215, 269, 272; World War I, 262,
    ; World War II, 170, 285
Water diversion, 168, 169, 170
Water rentals, 160, 162
Waterworks, Municipal, *31, 35*
Welland Canal, 102, 243

Welland River, 101, 102; see also Chippawa Creek
Welland Securities Ltd., 51
Whale, Robert, paintings, *The Canada Southern Railway
  at Niagara, 25; Niagara Falls, 80*
Whirlpool, 174, 177, 178, 183, 184, *194*, 196, 197, 198,
  199, 200, *200, 201,* 202, *202,* 207, 319, *321*
The Whirlpool and the Electric Railway (painting; Wm.
  Armstrong), *199*
Whirlpool Farm (also called Thom(p)son Farm), 196, *197,*
  198, *198,* 202
Whirlpool Golf Course, 314, 319, *320, 321, 322,* 323, *323*

Whirlpool Point. see Thom(p)son Point
Whirlpool Rapids, 174, *175,* 176, *178,* 183, *183,* 184, *184,*
  185
Whirlpool Rapids Bridge, 176
Whirlpool Rapids Co., 174, 176
Whirlpool Rapids Incline, 174, *175,* 178
Whirlpool Rapids Park, 32, 35, 176
White Water Tours, 184, *184*
Wild Life and Crown Preserve, 238
Willoughby Township, 243, 249
Windsor Great Park, England, 281
Wintergreen Flats, 203, 205, *210,* 212
Women's Wentworth Historical Society, 272, 274, 276; see
  also Pioneer and Historical Society of the County of
  Wentworth: Ladies Auxiliary

York, Upper Canada, 272
York boats, 243
Youngstown, New York, 163, 269

Zimmerman, Samuel, 11, 139; estate, *11,* 41, 94
Zybach, John, 34, 35
Zybach and Brundage, 35, 84
Zybach and Co., 35, 93